THE S. MARK TAPER FOUNDATION

IMPRINT IN JEWISH STUDIES

BY THIS ENDOWMENT

THE S. MARK TAPER FOUNDATION SUPPORTS

THE APPRECIATION AND UNDERSTANDING

OF THE RICHNESS AND DIVERSITY OF

JEWISH LIFE AND CULTURE

The publisher gratefully acknowledges the generous support of the Jewish Studies Endowment Fund of the University of California Press Foundation, which was established by a major gift from the S. Mark Taper Foundation.

Speaking of Jews

Speaking of Jews

Rabbis, Intellectuals, and the Creation of an American Public Identity

Lila Corwin Berman

UNIVERSITY OF CALIFORNIA PRESS

Berkeley / Los Angeles / London

University of California Press, one of the most distinguished university
presses in the United States, enriches lives around the world by advancing
scholarship in the humanities, social sciences, and natural sciences. Its
activities are supported by the UC Press Foundation and by philanthropic
contributions from individuals and institutions. For more information, visit
www.ucpress.edu.

Monroe image [figure 11] by Milton H. Greene © 2008 Joshua Greene,
www.archiveimages.com.

University of California Press
Berkeley and Los Angeles, California

University of California Press, Ltd.
London, England

Library of Congress Cataloging-in-Publication Data

Berman, Lila Corwin, 1976–
  Speaking of Jews : rabbis, intellectuals, and the creation of an American
public identity / Lila Corwin Berman.
        p.   cm.
  Includes bibliographical references and index.
  ISBN 978-0-520-25680-4 (cloth : alk. paper) —
  ISBN 978-0-520-25681-1 (pbk. : alk. paper)
    1. Jews—United States—Identity.   2. Jews—United States—Social
conditions—20th century.   3. Jewish leadership—United States—
History—20th century.   4. Judaism and the social sciences.   5. Religion
and sociology—United States.   6. United States—Ethnic relations.
I. Title.
  E184.36.E84B47   2008
  305.6′9609730904—dc22   2008025974

Manufactured in the United States of America

18 17 16 15 14 13 12 11 10 09
10 9 8 7 6 5 4 3 2 1

This book is printed on Natures Book, which contains 30% post-consumer
waste and meets the minimum requirements of ANSI/NISO Z39.48–1992
(R 1997) (*Permanence of Paper*).

Contents

Illustrations

Acknowledgments

This is a good place to offer public thanks to my teachers, friends, and family. At Amherst College, where I did my undergraduate work, I met professors, in particular Janet Gyatso and Susan Niditch, who took ideas and students seriously. The teachers I had in graduate school at Yale gave me the tools to do the same. Nancy Cott, Robert Johnston, Steve Pitti, and Harry Stout all modeled engaged scholarship. Matthew Frye Jacobson helped me craft a dissertation and then suggested ways to go beyond the dissertation. Finally, Paula Hyman and Jon Butler remain my teachers, a fact for which I am always grateful. Paula Hyman shared her acute historical sense and breadth of knowledge to make this project better and continues to invest herself in my work and well-being. Jon Butler, as anyone who has had the pleasure of getting to know him will understand, has an impeccable sense of what really matters, whether it comes to a historical debate or the practical matter of getting a job, and shares his wisdom with modesty and good humor.

The friends I met in college and graduate school all made it seem possible—and even reasonable—to follow one's intellectual passions. For their willingness to entertain any idea, debate any point, and tolerate (almost) any amount of absurdity, I am grateful to my fellow Lord Jeffs. Bree Grossi Wilde deserves particular mention for her unwavering support and friendship; she helped me move to New Haven and even read parts of my dissertation, but this just scratches the surface of how giving she is—and she's also often very, very funny. JooYun Kim let me stay at her place in New York when I was doing research and even carried my ridiculously heavy backpack through packed subway stations.

My graduate school friends—those who put up with my pitiful softball performances, fueled my love for teen television, and asked hard questions about whatever we were reading or studying—made the whole enterprise of writing a dissertation and trying to make it as an academic tolerable: Guy Chet, Becky Davis, Christine Evans, Kip Kosek, Carrie Lane, Bob Morrissey, Mark Oppenheimer, Aaron Sachs, Madeleine Weil, and my fellow writing-group participants. I mention Noam Pianko separately since he has probably read four versions of most parts of this book and tirelessly offers his insight and friendship.

Beyond Amherst or Yale, I have been fortunate to get to know a number of people who, even though they had no professional obligation to me, still allowed me to take up their time and benefit from their good sense. Foremost, Deborah Dash Moore—an accomplished scholar and a wonderful human being—has encouraged this project from its inception. Similarly, Michael Alexander, Susan Glenn, Karla Goldman, Andrew Heinze, and Riv-Ellen Prell have all provided sound suggestions and feedback. The scholars I've met at a number of conferences, including those of the Association for Jewish Studies, the Organization of American Historians, the American Historical Association, and the Biennial Scholars' Conference on American Jewish History, have also been essential in helping me develop the framework for this book. My gratitude extends to Avinoam Patt, a wonderful historian and the kind of person who you would want sitting next to you in Yiddish class, and Brettne Bloom, a dear friend who invested time and energy in this project and pushed me to think more and more about writing.

I have had the opportunity to meet incredible scholars of religion, Jewish Studies, and American history through various fellowships and working groups. I spent a wonderful week at Vassar College participating in the American Academy of Jewish Research graduate-student seminar, led expertly by Bob Chazan, Michael Fox, and Deborah Dash Moore. A little to the west, I sojourned in Indianapolis as part of the Center for the Study of Religion and American Culture's Young Scholars in American Religion Program. Judith Weisenfeld and John Corrigan set a tone of generosity and candor. A Wexner Fellowship supported much of my graduate education, and the community of Wexners continues to broaden my understanding of Jewish life. Yale also provided me with generous summer funding and a Robert M. Leylan dissertation fellowship. Finally, just as I realized that the last stages of getting a book ready for publication take far longer than I had imagined, I was given the opportunity to spend a year at the University of Michigan's Frankel Institute for Advanced Judaic Studies. My thanks to Deborah Dash Moore, Anita Norich, and the whole crew of 2007–2008 fellows for creating a stimulating and supportive environment, where one can finish a project and even start another.

Penn State has been a wonderful place to work and teach. I am grateful to Brian Hesse and Sally McMurry for their skill at navigating the Penn State system and for their enthusiastic and pecuniary support for my research. All of my colleagues have helped create an intellectually engaging and warm environment at Penn State. I especially appreciate the conversations I've shared about work and many other things with Greg Eghighian, Lyn Elliot, Lori Ginzberg, and Annie Rose. I want to mention Mal and Lea Bank by name: alumni of Penn State, they have generously supported the growth of Jewish Studies and shown remarkable investment in my and my colleagues' work.

The librarians at Yale and Penn State were unflagging resources, without whom I doubt I would have known where to start my research. A fellowship from the American Jewish Archives gave me the opportunity to use the collections housed at the Hebrew Union College in Cincinnati and permitted me to share some of my work with a receptive and informed group of scholars. Kevin Proffitt, Gary Zola, and a staff of skilled archivists helped me find whatever I needed and more. I am indebted to the directors and staff of the Jewish Chautauqua Society who opened their New York office to me, giving me a desk and unfettered access to their historical records and their own perspectives on the history of the JCS. The archivists at the American Jewish Historical Society in New York, the Blaustein Library of the American Jewish Committee, the New Haven Colony Historical Society, the Ratner Archives at the Jewish Theological Seminary, Connecticut College, Smith College, Stanford University, and University of Chicago were all knowledgeable and efficient. I also thank Joshua Greene for giving me permission to use a photograph from his father's estate, and Indiana University Press for allowing me to incorporate into chapters 3 and 7 excerpts from my article "Sociology, Jews, and Intermarriage in Twentieth-Century America," *Jewish Social Studies* 14, no. 2 (Winter 2008): 32–60.

Oscar Handlin and Nathan Glazer agreed to let me interview them and enriched this project immeasurably. I am also grateful to David Brody, Herbert Gans, David Kertzer, and Ruth Seidman (Rabbi Morris Kertzer's daughter) for talking to me about this project. Ruth Seidman, in particular, was a wonderful resource for her vivid memory and her commitment to maintaining records of her father's work.

A number of people and institutions have helped me publish this book, though I alone am responsible for its shortcomings. Most important, Reed Malcolm, at the University of California Press, has served as an expert editor. From our earliest e-mail exchanges to a conversation only days after my daughter was born (in which, he may not remember, he gave me a sound piece of advice about trying to be kind to one's spouse during those first sleepless weeks), Reed has supported this project. During his sabbatical from the press, Kalicia Pivirotto filled in wonderfully and conscientiously. She and Jacqueline Volin have answered every little question I have had about the book's production. I am also grateful to the National Foundation for Jewish Culture for awarding me the Sidney and Hadassah Musher Doctoral Dissertation Publication Prize in 2006, and the Center for Jewish History for selecting me for the Frederick P. and Sandra P. Rose Young Historian Award in 2005.

And then there's family, and I don't really know what to say. We live all over the place, but when I picture us together it's in Springfield, Massachusetts, at Bubbee's house. Aunts, uncles, cousins, brothers, parents—when we're all there, I can think of nowhere in the world I would rather be. In an environment of seamless love and warmth, we have debated and questioned most imaginable subjects; nothing is simply true. No one is more responsible for the depth of our connections to and engagement with one another than Goldie Newman, my bubbee. There's also the family you get to add along the way: Alex's wonderful wife, Lori, and my caring in-laws.

When I was younger I may have denied it, but my three brothers—Alex, Eric, and Ivan—have had a great deal to do with how I think about things: they are spirited, funny, and yes, occasionally caustic, and I can't imagine going through life without them. Sandy and Lee Corwin, our indefatigable parents, deserve more thanks than I know how to give. All I can say is that they have made me feel like I can do whatever it is I want to do, and that I will always have them to share in whatever I meet along the way.

Finally, I'm at home, with Dan, our toddler, Ella, and our new little one, Simon. They are the people who make each day matter in ways that can't be conveyed through any mere statement of gratitude. Dan went through the whole ordeal of writing a book first, and then read this one with the care and attention he gives to all that he does. Ella has not read any of this book, but she does love books, and I love reading them to her and her little brother. My husband and my young daughter and son make me smile all the time. What could be better? Thank you.

Introduction

Presenting Jews to America

Maybe you, reading these words, were the only Jew in your elementary school class, and maybe around Chanukah time, your mother would come in with a large shopping bag full of the wax-covered menorah from home, candles, plastic dreidels, and five pounds of potatoes. You would sit close to her, but not too close, as she explained what Chanukah was and why Jews celebrated it. And then you helped pass out dreidels and grate potatoes as your mom heated the oil in the electric frying pan. Or perhaps you grew up the child of immigrants who did not speak English at home, and when friends came over, you had to explain why your parents spoke a different language. Maybe you traveled through Europe or India and found yourself the only American in a crowded youth hostel lounge, fielding questions about what Americans do and think. You will likely understand that individuals, groups, and whole societies are pressed to explain themselves when they encounter people whom they are unlike. The way they explain themselves, however, is rarely static; it depends on to whom they are speaking, where and when the conversation is taking place, and whether the listener appears interested.

Over the course of Jewish history, Jews often thought of themselves as living among strangers. Through stories, rituals, laws, and folkways, Jews sought to understand their relationship to non-Jews. In the modern era, in a more sustained fashion than any other historical period, explaining—or presenting—Jewishness to non-Jews became a political necessity and an act of Jewish survival. For some Jews, the task bred ideological fervor, a sense that Jewishness was enacted only when

Jews were busy addressing themselves to the non-Jewish world. Even for those who were not so fervid, few Jews could navigate modernity without considering how to talk about being Jewish to non-Jews. This book is about some of the ways in which American Jews explained themselves to non-Jews and how the meaning of Jewishness became inseparable from their explanations.

In the United States, Jewish leaders—rabbis and intellectuals— sought to generate a public language of Jewishness, one that carried authority and was disseminated into an American public sphere. *Speaking of Jews* is a history of how these leaders talked about Jewishness in public from immediately after World War I through the civil rights era. As the most widely recognized spokespeople of American Jews, countless rabbis devoted themselves to creating an American language of Jewishness. Taking to the roads, the airwaves, the printing presses, university classrooms, and pulpits across the country, rabbis engaged in the central and as yet unexamined project of presenting Jewishness to the United States. Their task, as they saw it, was as much about defining a collective identity as it was about crafting an ideology about the relationship between Jews and non-Jews and the role that Jews could play in a non-Jewish society. At different times and in different contexts, rabbis claimed that Jews' religious ideals, their history, or their distinctive behaviors allowed the United States to forge ahead with its democratic experiment. When properly conceived, a public language of Jewishness, instead of marking Jews as outside of or peripheral to American life, enabled Jewish leaders to define Jews as indispensable to the United States.

Just as rabbis were developing new American ideologies of Jewishness, an intellectual revolution—what I call a social-scientific turn—irrevocably imprinted itself on the way Jews talked about their Jewishness. The stirrings of a new discourse of Jewishness emerged in the 1920s, when the social sciences offered a vital, nonreligious, nonbiological, and increasingly popular language in which Jews could explain themselves to Americans. Although the other social sciences, including psychology, anthropology, economics, and political science, were part of the social-scientific turn, sociological language and models became unrivaled sources of authority, sculpting the public language that American Jewish leaders used to talk about Jewishness.[1] Over time, rabbis filtered their own pronouncements about Jewishness through sociological language and even through prominent sociologists themselves. By the World War II era, sociological Jewishness had become the central framework through which Jews translated themselves to the United States.

In its universalization of communal distinctiveness, its commonsense functionalism, and its sheer popularity, sociological language endowed Jewishness with the kind of meaning and purpose for which American rabbis—and many other Jews—had searched. Refracted through a sociological framework, Jewishness was explained as a set of collective patterns and behaviors, many of which corresponded to the circumstances of one's birth into a Jewish family. Religion, according to this model, was a functional Jewish identity marker, no different from education level, occupation, neighborhood, or friends, all of which similarly could explain where a person fit in the structure of American society.

The Jewish social-scientific turn had deep American roots. Starting in the late nineteenth century, American universities had established sociology departments, which were thriving by the early decades of the next century. In the World War II era, the federal government recognized sociology as nationally valuable and channeled money to support sociological studies and institutes in hopes that they would illuminate the path toward social harmony and national strength.[2] Simultaneously, Americans increasingly relied on experts who used empirical and rational methods to make sense of daily life.[3] The Jewish attraction to the social sciences paralleled these trends, yet it was also a response to the particular circumstances of minority and Jewish life. Already in nineteenth-century Europe, Jews had distinguished themselves as crucial contributors to the nascent field of sociology, using its methods to makes sense of the political, economic, and religious upheavals afoot.[4] Whether in Europe or the United States, sociology offered minority groups an opportunity to integrate their experiences into larger national contexts. It also became a crucial political and ideological tool that members of minority groups used to influence the direction of social change.[5]

As a group, Jews were the subjects of a number of important sociological studies, and some of the most important American sociologists by the mid-twentieth century were Jews themselves. None of this was inconsequential. The fact that Jews helped mold the field of sociology is critical to understanding why sociological language became so useful in Jews' efforts to explain themselves to the United States, although this is far from the only reason sociology appealed to American Jews. For Jews, the ineffability of Jewishness had long pressed the questions of where they belonged and which categories of personhood—bodily, communal, or religious ones—best described them. Indisputably,

Mordecai Kaplan's revolutionary reformulation of Jewishness penned in the 1920s and 1930s was an essential foundation for the social-scientific turn and predisposed rabbis—many of whom considered themselves Kaplan's students—to feel comfortable in the idioms of sociology. Jews, Kaplan wrote in *Judaism as a Civilization,* should be understood as a "distinct societal entity."[6] Drawing in no small part on early sociologists, especially Émile Durkheim, Kaplan explained that what made a Jew a Jew was not what he or she believed, but how he or she lived. Religion, in other words, was a social phenomenon, and Jewishness, larger than religion alone, was a composite of social phenomena.[7]

What sociology seemed to offer was a functional way to define Jewishness that corresponded to the lived lives of Jews. Interpreted through midcentury sociology, Jewishness was a social fact that limned the kinds of interactions Jews could have with non-Jews. The original source of difference between Jews and non-Jews did not interest sociologists as much as the daily realities of that difference. Religion understood as a social phenomenon certainly marked people as different from one another, but it did so in remarkably consistent, even universal, ways. While rendered as description, sociological explanations of Jewishness came to exercise prescriptive force. Such explanations designated only certain patterns as normal, tying those to core American values. Behaviors inconsistent with this new language could simply be dismissed as deviant.

In the post–World War II era, as rabbis and Jewish leaders explained Jewishness more and more in sociological terms, counterexplanations were overshadowed. The language of sociological Jewishness became ubiquitous and could be found in popular articles and books about Jews, in sermons and lectures delivered in front of large audiences, and on radio and television broadcasts. It seeped into the everyday ways Jews and non-Jews talked about Jewishness, and it influenced how Jews thought about themselves and their future.

The Modern Jewish and American Histories of Difference

While Jews had been grappling with how to shape a particularly American Jewish identity since their earliest settlements on American soil, the period from the end of World War I through the civil rights era saw the flourishing of Jewish attempts to create a public and synthetic

American Jewish identity. By the 1920s a significantly expanded American Jewish population had started to stabilize because of new restrictions on immigration to the United States, and as European Jewish life crumbled, it became the central body of diasporic Jewry. In many ways, this process culminated by the end of the 1960s, when all measures indicated that Jews in the United States had achieved economic, political, and cultural success, and when the next generation—the baby boomers—started to rebel against the terms of their parents' success. Over these same years, a thriving world of Jewish popular culture developed: radio broadcasts, novels and short stories, films, theater and dance productions, music, and the visual arts were instrumental in shaping Jews' encounters with non-Jews.[8] Jewish authorities and intellectuals, the focus of this book, generated self-conscious explanations of Jewishness, aware—sometimes painfully so—of the cultural landscape in which they lived. In imagining and disseminating new modes for talking about being Jewish, they hoped to control how Americans understood Jews. At the same time, they worked to reshape the available language in which Jews themselves thought and talked about Jewishness. Most important, these leaders perceived their efforts to create public, popular, and American explanations of Jewishness as essential to the long-standing project of Jewish survival itself.

Being treated in law as individuals compelled American Jews to question the terms of their collective existence: whether it served an ongoing purpose, and on what foundation it could rest. Already Jews in Enlightenment-era Europe had started wrestling with these questions, as they were (or in some cases, imagined themselves to be) on the brink of emancipation into full citizenship. Jewish Enlightenment thinkers sought to define Jews as guides for the process of modernization and, in effect, positioned Jews as avant-garde. Initiating an explosion of new cultural and political movements, many of these thinkers conceived of Jewishness as an ideology to mediate between Jews and the non-Jewish world. Yet for the most part, European nations and thinkers defined modernity in opposition to Jewish religion and culture, designating Jews as a problem or obstacle along the path toward social improvement.[9]

America, a polyglot, heterogeneous society even well before nationhood, took a very different route to modernity.[10] An open immigration policy, a thriving slave economy, a denominational—not centralized—ecclesiastical structure all made difference an indelible part of American life. Figuring out how to balance aspirations for national unity with the reality of diversity was an American obsession. The solutions that policy makers and thinkers proposed—creating hierarchies of belonging and not belonging, establishing assimilationist and Americanization programs, waging campaigns to teach Americans how to appreciate difference and how to be different—shaped the political, economic, and cultural life of the nation.[11] Jews were neither the originators nor the primary subjects of these debates about diversity. Rather, they entered into an ongoing conversation. But, as in many European countries, Jews also had a particular stake in guiding discussions about the role of difference in modernity. Jewish leaders in the United States realized that Jewish survival could not be taken for granted, though not for the same reasons that challenged it in Europe.

American citizenship law, in theory, promised to protect Jews as individuals, but it extended no similar protections over Jews as a group. The social prejudices and discriminatory policies that American Jews experienced never issued a persistent threat to Jewish survival. America's commitment to liberal individualism, however, accosted the collective dimensions of Jewish life. Jews became deeply invested in producing and revising American ideologies about social diversity, like pluralism, liberalism, and individualism, for the simple reason that these ideologies held promise to sustain or disrupt Jewish life. Scholars and commentators on American Jewish life have explained why Jews have maintained such a strong tradition of liberalism and, alternatively, why some shifted away from that liberalism.[12] Yet in drawing attention to the ways Jewish leaders crafted a public language of Jewishness, I necessarily raise a different question about Jewish liberalism: how did Jewish leaders rearticulate American liberalism and embed it in their efforts to conserve group identity?

In the same years when many Jewish thinkers were suggesting the ways that group distinctiveness could play a vital role in American democracy, most Jews were learning to look and act like Americans—through their worship styles, their consumer habits, their political loyalties, and their leisure patterns. This has been richly documented by a number of historians.[13] Absent from most studies of Jewish life in the United States, however, is a consideration of the language that Jews crafted to explain themselves into American life. While this book does not ignore popular culture sources—like films, television programs, and novels—as channels through which non-Jews encountered Jewishness, its aim is to explain the intellectual framework Jewish leaders created to make Jewishness intelligible to the American public.

By showing how Jewish leaders attempted to formulate Jewishness as an ideology to mediate between Jews' desire for acceptance into the United States and their commitment to Jewish survival, I hope to contribute to a larger historical and political discussion about how people, communities, and nations have encountered the tension between humanism or universalism on the one hand, and particularism or distinctiveness on the other.[14] American Jews were forced to be self-conscious of their differences from other Americans, but they were also given the freedom to eradicate many of those things that made them different. Jewish leaders used their stature and authority to propose a public language of Jewishness, broadly accessible and even attractive to non-Jews, that could nonetheless articulate an ongoing purpose for Jewish distinctiveness. By no stretch did Jewish leaders arrive at perfectly balanced formulations of Jewishness. Depending on one's perspective, they may have even failed miserably. Yet what interests me is how they again and again revised the terms of Jewishness, responding to demographic, political, and cultural transformations in American and Jewish life.

Who Spoke, Who Listened

The rabbis and intellectuals portrayed here were, of course, not speaking for every Jew. Nonetheless, the figures I chronicle in this book imagined that their understandings of Jewishness corresponded to realities of Jewish and American life. They also believed that, through their public authority and the positions they occupied, they could reshape those realities. Often their conversations were insular—taking place at academic conferences or meetings with other rabbis—but these rabbis and intellectuals were also committed to speaking in places where Jews and non-Jews would hear them: synagogues, college campuses, summer camps, brotherhood meetings, fund-raisers, historical commemorations, rallies, Jewish newspapers, American popular magazines, highly publicized books, radio shows, and television programs.

The fact remains that they were an elite group. While women certainly joined these public conversations about Jewishness, the majority of the historical actors in this book are men, a function of the gendered nature of the rabbinate and academy during the time in which they lived. Their efforts to explain Jewishness were enmeshed with gender ideals and anxieties. These leaders were also among a set of educated

Jews who lived at a time when many Jews were not formally educated. Furthermore, until World War II, among the rabbis involved in rethinking the language of Jewishness, Reform rabbis figured disproportionately, for many reasons. First, with two-thirds of Reform rabbis ministering to small Jewish communities outside the northeastern corridor, they were pressed more than other rabbis to explain Jewishness to curious, incurious, and sometimes hostile onlookers.[15] Second, the Reform movement had the deepest institutional roots in the United States, established before the massive wave of eastern European immigrants invigorated the American Orthodox and Conservative movements. As a result, Reform Judaism developed an infrastructure for interacting with the non-Jewish world far earlier than the other movements. Finally, ideologically and intellectually, Reform Jews tended to be more concerned with life outside a purely Jewish context.[16] By the World War II era, many Conservative rabbis took their place alongside Reform rabbis and devoted themselves to explaining the relationship between Jews and non-Jews. As hundreds of Conservative synagogues sprouted in the burgeoning suburbs, Conservative rabbis became the face of Jewishness to postwar America. Rabbis were joined by Jewish intellectuals, especially, as I argue, social researchers in the pursuit of creating Jewishness as an exportable, comprehensible, and indispensable American idea.

With attention to who was speaking, who may have been listening, and in what context, I trace how rabbis and intellectuals crafted a public language of Jewishness to communicate the relationship between Jews and the non-Jewish world in which they lived. In the first chapter, I explore two avenues through which Reform rabbis formulated Jewishness for the United States in the 1920s: their lecture tours to college campuses, and their efforts to create a Jewish missionary movement. Whether talking to predominantly non-Jewish college students or imagining the terms of missionary Judaism, these rabbis tended to define Jewishness as a set of ethical precepts that could guide anyone in better apprehending and inhabiting the world. Jewishness, they asserted, could help an individual in need just as ably as it could revitalize a nation suffering from the malaise of a brutal and seemingly meaningless war. These same years, however, saw the emergence of a new vocabulary of Jewishness formulated in sociology departments and Jewish research institutions. In chapter 2, I argue that, instead of defining Jewishness as an ethical force, sociologists observed it as a social force.

The utility of sociological Jewishness as a public discourse through which Jews could explain themselves to non-Jews became abundantly clear in the decades following the 1920s. Chapter 3 illustrates the efficacy of sociological language for explaining Jewish distinctiveness and Jewish Americanness by exploring how rabbis and sociologists talked about Jewish marital patterns in the interwar years. As sociologists increasingly equated social harmony with family harmony, many rabbis learned to position Jewish endogamy (or inmarriage) as an American value. Sociological vocabulary filtered into rabbis' normative pronouncements against intermarriage, while at the same time religious norms sculpted sociological models, eroding boundaries between a so-called sacred realm and a secular realm of human inquiry.

By World War II, Jewish leaders were convinced that Jewish survival in the United States depended on sociological explanations of Jewishness. A cadre of Conservative rabbis, the subjects of chapter 4, maintained that the ultimate purpose of Jewishness was its function outside the Jewish world. Even while some rabbis highlighted Jewish spiritual insights, they still explained Jewishness through its instrumental and social terms: Jews, as a group, served the public good by mirroring and confirming nationalistic goals. In the cold war era, a number of Jewish intellectuals were motivated to align Jewishness and national goals even more precisely. Chapter 5 describes how they helped reformulate sociological thought to reflect what some termed an essential American ethnic pattern, simultaneously recrafting the meaning of Jewishness and Americanness.

While rabbis and Jewish intellectuals put their faith in the ability of a sociological vocabulary to guard Jewish survival, some started to sense the limitations of this model of Jewishness. Chapter 6 argues that the postwar resurgence of missionary thought among some Reform rabbis and the growth of a more general outreach movement to non-Jews pushed the boundaries of Jewishness and threatened to disrupt its assumed sociological fixity. The final chapter describes a new kind of stumbling block to Jewish leaders' efforts to explain Jewishness: rising rates of intermarriage. Indicative, perhaps, of their success in explaining Jewishness as being both attractive and fundamentally American, marriages between Jews and non-Jews seemed to call into question the very project of making Jewishness knowable and familiar to the non-Jewish world. A community that had come to articulate itself as a product of social facts became embroiled in a survival crisis when those social facts proved impossible and undesirable to sustain. Living in a time when integrationist ideals pervaded American culture and politics, and bombarded by studies about ever-increasing intermarriage rates, rabbis and Jewish leaders found themselves without a vocabulary of Jewishness that could make sense of their times. This book ends with leaders searching for a new language of Jewishness and experimenting with what I term a language of volition: a language that describes Jewishness as a choice, not a social fact, not a religious mandate, and not a biological rule. Yet blood, God, and community are tough to replace or discount, as anyone thinking about Jewishness in the beginning of the twenty-first century would likely admit.

Much of this book is about changes in Jewish self-understanding. Still, Jewish leaders and intellectuals consistently drew analogies between Jewishness and the United States. The Jewish story, they proclaimed, was a metonym for the American story. Such was their faith in America's inclusiveness, and their willed attempt to subvert narrower or less tolerant narratives of America's heritage. But the same statement could produce a new mechanism of exclusion, suggesting that other Americans, particularly other new Americans, who did not follow the same social, economic, and political patterns as the Jews, were perhaps less worthy exemplars of the American story. Clearly, Jews suffered social exclusion in the United States, but this fact did not negate the parallel existence of Jewish pride and even feelings of superiority.[17] The conviction—of faith and of necessity—that Jews and Judaism had a uniquely meaningful message to give the modern world sustained Jewish life in modernity and fueled Jews' efforts to explain themselves to, and as, America.

CHAPTER I

Spiritual Missions
after the Great War

*The Reform Movement and the
Jewish Chautauqua Society*

Missionary Rabbis

Rabbi Kaufmann Kohler planned to travel to Cincinnati in April 1919. There, in the cradle of American Reform Judaism, the eminent seventy-six-year-old rabbi hoped to persuade his colleagues to return to their long-forgotten missionary task. Illness dashed his hopes. Instead of striding to the front of the hall and delivering his pronouncement to the rabbis gathered for their annual conference, he asked his friend Samuel Schulman to read his paper, "The Mission of Israel and Its Application to Modern Times."[1]

"At no time and in no country," Kohler wrote, "has the opportunity come to the Jew to again mount the watchtower of prophecy, and in working out his mission to unfold the banner of the highest idealism for all humanity as at the present . . . in America."[2] Americans living in the wake of World War I, in his estimation, were searching for a salve to widespread spiritual depression, the unhappy outcome of a war that had produced immense casualties and few answers about the fate of modern life. Here was an opportunity for a small and benighted people, the Jews, to rise to the position of spiritual and ethical guides. "Never before," Kohler explained in his 1919 address, has "the outside world [been] so eager to listen to the view of progressive Judaism and to accept its doctrines as it is today."[3]

That same year, a group of Reform rabbis traveled to American colleges and universities to explain Jews and Judaism to predominantly Christian student bodies. Their visits were sponsored by the Jewish

Chautauqua Society, a national organization that by the early twentieth century had committed itself to spreading knowledge about Jews and Judaism throughout the United States. One of the rabbis, after returning from a university visit, remarked that his lectures and class discussions offered non-Jewish Americans a chance to encounter "the outstanding features of Judaism as a spiritual force in the life of the Jew and the world."[4]

To this day, it remains common wisdom that Jews are not a missionary people. For centuries, the confluence of anti-Jewish sentiment, Jewish insularity and self-definition, and Jewish insecurity had overshadowed occasional missionary proposals and attempts. Christian doctrine made it dangerous and, in many places, illegal for Jews to proselytize.[5] But starting in the early twentieth century, Jews in the United States had an unprecedented opportunity to question the wisdom and necessity of their centuries-long disavowal of missionary activity. Undoubtedly, American Jews inherited and often elaborated on statements that dissuaded Jews from missionizing or making converts. Yet the American environment—founded on a religious "errand" or mission and eventually premised on a free market of ideas and beliefs—had the power to undermine an ideology that, throughout most of the millennium, had seemed like a necessity of survival.[6]

In the 1920s and 1930s, rabbis, particularly liberal ones, devoted energy to creating Jewish missions to non-Jews. Some of the rabbis dreamed of converting non-Jews to the beliefs and doctrines of Judaism, while others were far more intent on educating non-Jews about Jews and Judaism. Either way, they interpreted American liberalism as granting them permission to speak openly about Jews and Judaism and what they could offer to Americans. These rabbis maintained that their efforts to translate Jews and Judaism into accessible American terms were as good for the United States as they were for the Jews. In their missionary tasks, rabbis sought to ingrain Judaism at the core of American values and experiences.

Interwar rabbis employed a fundamentally religious vocabulary to convey Jewishness to Americans. Whether speaking to would-be converts or to non-Jewish students, rabbis tended to explain Judaism in terms of its beliefs, not its practices or community structure. Not coincidentally, the beliefs that the rabbis highlighted, like monotheism and ethical conduct, were easily equated with Christian ones. Yet few rabbis were interested in dissolving the barrier between Jews and Christians entirely. Instead, they contended that Jews and Judaism had particular insights from which the modern world could benefit. The rabbis found themselves stuck between an attraction to the universal dimensions of Jewish faith and a fidelity to the particular elements that defined it. Would Judaism survive in the United States because it could fit itself into certain universal religious categories and concerns, or because it offered something new? Did it reflect what already existed, or could it situate itself as avant-garde, poised to offer new alternatives to a country searching for something better? As rabbis debated Jewish missionary possibilities with one another and told their congregants about their visits to university classrooms, it was clear that, as much as the objects of their efforts were non-Jews, their audience often consisted of Jews. In addition to working out their own questions about modern Jewish life, rabbis sought to convince Jews that they had access to a special tradition, and that it was their obligation to enact it as part of—and not apart from—American public culture.

In their daily lives, the America that many Jews encountered was not the America that rabbis idealized as yearning for Jewish spiritual guidance. There was clearly a disjuncture between the rhetoric of Jewish missionary campaigns—whether educative ones or potentially proselytizing ones—and American social realities. Many rabbis hoped that a true Jewish mission could help steer American social and political policy onto a path of greater tolerance. While the language they used to talk about Jewishness was consistently grounded in religion—specifically as a set of beliefs about ethical conduct—their goals were in many ways sociological. They hoped to legitimate Jewish collective existence in the United States by communicating to all Americans the purpose of that existence. They reasoned that explaining themselves to non-Jews could serve as both the purpose and method of Jewish group survival. An interest in the relationship between the group and the larger American nation underlay their missionary activities, but few rabbis possessed the vocabulary to talk about Jewishness as a sociological identity. That vocabulary was only starting to develop in young sociology departments, and most rabbis would not become versed in it until the 1940s and 1950s. Many knew intuitively, however, that religion, no matter how high-minded its ideals and codes, was also an instrument for social acceptance in the United States. In hopes of proving that America needed Jews as much as Jews needed America, these rabbis drew Jewish survival into a broader narrative about American democracy and the national good.

A Missionary Plan

By 1919, Kaufmann Kohler was a mainstay of the American Reform movement. Born and educated in Germany, the rabbi came to the United States in 1869 and became a protégé of David Einhorn, one of the two giants of American Reform Judaism. (He also, incidentally, married Einhorn's daughter.) In 1918, Kohler published *Jewish Theology,* a seminal explanation of Judaism based on decades of reflection. Kohler, like so many other Reform leaders, was shaped and haunted by his Orthodox upbringing. Throughout his life—which ended seven years after his mission paper was read at the Central Conference of American Rabbis (CCAR)—he could never shake the importance of a Jewish community defined by tradition, symbol, and birth.[7] He spent a lifetime trying to understand how Judaism could possess universal value and still maintain a special relationship with the Jewish people, a dilemma that his theological tome could not solve. In his introduction, Kohler wrote emphatically, "Judaism, accordingly, does not denote the Jewish nationality."[8] In other words, Judaism did not depend on a specific Jewish people for its existence. Yet, many chapters later, he qualified his statement: "In fact, the soul of the Jewish people reveals a particular mingling of characteristics, a union of contrasts, which makes it especially fit for its providential mission in history."[9] The Jewish people as a collective entity, then, were of unique importance to the historical value of Judaism.

Working one's way through Kohler's treatise, it is impossible not to feel the weight of his warring ideals—the universality of Judaism on the one hand, and its deep connection to a special people on the other. The same tension coursed through Kohler's address to the Reform rabbis in attendance at the 1919 CCAR convention. At one moment, he suggested that Judaism's mission was fulfilled by the fact of Jewish survival. A specific people, the Jewish people accomplished what he termed a "passive mission" by maintaining an allegiance to God, ethics, and morality even in dark and inhospitable times and acting, therefore, as an example for the world.[10] If the passive mission signaled the value of a distinctive Jewish community, however, the active mission—characterized by efforts to draw non-Jews toward Judaism—implied a far more universal Jewish purpose. For Judaism's mission to be truly fulfilled, Kohler explained, it had to synthesize passive and active, distinctive and universal. The passive mission sanctioned the ongoing survival of a small group of people; the active mission was the rightful claim of a universal system.

Mission theology, a component of Reform ideology since its early development in nineteenth-century Germany, was a product of the merging of Enlightenment thought with traditional notions about Jews as God's chosen people.[11] Some Jews found it uncomfortable or impossible to square Jewish claims of chosenness with their aspirations to modern citizenship. For others, however, the task of reconciling these two ideas grounded a new and modern theory of Jewish identity.[12] Understanding chosenness as a mandate placed on Jews to improve the world, and not to live as an insular and law-bound community, enabled late-eighteenth- and nineteenth-century Enlightenment and Reform thinkers to assert a bond between Judaism and modernity. Termed mission theology, the notion of an outward-looking and world-bettering Jewish purpose gave Reform thinkers a way to explain why Judaism should thrive, not recede, in the modern world.

Kohler, drawing on his intellectual forbears, sought to prove that the Jewish mission was not simply a modern fantasy or a product of apologetics. Instead, he argued, it was at the core of Jewish tradition. The teachings of the prophet Isaiah, who had instructed the Jews to spread their "light" throughout the world, provided the ultimate proof for Kohler.[13] Even during the times when Jews were persecuted and tortured, Kohler maintained, simply by remaining Jewish they had fulfilled Isaiah's commandment. Yet as Jews emerged from centuries of oppression, they had the opportunity to illuminate the world with their Judaism, both by living it themselves and by sharing it. For Kohler, like others who followed him, anchoring the mission to the long sweep of Jewish history proved its authenticity and power. Kohler's intentions, however, went beyond a mere textual and historical analysis of Judaism and the Jewish people.

Judaism, in Kohler's mind, was a gift to the United States. He hoped that, through a missionary program, Jews would learn that their Jewishness itself was a service to the United States that would spur a new era of tolerance and ethics. Already, starting in the last years of the nineteenth century, Kohler had worked to translate (quite literally) Jewish ideas into American life. As part of a committee formed by the Jewish Publication Society, Kohler and several other prominent rabbis endeavored to create "a new and popular English rendition of the book which the Jews have given to the world, the Bible."[14] By claiming authority over the Bible—really, the Hebrew Bible—these men hoped to position Jews and Judaism at the core of American values and even American Christianity. For Kohler, the missionary idea held the same promise.

FIGURE 1. Kaufmann Kohler and the editors of the Jewish Publication Society working on the English translation of the Hebrew Bible, November 1915. Left to right: Joseph Jacobs, Solomon Schechter, Max Margolis, Cyrus Adler, David Philipson, Kohler, and Samuel Schulman. Courtesy of the Jacob Rader Marcus Center of the American Jewish Archives.

Rabbi Kohler's plea for a new missionary movement, however, was marked by an idealism and abstraction far removed from the daily circumstances of American and Jewish life.[15] While he highlighted religion as the crux of who Jews were, most Americans apprehended race as essential to identifying Jewish and, more generally, human difference. Jews themselves had helped construct racial typologies that classified Jewishness as a biological variant. Indeed, race language was a useful way to talk about Jewishness: it demanded little in the way of specific practice from Jews, and it seemed to guarantee Jewish survival as long as Jews continued to reproduce themselves.[16] Race assumptions marked human difference in powerful ways, but they were also often employed to naturalize hierarchies among social groups. By the mid-nineteenth century, popular racial terminology in the United States characterized Jews as being among the most inferior of all classes of people, rivaled only by African Americans, who stood even lower on the racial hierarchy. Many so-called race scientists suggested that Jews were unable to escape this bitter fate of their biology and, thus, there was little they could do to become true Americans.[17]

Kohler's attraction to the Jewish mission was fueled by his desire to unseat a racial model of Jewishness to which many Jews and non-Jews subscribed. In line with his Enlightenment-era predecessors, he suggested that Jews would no longer suffer from social exclusion or allegations of clannishness if they could only convince Americans that they were members of a religion, not a race. Simply put, a non-Jew pledging himself or herself to Judaism would serve as irrefutable proof that race had nothing to do with Jewishness. Additionally, by highlighting the openness of Judaism to converts, a missionary-style Judaism would more closely hew to the Christian majority's presuppositions about how religion worked.

By 1969, fifty long years in the future, Kohler prophesized, Judaism would "become the common property of the American people."[18] Kohler's idyllic view of American liberalism and tolerance mirrored his proposed version of a permeable and world-enlightening Judaism. By the second decade of the twentieth century, the progressivism of liberal America embodied a contradiction that made the comparison between it and a Jewish mission apt, although perhaps not for the reasons Kohler had intended. American progressives embraced Americanism as a force of universal good, even as they simultaneously patrolled the boundaries of Americanism.[19] In 1919, when Kohler suggested that the Reform movement adopt a missionary mentality, the United States Congress had already passed the first of three immigration restriction acts in the name of preserving true Americanism, a remarkably less elastic category when the economy sank and antiforeign fears erupted. American liberalism and liberal Judaism proudly made universal claims that fueled adherents' sense of superiority and their missionary mandates, whether to heathen people throughout the world or non-Jews in the United States. Yet both systems defined themselves by the boundaries they maintained.[20]

Kohler's encounter with American liberalism gave him hope in the viability of a universal doctrine, but it also chafed against his missionary fantasy. Could missionary Judaism thrive without challenging American liberalism and its voluntarism, freedom of affiliation, and individualism? In one rhetorical flourish, Kohler instructed his rabbi colleagues to abandon their defensive tactics and to instead aggressively assert "our birthright."[21] He was clear about what this meant: "Let the world learn our view of Christianity and its founder. Let the New Testament teachings be shown in the true light of historical development and so-called Christian civilization presented from the Jewish point of view."[22] But, within only a few paragraphs—as if he had taken a deep breath, wiped his brow, and reconsidered—his paper admonished the audience of rabbis that divine truth can be "reflected in many systems of belief and thought, just as the diamond reflects light by its many facets."[23] There was no singular path to salvation, to the "mountain of God," and the mission was perhaps best enacted "within our own circle."[24] Kohler realized that, if the missionary idea clashed with American values, it had no hope of succeeding. The Jewish mission had to be an American mission as well.

Listeners that day were able to hear what they wished in Kohler's paper. For some, it was a call to the cause of social justice, a call to fix the world. For others, it was a reminder to attend first and foremost to their own congregants and educate their own people. And for still others, it was a clear statement about the seamless union between Judaism and Americanism. One rabbi responded enthusiastically, "I believe in Judaism and I think the principles which it teaches are such that it can become universal. I believe in Americanism because I find therein also the principles which are destined to become universal."[25]

"Let us not waste our efforts on discussion only," another rabbi remarked. "Let us try to do something definite, something that will stimulate thought—something that will bring results."[26] Doing "something" was difficult, even dangerous. Rabbis listening to Kohler's paper were living on the brink of a new decade that historians have termed the "Tribal Twenties" for its antiforeign sentiment, anti-Catholicism, antisemitism, and racism.[27] From the publication of the scurrilous *Protocols of the Elders of Zion* in Henry Ford's *Dearborn Independent* to the new immigration restriction acts, the 1920s were hardly an ideal time to suggest Jewish outspokenness.[28] Despite some of the rabbis' grand pronouncements to the contrary, most Americans did not seem eager to glean wisdom, truth, and perhaps a new religion from the Jews in their midst, and few Jews were prepared to step into a missionary role.

Four months after the 1919 CCAR meeting, the *Literary Digest*, a Christian journal, published "Why the Jews Are Not Missionaries." The editorial reported that Jews do not and have never sought prose-lytes and praised a recent article from the Jewish press for disavowing missionary activity. The *Literary Digest* concluded: "It is the zeal [of missionary faiths] which has brought into the world so much misery, and cruelty, and torture."[29] Jews, of course, knew the trauma that missionary movements could unleash. Religions that claimed exclusive access to salvation often inspired their adherents to acts of coercion and violence. By the 1920s, some liberal Christians, like the editorial writers of the *Literary Digest,* rejected missionary work and instead devoted their energy to "goodwill" or interfaith efforts.[30] Yet the fact remained that, by the same decade, almost every major urban area had Christian missions directed to Jews. Ever since Jews had created settlements in the United States, rabbis of all stripes had opposed such Christian proselytizing efforts.[31] Support for a passive mission, a mission that was about setting an example to the world, not leading or converting the world, was deeply connected to an aversion to Christian missionary practices. One Jewish commentator in 1925 explained, "The Jew's mission on earth is 'Religion.' . . . As such, he is the divinely appointed missionary: and cannot, of course, be confounded with the type of the perverted convert, blossoming forth into a missionary: whose palms have been greased with silver: and from whose lips 'bribery' talks— whose very presence is offensive!"[32]

A Jewish mission of any kind would be meaningless unless Jews could explain their purpose to the non-Jewish world. Rabbi Samuel Goldenson of Pittsburgh, who attended the 1919 CCAR conference, had come home excited and troubled by the missionary idea. He struggled to understand how one group of people could be elected to communicate truth to the rest of the world. It seemed a mark of utmost conceit, he admitted to his congregation in 1923: "You and I should have a mission," he asked. "Think of it. . . . Why it is too arrogant, too conceited and egotistical."[33] He concluded instead that the best mission was one that led by example: "I say to the extent in which we incorporate the consciousness of God in our businesses, in our human relationships, in the things we say, the things we feel, the things we do, to that extent we are missionaries."[34]

In 1924, the *Menorah Journal,* an intellectual Jewish journal, published a forum about the Jewish mission. Samuel Schulman, Kohler's friend who read his address to the CCAR, endorsed the idea of a Jewish mission. "It means for us American Jews," he explained, "the carrying into our American national life . . . of the heritage of [our] religious community."[35] He noted enthusiastically, much like Kohler, that a "glorious prospect" existed for Jews to spread their Judaism now when "the world is hungering for a new revelation of religious sentiment."[36] Yet the forum's other writer, an author and Zionist, saw the Jewish mission as a thin veneer for assimilation. Really, he wrote, the Jewish mission was a sorry attempt to portray Judaism as just another variety of Americanism. He elaborated: "'Patriotism of the Jew,' 'The Jews as Philanthropist,' 'Jewish Americanism,' the hundred-per-cent-this-or-that Jew; who has not been shamed and humiliated by these topics in book and speech, article and sermon throughout the land?" In the act of explaining "that we are even as other men," true "Jewish characteristics" were abandoned, and, the author concluded darkly, the Jew remained no more loved than before.[37]

Irrefutably, none of the rabbis who listened to Kohler's paper heard a call to usher non-Jews into the ritual or legal (halakhic) patterns of Jewish life. Few Reform rabbis in the 1920s were themselves interested in the visible symbols of Judaism—like wearing a yarmulke or keeping kosher. Religion, they suggested, should be based on creed or belief, not arcane practices. Furthermore, the assumption that Judaism could have universal import undermined the specific practices of Judaism that depended on a distinctive, law-bound Jewish community.

Often when rabbis spoke about a Jewish mission, they did so in the absence of real overtures to non-Jews. Still, the notion of a Jewish mission was not easily dismissed, because it spoke to a deep concern, particularly among Reform rabbis, about whether Jews could communicate who they were and what they did. If Jews were unable to convey these things to America, then they would either be boxed into categories not of their choosing, or they would slip mutely into the world, unable to explain what made them different or special.

A Guide for Missionary Judaism

American rabbis were attracted to the idea of missionary Judaism because it offered an opportunity for them to redefine Jews and Judaism for themselves as much as for the audience of Americans they may have imagined. In 1924, a group of Reform rabbis, constituted as the Committee on the Preparation of a Manual for the Instruction of Proselytes, had been asked to develop new guidelines for what a non-Jew would need to do and believe in order to become a Jew. A desire to spread Judaism beyond the existing boundaries of the Jewish people rested at the foundation of the manual. The committee members emphasized that their goal was "to show to those who are interested in becoming one with us in religious fellowship that our religion is whole-heartedly open to anyone who wishes to make it their guide of life, labor and hope."[38] The manual the committee presented at the 1925 convention of Reform rabbis had three main sections: the history of Judaism's attitudes toward non-Jews, the cardinal teachings and rituals of Judaism, and the conversion service. More than anything else, the manual was a text about self-definition. In outlining conversion requirements, the rabbis sought to characterize Jewishness as universally accessible—in other words, not determined by birth—yet distinctive from the faith, generally Christianity, in which a convert would have grown up. The result of this double-sided agenda was that Jewish practices—the demands made on the daily life of a Jew—were diminished in favor of large, often abstract principles that were then designated as somehow particular to Judaism.

Even Reform rabbis, who by their very affiliation admitted to a desire to change the form of Judaism, consistently lodged their vision of change in an overarching narrative of historical continuity and authenticity. It was imperative to the committee members, as it had been to Kohler, to prove that their openness to accepting converts, and even their desire to seek them out, had historical and traditional scriptural backing. The rabbis all concurred with the committee's suggestion that a historical section be included in the manual, and that it conclude "with a strong statement in clear and simple language inviting those to whom Judaism is the highest expression of religious life to join us and be heart and soul with us in our faith."[39]

The committee's recommendation that the historical section also offer an explanation of why Jewish proselytizing activities had waned over the past millennium, however, generated debate among the rabbis. Only when the opportunity that modern America offered Jews was viewed against the years of ugly repression, some rabbis believed, could one appreciate it and account for the many centuries during which Jews eschewed any missionary purpose. Rabbi Schulman, who spoke with an air of authority in the discussions about a Jewish mission—after all, he had read Kohler's germinal paper and had been a close friend of the now ailing rabbi (Kohler died the next year)—objected strenuously. Reviewing a draft of the manual as late as 1927, he wrote to the chair of the committee, "I am uncompromisingly opposed to any attempt to write a history of the Jew . . . for this Manual. . . . If a convert, in good faith, accepts what we teach him of our religion, we can leave the reading of Jewish history to him or her."[40] The manual, Schulman believed, should offer only "positive statements."[41] Nonetheless, in the years to

follow, rabbis wove historical claims into their missionary pronouncements, both to argue that Jews had once been a missionary people and
to explain why they had abandoned the task for so many years.

In the section of the manual that addressed the procedure of conversion, the rabbis were pushed to define the precise boundary between
Jews and non-Jews. As an unequivocal indication of their commitment
to making Judaism easily accessible and palatable to Americans, the
framers suggested creating a new ceremony that would eliminate the
traditional question asked of converts: "Are you ready to sever your
allegiance to the religion in which you were born and reared?" "Isn't it
enough," they asked beseechingly, "to be one with the new religious
love without disclaiming the old?"[42] For many rabbis, even those who
heartily endorsed a Jewish missionary agenda, this suggestion that converts need not publicly disavow their former faith went too far. These
rabbis may not have been particularly concerned about what one did
once he or she became Jewish, but they did believe that one had to
commit fully to being Jewish. In the end, the committee compromised
and rewrote the traditional question. Now converts were asked to
"renounce," not "sever" their allegiance to, the faith in which they
were born.[43]

When asked how many teachings of Judaism a potential convert
should be expected to learn, the framers curtly responded, "These
should be as few as possible."[44] They proposed a brief overview of the
Sabbath and Jewish holidays, but urged that the manual omit any mention of the laws of Kashruth or the differences between the Orthodox,
Conservative, and Reform movements. When the CCAR reconvened in
1927 to finalize the manual, two rabbis fought a losing battle to include
a section on keeping kosher and another on the different movements in
contemporary Judaism. Theology and doctrine, they argued, were
hardly the most important concerns for converts to Judaism, who more
often than not elected to become Jewish because they were marrying or
had married a Jew. One explained, "Such a person wants to know how
to conduct a Jewish home for the purpose of establishing happier relationships with husband or with wife."[45] Even Schulman had acknowledged this when he supported adding a statement about the practice of
lighting candles on the Sabbath. He wrote to the chair of the manual
committee, "There should be some reference made, especially as most
of our converts are women who marry Jewish men (what is the use of
beating around the bush?), to the beautiful custom of kindling the
Sabbath light."[46]

Perhaps what one *did* as a Jew, and particularly what a Jewish woman did, and not what one believed or did not believe, was the true education that a convert needed. Rabbi Julian Morgenstern, the American-born president of the Reform movement's Hebrew Union College, was incredulous when he heard the suggestion to include a section on keeping kosher: "Since when do we Reform rabbis believe or contend that the essential quality for maintaining a Jewish home is to observe the laws of Kashruth?"[47] Indeed, most of the rabbis were concerned with presenting Judaism as an accessible religion that offered ethical wisdom without nitpicking about what one ate. Furthermore, few of them were particularly interested in attracting or instructing female converts, despite demographic realities. They assumed that women, especially those who converted for marriage, would likely do little to enhance the intellectual and spiritual vigor of Judaism in early-twentieth-century America.[48]

Practice was minimized because by its very nature it was not universal. In fact, much of Jewish practice focused on drawing distinctions—dietary, physical, spatial—between Jews and others.[49] Instead, the rabbis sought to articulate the most general principles that they believed guided liberal Judaism, including revelation, ethical monotheism, "the spiritual unity of Israel," and most vaguely, "Judaism's place and purpose in the world."[50] The framers of the manual asserted that these core ideas would distinguish Judaism from Christianity and teach potential converts that the moral and ethical ideals that Christianity claimed as its own "are all of Jewish origins."[51] In a sense, then, a convert from Christianity would not need to relearn these teachings; instead, he or she would be receiving them in their original and, the rabbis believed, truer form. In this way, the rabbis attempted to move one step closer to realizing Kohler's prediction that Judaism would eventually become the common inheritance of all Americans. The new manual represented the rabbis' belief in the instrumentality of Judaism for the survival of the Jewish people in the modern world. They placed Judaism at the center of modern-day ethics and formulated it as a guide for Jews and all people wishing to live a moral life.

In his 1934 book *Judaism as a Civilization*, Jewish thinker Mordecai Kaplan encapsulated the Reform movement when he described it as seeking to shift "the center of gravity from interest in the hereafter to interest in transforming the world we live in."[52] Certainly, the goal of world betterment was not the exclusive possession of liberal Judaism. The Jewish principle of *tikkun olam*, literally "repairing the world," appeared as an essential value in more orthodox strands of Judaism as well. For example, in a 1920 article about the future of Orthodox Judaism in the United States, Rabbi Henry Pereira Mendes pledged it to the task of "world up-lift."[53] Yet Reform leaders, along with many liberal Christians, drew religion closer to this-worldly human progress. These religious modernists argued that God and religion were meaningful only if they could address immanent concerns and help human beings figure out how to encounter their world.[54] Judaism could do so by extending itself throughout the world, a strategy that would ensure Jewish survival without exacting Jewish insularity and segregation as its price.

Critics, who generally aligned with some form of orthodoxy, accused religious modernism of replacing God with human progress and culture and, ultimately, sounding the death knell of religion. Although not an orthodox of any variety, Kaplan similarly feared that, in "reconstruct[ing] its teachings in the light of the new developments of human life" and viewing history as "a progressive movement toward the kingdom of God," Reform Judaism had ceded its own sustainability.[55] Kaplan interpreted the Jewish mission as a last-ditch effort on the part of Reform rabbis to give Jews a purpose for surviving: to spread the ideals of Judaism, conceived as the highest human truths, to the world. Those ideals, when divorced from the daily practices of being Jewish, often appeared ethereal and, in fact, were rather difficult to communicate. Yet Reform rabbis hoped that, as much as Jews might sustain a mission to the non-Jewish world, the mission would sustain the Jews.[56] They were not alone in perceiving the generative force of a Jewish mission.

The Jewish Chautauqua Society

From its origins in 1893, the Jewish Chautauqua Society (JCS) similarly believed Judaism was driven and sustained by a mission. Although in its earliest phases the organization directed its efforts toward educating Jews about Judaism, by the first decades of the twentieth century it reconstituted its purpose as providing non-Jews with accessible explanations of and experiences with Jewishness. Founded by a Reform rabbi and led mainly by Jews affiliated with the Reform movement, the JCS understood the Jewish purpose in the United States as primarily educative. This conviction was grounded in the social circumstances of Jewish life: unless non-Jews learned to appreciate Judaism, Jews could expect to be the objects of hatred and intolerance as they had been so often in the past. In proposing that Jews had a mandate to educate the world, JCS leaders also created a framework for characterizing Jews and Judaism as indispensable to progress and modernity. JCS leaders, much like missionary rabbis, explained that Jews were heirs to a system that could improve the world, and therefore they were obligated to share it. Similar to the Reform movement's missionary proposals, the philosophy of the JCS respun the traditional doctrine of Jewish chosenness into a doctrine of universalism, not exclusivity.

People familiar with the history of Methodism, adult education, or Christian revivalism will no doubt recognize that something markedly not Jewish—the Methodist Chautauqua Society established in 1874—had been converted into something distinctly Jewish. In 1892, Henry Berkowitz, a Reform rabbi in Kansas City, was invited to attend the Christian Chautauqua Society's summer program in western New York.[57] He was impressed by the group's popular success and its strategy of pairing educational activities with leisure ones. The next year, Berkowitz received permission to use the Chautauqua name for a new Jewish organization that would wed turn-of-the-century American middle-class culture to the "rich sources of Jewish lore and the treasures of Jewish wisdom and experience."[58] For two decades, the JCS invited middle-class Jews to vacation on the sunny shores of New Jersey while taking courses about Judaism, learning how to create Jewish reading circles, and receiving training to teach religious school.

Testimony to the success of the summer programs was the celebrity they drew. In late July 1900, the victorious war general and president-to-be Theodore Roosevelt traveled to Atlantic City to address participants at that year's summer institute. He spoke to an adoring crowd about his experience commanding the indomitable Rough Rider battalion during the Spanish-American War.[59] According to a summary of his speech, the future president described his unit as "made up of men of all different creeds, men of every occupation, rich and poor. All were treated alike."[60] The process of Americanization, according to Roosevelt, had succeeded brilliantly. Difference mattered little compared to the unity of purpose that his troops felt.

The early leaders and members of the JCS shared Roosevelt's passion for Americanization. They were on the whole German-born or German-descended Jews who tended to be middle class and affiliated with the Reform movement.[61] Like other Jews who had come to the United States in the middle decades of the nineteenth century, many of them

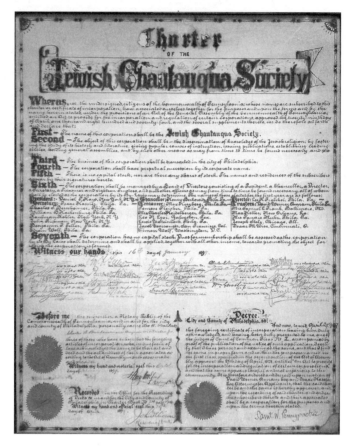

FIGURE 2. The charter of the Jewish Chautauqua Society. Photo by Eric Corwin.

felt ambivalent about the recent influx of eastern European immigrants. Some attempted to distance themselves from the new immigrants, but others believed this was impossible or irresponsible. These German Jews hoped instead that, through education and social services, new immigrants could be uplifted to American middle-class standards and would not taint their own precarious status in American society.[62] Yet the truth of the matter was that the JCS was most active in areas of the country— Akron, Ohio, and Wheeling, West Virginia, for example—far outside the zones of eastern-European Jewish settlement. Other Jewish benevolent organizations, like the National Council of Jewish Women (also founded in 1893), were clearly better situated and equipped than the JCS to address the needs of new Jewish immigrants.[63]

The JCS avoided an almost certain fate of institutional decay by creating a new mission: to educate non-Jews about Jews and Judaism. When JCS leaders decided to shift their attention from Jewish to non-Jewish audiences, they did not repudiate their earlier concern with Americanization. Instead the leaders of the organization came to believe that Americanization had two vectors: Jews adapted to American culture, but they also could mold American culture to embrace Jews and their Judaism. In 1909, a rabbi from New Jersey spoke to the members of the JCS about "the mission idea in Judaism" and suggested that Jews could guarantee their ongoing survival only if they felt propelled by a sense of duty to share their gifts with the broader world.[64]

The Jewish Chautauqua Society was not alone in believing that Jews would gain a more secure position in the United States if they learned to reach out beyond the Jewish world. In the early decades of the twentieth century, organizations like the American Jewish Committee and the Anti-Defamation League were formed to defend Jewish rights in the United States and abroad.[65] Unlike these organizations, however, the JCS did not systematically study antisemitism or lobby for legal measures to guard against the infringement of Jewish civil liberties. Instead, in narrowing its work to a specific population—youth—and to specific locales—universities (and later summer camps)—it attempted to offer the next generation of non-Jews firsthand encounters with Jews and Judaism.

It was one thing to decide that non-Jews should learn about Jews and Judaism, but it was quite another to find non-Jews who were willing to do so. Fortunately for the leaders of the JCS, a non-Jew offered them an initial point of entry into the non-Jewish academic world. The chain of events leading to the first JCS lecture to non-Jewish students enabled the organization to avoid stereotypes of Jewish pushiness or aggression: the JCS simply answered the call of duty.[66] In 1909, Rabbi Berkowitz, the founder of the JCS, was put in contact with Philander P. Claxton, the eventual U.S. commissioner of education under Presidents Taft and Wilson. At the time, Claxton was head of the Summer School of the South at the University of Tennessee in Knoxville. A longtime admirer of Judaism who claimed to have realized the "genius of the Jew" from reading Jewish Publication Society books, Claxton wanted his students, mainly public school teachers, to learn about Jews and Judaism from a respected Jewish scholar.[67] News of Claxton's request reached Berkowitz, who then dispatched Julian Morgenstern, a young rabbi then and an instructor at the Hebrew Union College, to Tennessee.

Rabbi Morgenstern taught two courses—one on Jewish history and the other on the prophets—and delivered a series of public lectures during the summer of 1909. In his midsummer report back to the JCS, Morgenstern was upbeat: "I believe judging from small signs and indications here and there, that I have succeeded in winning the approbation of a great many people here."[68] Anticipating the later policies of the JCS, he tried to avoid controversial topics in his lectures while still teaching students about the positive contributions of Judaism and the Jewish people. Yet according to other sources, Morgenstern's visit unleashed a torrent of prejudice by local groups who felt that "the presence of a rabbi on the campus was an insult to Christianity and demanded that he be sent away."[69] These reactions may have only strengthened Claxton's resolve to educate his students about Jews and Judaism. The steady stream of Jews immigrating to the United States was a guarantee that more and more non-Jews, even those living below the Mason-Dixon Line, would come into contact with Jews and Judaism.[70] Yet non-Jews had limited opportunities to learn about Jews in the early twentieth century. In 1909, when Claxton approached the JCS, no American universities offered a systematic way to study the Jewish people or Judaism. A non-Jew might have taken a course on the Hebrew Bible or turned toward philology and the study of Hebrew. But until the 1960s, most non-Jewish university students would have been hard pressed to study the history, beliefs, and practices of the Jews.[71]

Whether or not he sugarcoated his experiences, Morgenstern, later the president of Hebrew Union College, convinced Chautauqua leaders to develop a full-fledged program to send rabbis to lecture and teach courses at universities. The process was slow, interrupted by World War I. In the summer of 1919, however, the JCS dispatched rabbis to lecture at ten university summer programs. One of the rabbis, Louis Wolsey, traveled from his home in Cleveland to the University of Michigan, where he delivered three lectures about the misrepresentation of Jews in literature. Expertly navigating the plotlines of a number of books, Wolsey offered the students, in his words, "a specifically Jewish interpretation, to show the essentially Jewish basis of each subject, the Jewish message which they convey and the Jewish doctrine they illustrate."[72] He concluded that Jews were "normal" and did not embody the exaggerations of their fictional counterparts. Yet he also explained to the students that Jews had special insight about the world that they could use to "teach tolerance."[73]

The JCS tread dangerous ground by seeking American acceptance by enhancing Jewish visibility and, often, emphasizing the superior wisdom of Jewish traditions. Henry Ford's newspaper, the *Dearborn Independent,* alleged in May 1921, "The Jewish Chautauqua, which works almost exclusively through colleges and universities, together with Bolshevism in art, science, religion, economics and sociology, are driving straight through the Anglo-Saxon traditions and landmarks of our race of students."[74] As objectionable as the newspaper's perspective was, the writer correctly perceived that the JCS was trying to claim American values as being concordant with and even emerging from Jewish values. Like the Reform rabbis who advocated a missionary agenda, the leaders of the Chautauqua Society hoped that their Judaism, presented as a cultured and modern value system, would serve as a pathway to American middle-class respectability. Such a conception of Judaism would replace the increasingly prevalent images of Jews as impoverished, uneducated, primitive, and clannish.

Throughout the 1920s, the JCS worked to present itself as an authoritative voice on Jews and Judaism; publicity statements described the group as representing "national, not sectional, Judaism."[75] For the most part, however, the rabbis were Reform, and, already in the 1920s, Jewish institutional life was moving toward greater Jewish fragmentation and denominationalism, so claims of unified Jewish values or beliefs were certainly overblown.[76] In the late 1930s, the JCS merged with the National Federation of Temple Brotherhoods, an official organ of the Reform movement. Still, the JCS wanted to preserve the semblance of a unified Judaism that Americans could come to understand and appreciate as a coherent entity.

From the start of the JCS's efforts to send rabbis to lecture at universities, Jeannette Miriam Goldberg, a Texas-born Jew and a Vassar graduate, had supervised rabbis' visits and made certain that they did not present any potentially controversial or divisive views.[77] In 1923, Goldberg asked Rabbi Abraham Feldman to deliver a series of lectures at Pennsylvania State College. Feldman, who lived in Philadelphia, agreed to take the journey halfway across the state. The opportunity to speak at a university appealed to him as it did to many rabbis who felt attracted to the prestige of university life. The JCS invitation, however, came with clear parameters. In a letter she sent to every rabbi before his visit to a university, Goldberg explained, "The specific purpose of the Society in introducing these lectures to the various Universities is to promote a better understanding of Jews and Judaism, and to emphasize our desire to avoid controversial and doctrinal discussions. . . . We make this request in view of the fact that in the past some of our lecturers have created discussions of this [controversial] nature, not to the advantage of the work."[78]

Goldberg promptly rejected the first two lecture topics Rabbi Feldman proposed for his Penn State visit. Both—one about Jewish sects and another about Jews in the United States—were too "controversial" and not "in accordance with academic procedure."[79] Doubting that Feldman was capable of choosing appropriate subject matter, Goldman suggested two new topics: "Jews of Spain as Cultural Forces" and "Many Sided Contributions of Jews to the Discovery of America." She even outlined precisely what he might say: "You could take up the astronomical work done by Jews in Spain, of which Columbus availed himself; the money for Columbus' expedition, which came from Jews; the Jewish personnel in the crew of Columbus; and, finally, the theory that Columbus himself was a Jew, and, if not a Jew, at least of Jewish extraction."[80] Feldman was insulted by her suggestions, and he tartly responded that the "Committee" seemed a "bit shy" about discussing important matters. Furthermore, the two subjects she had proposed were "worn threadbare" and "meaningless."[81] Nevertheless, he agreed to avoid any topic that could spur controversy. In late June 1924, Rabbi Feldman took a train and then a bus to State College and delivered a lecture on Jews in Russia and Poland and a second on Jewish immigrants in the United States. The audience, he concluded, had learned a great deal from his much-revised presentations.[82]

Throughout the 1920s, Jewish Chautauqua rabbis tended to highlight the contributions that Jews and Judaism made to the United States. They described these contributions as embodying the essence of Judaism and portrayed Jews as a people fundamentally committed to enhancing American values. Specific Jewish practices or behaviors were almost never mentioned, since they seemed unconnected—and perhaps antithetical—to Jewish attempts to prove themselves indispensable to the United States. Rather the more universal elements of Judaism—its conception of God or its ethical insights—and the most triumphant renderings of Jewish history stood for the whole of Jewishness.

Guardians of American Democracy

By the mid-1930s, JCS rabbis had lectured at more than forty universities.[83] As the threats of totalitarianism and fascism rose in Europe, they honed their explanations of Jewishness to reflect the ideals of American democracy. Rabbis explained to their non-Jewish students that Jews and Jewish ideals were some of the staunchest defenders of democracy, pointing to traditional Jewish texts and Jewish history as the foundations for democracy. They also argued that the very existence of Jews in the United States was proof of the enduring strength of America's democratic values. Jews, in other words, helped the United States recognize and live up to the ideals of democracy. A decade later, Louis Finkelstein, a leader of the Conservative movement, would pursue a similar logic, though with a new vocabulary for talking about Jewishness.

JCS rabbis' presentations of Jewishness were not about the daily or sociological realities of being Jewish; they instead focused on equating an idealized version of Judaism and an idealized version of the United States. The more that Jews could formulate their own survival as a manifestation of American ideals, the less likely they were to be blamed for national woes and the more likely their rights were to be safeguarded. A few rabbis went so far as to chastise certain American leaders, especially those who stifled individual freedoms, for weakening democracy. For example, in the summer of 1935, Rabbi Adolph Fink, a thirty-six-year-old Hillel director at the University of Washington, spoke to university students throughout the Northwest. He alerted them to the dangerous drift away from true democracy exhibited in government-sanctioned efforts to silence dissent. If these trends were left unchecked, Rabbi Fink warned, then "you have Fascism in the making."[84] Fink explained that Jews were particularly sensitive to encroachments on true democracy, since their traditions formed the core of democratic ideals.

JCS rabbis, much like advocates for missionary Judaism, frequently explained that the Torah and other traditional Jewish texts were blueprints for democracy. Rabbi Theodore Lewis, another JCS lecturer in 1935, informed a group of Iowa students that the Talmud resembled the American Constitution in both form and content. Speaking from an evidently nonorthodox perspective, he argued that both documents were flexible and responded remarkably well to social change.[85] Another rabbi spoke about the social teachings of the Hebrew Bible to students at the University of Virginia; and at the University of Kentucky, students listened to a lecture titled "The Conception of Social Justice as Found in the Bible."[86]

As much as the Chautauqua rabbis set their sights on non-Jews, they also participated in reeducating Jews about what it meant to be Jewish. It was, indeed, one of the rabbis' tasks to reconstruct the way Jews thought about being Jewish in the United States. Unless Jews came to

accept and reflect the values that Chautauqua rabbis described as particularly Jewish, then a gap would grow between the realities of Jewish
life and the outward presentation of it. One of the primary ways that
Chautauqua rabbis educated Jews was through frequent fund-raising
events. Usually held at a synagogue, each event generally showcased a
rabbi reenacting a lecture he had given to non-Jewish students. Jews in
attendance were then asked to open their wallets and give generously so
that non-Jews "in practically every state of the union" could have the
opportunity to learn about "your history, your value to America, eco-
nomically and as a citizen and patriot as well as a Jew."[87] By occupying
the role of a non-Jew, then, Jews were taught about what it meant to be
a Jew. They learned, for example, that of all Jewish beliefs, traditions,
and practices, the ones that rabbis most often highlighted had to do
with monotheism and ethical conduct. Far less important were the rituals of Jewish observance and the daily practices of Jewish life.

Missions and the Everyday

The fact of the matter was that the Reform rabbis who advocated missionary Judaism and the leaders and rabbis involved in the Jewish
Chautauqua Society were not particularly interested in giving
Americans a glimpse into the daily life of a Jew. Both envisioned the
long history and scriptural tradition of the Jews as the true foundation
of the relatively young nation and, thus, Judaism as the basis of
American values. These early-twentieth-century rabbis and Jewish leaders believed that, by Judaizing America, they could Americanize Jews.

A commitment to ensuring Jewish survival rested at the foundation
of missionary fantasies and Chautauqua activities. Yet both movements
created explanations of Jewishness that seemed destined to undermine
the existence of a distinctive Jewish people. What consistently mediated
against the dissolution of Jewish life into a set of universal ethical ideas
were the daily realities that Jews experienced as a non-Christian minority in the United States. Indeed, these realities gave rabbis license to
draw close parallels between Judaism and Christianity and between
Judaism and American values without worrying about actually eroding
the boundaries of Jewish life.

Neither missionary rabbis nor Chautauqua rabbis articulated the
elements of Jewishness that continued to distinguish Jews from non-
Jews. The professions that Jews entered, the family relationships they

developed, the neighborhoods they lived in, the languages they spoke, and the social activities they participated in: none of these were defined solely through religion or ethics, yet all of them were part of Jewish life in the United States. Missionary rabbis and Chautauqua rabbis and leaders were often self-conscious about their neglect of these sociological elements of Jewishness. Echoing Jewish Enlightenment beliefs, many thought that Jews would be accepted in the United States only if they defined their differences in religious terms and if they simultaneously formulated Judaism as consonant with American ideals. The vocabulary of sociology was still in its infancy in the United States. Very few rabbis, at least until the mid-1930s, had access to words—such as *culture, peoplehood,* or *ethnic identity*—that would eventually enable them to construct alternative models of Jewishness and draw new kinds of parallels between Jewishness and Americanness.

In the same years that American rabbis worked to explain that Judaism, as a set of religious and ethical ideals, rested at the foundation of American values, a new intellectual vocabulary was sweeping through American universities: that of social science. Like other Americans, rabbis and Jewish leaders could hardly avoid listening to what social researchers, especially sociologists, had to say about American life. Particularly when sociologists turned their attention and methods to characterizing American Jewish life, they helped create the new terms of Jewishness that came to overshadow all other explanations of Jewishness. Based on empirical research into daily Jewish life, social researchers' vocabulary of Jewishness was far more concerned with the daily experience of being Jewish in the United States than Chautauqua or missionary rabbis' explanations of Jewishness had been in the 1920s and 1930s. These new terms, grounded in social science, came to influence the way a new generation of rabbis and Jewish leaders talked about being Jewish.

CHAPTER 2

The Ghetto and Beyond

The Rising Authority of American Jewish Social Science in Interwar America

The Social-Scientific Turn

Louis Wirth had done very little to endear himself to the organized Jewish community. The sociologist had argued in his first book that Jews were perennial ghetto-dwellers. Whether or not the places they lived were walled in reality, he wrote, the mentality Jews carried with them was one of insularity. At the time of the book's publication in 1928, and for many years after, Jewish leaders were cool to Wirth's conclusions, and as a secular intellectual married to a non-Jewish woman and immersed in the non-Jewish academic world, Wirth was hardly a likely candidate to lead or advise the Jewish community. Yet by the 1940s, he had come to occupy a crucial role in American Jewish life: the expert social researcher.

Social researchers seemed to succeed just where liberal rabbis failed when it came to explaining Jews to the United States. Although most social researchers were tone deaf to religion and theology, they had a good ear for lived experience. Thus, unlike the rabbis who sought to explain Jewishness through religious precepts—like ethical monotheism— and often found themselves well off the mark of the daily realities of Jewish life, social scientists issued explanations based on social patterns: Jewishness was the sum of what Jews did. For some, like Wirth, this strict brand of functionalism edged into nihilism. Replacing a faith in Jewish chosenness or a divine mandate with a faith in social function, social-scientific explanations of Jewishness did not carry a self-fulfilling logic for Jewish survival. Yet by defining Jewishness through the patterns of Jewish social existence, Wirth and other social researchers sculpted heartier and more descriptive explanations of Jewishness than those offered by most liberal rabbis.

Social science, particularly sociology, provided Jews with new tools for balancing their own particularism with universal ideals. In the interwar years, when Wirth started his career as a sociologist, social scientists were revolutionizing the study of American life. Their studies were increasingly guided by the belief that American social structure was composed of many different, yet similar-acting, social groups, and that to study one group was to gain insight into the social system more generally. In the post–World War II era, this method of moving from the local to the universal would emerge as the governing premise of the ethnic idea in the United States.[1] Decades before the Second World War, however, Jews found the social-scientific method an attractive one for thinking about their place in America. After all, it offered them a way to position themselves as central to—not on the margins of—modernity and American society.

Whereas liberal rabbis turned to the ideals of ethical monotheism and mission theology to help them assert a universal purpose for the particular survival of Jewishness, important twentieth-century Jewish intellectuals drew on social science and especially sociology to make similar claims. In the correlations that sociologists drew between the workings of small groups and the overarching texture of modern society, Jewish experiences were validated as consonant with and constituent of the rules of American social life. In other words, even what was most distinctive about Jewish life was also indicative of larger—or universal—American social patterns.

By the 1930s, prominent Jewish leaders pledged fealty to social science as a means for Jewish redemption. In the face of Hitler's growing power, these leaders clung to the expectation that certain immutable social rules would guard against total social chaos and worse. They hoped that they could fit Jews into prevailing social models and prove that Jews upheld—and did not threaten—social order. In these years, Jewish social researchers, like liberal rabbis, served as messengers of sorts to the non-Jewish world, developing a discourse of Jewishness that related Jewish life to larger non-Jewish patterns. This same discourse of Jewish identity also gradually filtered into the ways rabbis and lay Jews talked about being Jewish. Increasingly, explanations of what it meant to be Jewish in the United States addressed questions about the social existence of Jews: were all Jews necessarily part of the Jewish social group, what did Jews do to mark themselves as different from non-Jews, and how might group boundaries be expected to change over time? By the postwar years, Jewish leaders tended to focus their public explanations of Jewishness on its sociological dimensions, articulating what might be best called sociological Jewishness.

Though sociological vocabulary held a special position in the emerging public language of Jewishness, the divide between sociology and other social-scientific modes was often not distinct, and insights from the other social sciences also were woven into new explanations of Jewishness in America. Psychology, for example, informed many core sociological ideals, like that of marginality and even assimilation. Furthermore, as a vocabulary itself, psychology provided an important means of translating Jewishness into American terms.[2] Demography and anthropology also overlapped significantly with sociology while retaining their own methodological integrity, and historical scholarship, though not strictly social-scientific, was integrated into almost every social-scientific framework. The particular history, goals, and methods of sociology, I believe, situated it to become central in the twentieth-century public language of Jewishness. I acknowledge, however, that a broad constellation of social-scientific scholarship—or social research—shaped the way Jewish leaders and intellectuals publicly defined Jewishness.

Louis Wirth, one of the first sociologists of American Jews, provides a point of departure for understanding how Jewish intellectuals harnessed the methods of social science to translate Jewishness into modern American terms. Other prominent Jewish intellectuals, including Morris Raphael Cohen (trained as a philosopher) and Salo Baron (a historian), similarly put their faith in social science as a means for ushering Jewishness into modernity. All were driven by the conviction that Jewishness needed to be—and could be—presented to the United States through the language of social science. Their efforts, combined with the rising popularity of surveys and other social-scientific studies of American life, set the stage for a social-scientific turn in how Jews described Jewishness. In the long span of Jewish history, the social-scientific turn represented another instance in which Jews sought to resolve the tension generated by universalistic aspirations stemming, paradoxically, from a passionate sense of distinctiveness.

Preaching from the Altar of Sociology

When Louis Wirth set out to write his dissertation, his advisor, the famed sociologist Robert Park, instructed him, as he did all of his students, to write about what he knew.[3] What Wirth knew most intimately was his experience as a first-generation Jewish immigrant to the United States. Born in Gemünden, Germany, at the end of the nineteenth century, he grew up in an upper-middle-class family. In 1911 his uncle, who had moved to the United States to avoid military conscription, returned for a visit. When his uncle learned that Wirth was on the brink of completing his eight years of compulsory education at a Protestant evangelical *Volksschule*, his uncle offered to bring Wirth and his sister to the United States so they could continue their education. Committed to education—so much so that they had allowed their children to attend a Protestant school—Wirth's parents agreed to let their two children go to the United States. They may have guessed that the children's weekly Jewish lessons would not continue in their new lives in Omaha, Nebraska (where the uncle lived), but they also must have believed that America would ultimately offer their children a better life. In Omaha, Wirth excelled as a student and became a skilled debater, even winning a dinner invitation to the home of the populist activist and onetime presidential hopeful William Jennings Bryan, where Wirth was required to sign a temperance pledge. In 1916, Wirth won a scholarship to the University of Chicago (no temperance pledge required). There, he imbibed the radicalism of the moment, attending lectures on Marxism and becoming involved in the antiwar protest movement. At the same time, the young, diminutive man (Wirth was only five feet, two inches tall) became a disciple of Robert Park.[4]

American sociology had emerged as a discipline at the end of the nineteenth century in the midst of massive social changes. The daily arrival of new immigrants, the growth of American cities, and the rise of an industrial economy transformed American life. Early American sociology, almost entirely a discipline composed of Christian men with so-called Anglo-Saxon ancestry, represented an attempt to understand these changes. Many early sociologists were influenced by the turn-of-the-century social gospel movement's belief that it was a Christian duty to help people endure social change and to work toward the betterment of society. Sociology, a method for classifying social change, offered a way to think about change as orderly—not disruptive—and to help individuals adapt themselves to changing realities. Unlike European sociology, which emerged from a Marxist interpretation of social change, American sociology focused on reform not revolution as the path toward social good. American sociologists tended to believe that the precise study of social patterns would generate the knowledge needed to regulate a rapidly changing world.[5]

If a person in the 1920s wanted to study sociology, there were few better places to do so than the University of Chicago. There, men like Albion Small, Charles Henderson, and Ellsworth Faris (all of whom had been trained as clergy) established a department attuned to the urban community surrounding it. The line between social work and sociology certainly blurred for some. Especially under the sway of Robert Park, however, a more detached scientific method came to define sociology, even though reform remained intrinsic to the discipline. Park, who joined the department in 1913, was committed to fusing social theory with empirical data generated from community studies, often of urban dwellers. These studies generally illustrated the inexorable, if bumpy, process by which immigrant and minority groups learned American norms and customs. Segments of the American population—such as ethnic and racial groups or adherents of specific religions—which otherwise were difficult to survey became the focus of the Chicago school's research. Reflecting progressive-era reform, many sociologists understood minority experience as a progression along a series of stages toward full assimilation. At the same time, they validated the daily struggles of immigrant and minority life by formalizing those struggles into predictable stages of a grand process of assimilation.[6]

By the early decades of the twentieth century, sociology branched out beyond its white Protestant roots. Jews and African Americans in particular gravitated toward the field, and the field, in a sense, gravitated toward them. For one, both Jews and African Americans were accepted into the discipline of sociology earlier and more completely than they were into other academic fields.[7] Park, not a trained sociologist but a student of social theorists John Dewey and William James, was instrumental in this. He joined Chicago's sociology faculty after having spent time working with Booker T. Washington at the Tuskegee Institute in Washington, D.C. Upon accepting the position at the University of Chicago, Park wrote to Washington that he had come to feel as if he belonged "in a sort of way to the Negro race."[8]

Under Park's leadership, immigrants and African Americans became central to narratives of social theory, both as the subjects and as the authors of it. Park fostered relationships with minority students, whom he then encouraged to explore their own social backgrounds. During his tenure at the University of Chicago, he mentored some of the most notable African American sociologists, including Charles S. Johnson and E. Franklin Frazier, and Jewish sociologists. Faculty and graduate students, no matter their backgrounds, tended to use the city around them as their field site. By the interwar era, Chicago was home to count-less immigrant groups and also had attracted a number of African Americans who were moving north for jobs and in hope of escaping the racism of the South.[9] As a body, Chicago sociology drew a new focus to urbanism and minority life, arguing that the true workings of American society were most visible among those people seeking acceptance into it.

In 1928, the year Wirth published *The Ghetto,* Park wrote a medita-tion on the "marginal man," a person, he explained, who "learns to look upon the world in which he was born and bred with something of the detachment of a stranger."[10] While the idea of the marginal man had roots in Georg Simmel's writings on the stranger, it also served as an apt description of many of Park's students.[11] According to Park, the marginal man often left the comfort of his community (a place Park termed a ghetto) in search of a more cosmopolitan world. Although clear psychic strain—the feeling of being part of a new society without being fully accepted into it—accompanied his move into a new world, the marginal man, Park later wrote, was the source of progress and civi-lization: "Inevitably he becomes . . . the individual with a wider horizon, the keener intelligence, the more detached and rational view-point."[12] Marginal men were no more capable of fully integrating into their new world than they were of returning to the world they had left, and thus their liminality gave them an acute perception of both worlds.

"The emancipated Jew," Park suggested, "was, and is, historically and typically the marginal man."[13] Jewish social researchers, indeed, often claimed that their marginal status positioned them as self-conscious and objective observers of society. The posture of marginality grew in sig-nificance particularly as sociologists and anthropologists attempted to use their methods to study places close to home. Hortense Powder-maker, for example, a Jewish anthropologist who did her earliest field-work on an island in Papua New Guinea, focused her second study on race relations in Indianola, Mississippi, in the 1930s. In later writings, she claimed she was able to apply the same method of participant-observation in the American South that she had used in the South Pacific. Her experience growing up Jewish and female had marked her as an outsider and helped her hone the ability to "step in and out of society and to study it."[14]

Whether or not it was a sense of marginality that propelled Jews toward the social sciences, their large presence especially in the field of sociology was irrefutable. Already at the turn of the century in Europe,

Jews were recognized as instrumental in shaping the discipline, to the point that some commentators considered sociology a Jewish science. In the United States, Jews continued to be numerically and individually significant to the field. A survey done in the 1930s found that almost one-third of rabbis who had a graduate degree had earned it in the social sciences (which included history, economics, and sociology), and by the 1960s close to 20 percent of the membership of the American Sociological Association was Jewish.[15]

Ghetto Research

Wirth once remarked that personal circumstances and "values," while they may not be the stuff of science, "determine our intellectual interests, the selection of our problems for analysis, our selection and interpretation of the data and, to a large extent, also our generalizations and, of course, our application of these generalizations."[16] Without a doubt, the kind of research he did was inseparable from his place within and outside the Jewish world. After completing his undergraduate degree at Chicago, too poor to devote all of his time to schooling, Wirth took a job as a caseworker with the Jewish Charities of Chicago and enrolled as a part-time graduate student. Aside from paying him a living wage, Wirth's job complemented his growing interest in urbanism and immigration. Daily, he met Jewish immigrants who felt profound dislocation from the places they had left, from the United States, and from any sense of community. For his master's thesis, which he wrote in 1925, Wirth drew on his contact with these immigrants to argue that immigration disrupted family life. Immigrant family structures, he believed, weakened when traditional patterns conflicted with new and modern opportunities. He mused that this problem was felt more acutely by Jews than others: "Deviations from customs, the traditions and norms of conduct . . . often constitute serious problems in the Jewish family and community, when similar violations of the code would be regarded as trifling incidents . . . by other groups."[17]

Wirth, however, did not linger long in his sense that Jews experienced modernity and immigration differently from non-Jews. Instead, he went on to produce a study of Jewish life that drew its significance from the generic quality of immigration and assimilation. Wirth's dissertation, which he turned into his book *The Ghetto,* was an attempt to understand why it was so brutally difficult to leave one's home. He sought to answer this question in the most personal of ways: by tracing the relationship between Jews and the non-Jewish world. Yet he had no desire to write a dissertation itself encircled by ghetto walls; rather, he intended his work to "throw light on a much broader subject—on human nature and on culture."[18] In the final pages of *The Ghetto*, he wrote, "The Jews drift into the ghetto . . . for the same reasons that the Italians live in Little Sicily, the Negroes in the black belt, and the Chinese in Chinatown."[19] Park, in a short foreword to the book, emphasized, "Every people and every cultural group may be said to create and maintain its own ghetto."[20] In other words, the cyclical story of Jews struggling to leave the ghetto, and yet always feeling pulled back to its familiarity, was replicated in the experiences of all American minority groups. Centuries of ghetto-dwelling, according to Wirth, had calcified certain traits as seemingly uniquely Jewish. As such, these traits came to carry an aura of biological inevitability.[21] Yet historically and sociologically produced Jewish distinctiveness was not to be confused with hereditary difference.

Sociology, as a method, challenged the rigidities of race science, which was both a forerunner and a contemporary of sociology. Whereas race scientists studied immigrants to support theories of human immutability, sociologists—following the lead of anthropologists—turned to immigrants to confirm a liberal vision of human progress. Jewish-German immigrant Franz Boas stood at the vanguard of a movement to separate biology from what he termed culture. Charting a new course in anthropology, Boas sought to prove that even immigrants' physical characteristics changed with exposure to new living conditions. His success in defining culture—not biology—as the most crucial determinant of human experience was visible across the social sciences by the interwar era.[22]

Wirth encouraged social scientists to see that cultural forces could be almost as difficult to shed as biological traits. Many Jews, he explained, found it nearly impossible to escape the clutches of the ghetto, even after historical and social circumstances no longer demanded that they remain inside ghetto walls. The Jew who attempted to live outside the ghetto often "bec[ame] conscious of his inferior status" in the eyes of the outside world.[23] In elegant yet searing terms, Wirth described the lonely ghetto-less Jew, who, after fleeing the ghetto, quietly slips back in, choosing comfort and acceptance over cosmopolitanism. He argued that Jews preserved the form of the ghetto even as they shrugged off the laws and customs of Judaism and lived much of their daily lives outside of Jewish structures. Wirth concluded, "It is [the] ghetto which keeps the Jew, who does not himself live in it and perhaps never has lived in it, from completely merging and being accepted in the non-Jewish community."[24]

Still, Wirth did not regard assimilation as a hopeless task. To the contrary, he believed that Robert Park's model of assimilation would ultimately operate for all American groups. Wirth, it seems, saw his own life as a testament to the eventuality of full Jewish assimilation. In 1923, he married Mary Bolton, a classmate of English descent, whose childhood had been spent in Paducah, Kentucky, where she attended the Baptist church of her Fundamentalist father's choosing.[25] Four years later, in 1927, Wirth was naturalized as an American citizen.[26] One of his daughters recalled in detached prose, "Wirth's assimilationist inclinations and principles, like those of his wife, partly derived from their common reaction against dogmatism and provincial ethnocentrism. Their two daughters were to be encouraged in agnosticism with audible atheistic overtones, at the same time that they were to acquire a 'generalized minority' ethnicity identification."[27]

Yet even for Wirth, full assimilation remained an elusive goal. No matter how far he thought his marriage, education, attitudes, and life practices had transported him away from the ghetto, Wirth could not change the fact that he was still considered a Jew and, thus, was subject to the repercussions of being Jewish in interwar America. After completing his degree and securing a book contract for his dissertation, his home department at Chicago voted against hiring him for a recently opened faculty position. For a brief time, Wirth taught at Tulane, and then he took a research fellowship in Germany from 1929 to 1931. That he published a book about Jews, even if he intended the import of the book to be broad, and that he himself was recognized as a Jew, made his journey into the American university uphill and, likely, disheartening. Despite the popular attention the book received from the Jewish and non-Jewish press, the scholarly world largely ignored it. To certain critics *The Ghetto* appeared too historical and not theoretically engaged; it also was too concerned with Jews for many scholars' tastes.[28] Wirth's academic homelessness ended in 1931, when Park finally convinced Chicago's sociology department to offer him a job. Wirth returned to Chicago and joined a department whose chair had once described him as "keen," and then had qualified, "He is a Jew, however."[29] Learning from his experience, Wirth shifted his scholarly interests away from the Jews.

FIGURE 3. Louis Wirth conducting a seminar at the University of Chicago, 1945. Courtesy of the Special Collections Research Center, University of Chicago Library.

The question remained, however, whether complete assimilation was the sure outcome of contact with American society, or whether minority experience operated within an alternative framework. Whatever, the answer, Jewish intellectuals were increasingly certain that it could be discovered only through social-scientific inquiry.

Placing Faith in Social Science

By the interwar years, Wirth had become convinced that social science was "indispensable" in the modern world.[30] In the same years, a number of American Jews were similarly struck by the indispensability of social science—an insight borne out of faith in rationalism and empiricism on one hand, and desperation on the other. Jews watched their world spiral out of control as events in Europe and the United States jeopardized Jewish security.[31] The social-scientific method of taking specific experiences and explaining them through universal social models, whether behavioral, structural, or even psychological, offered a new kind of order that challenged much of the animus against Jews. If Jews were classified according to the same patter█████████her people, then the logic of singling them out as being devia█████ial norms and destructive to society would collapse, or so Je█████hoped. A decade and millions of atrocities later, it was clear █████ience had no more saved the Jews from systematic destructi███████d international diplomacy. But it had given some Jewish le████████scholars a sense of hope and control and had sculpted the w██████generation thought about Jewishness.

Morris Raphael Cohen, a philosophy professor at City College of New York, led a movement to anchor social-scientific scholarship to Jewish self-preservation when he founded the Conference on Jewish Relations. In 1933, the year Hitler rose to power, Cohen organized this new organization to coordinate, carry out, and disseminate Jewish social research. Years later, he asked, "Were we to face a cunning enemy with bare breasts and blowing trumpets, or could we make use, in the cause of freedom, of the tools of science that freedom of thought had called into being?"[32] Cohen's faith that scientific inquiry could save the Jews from the "cunning enemy" of Nazism reflected the broad trends of positivism that shaped 1930s social science. His lofty expectations for scientific research into Jewish life also built on Enlightenment-era Jews' attempts to use scientific inquiry as a means to ease Jews' journey into modernity.[33]

In the early nineteenth century, German Jews had developed the so-called scientific study of Judaism and Jewry (*Wissenschaft des Judentums*) amid a hotbed of ideological questions about modern Jewish identity.[34] For many years, Jews in Europe had been counted and classified through surveys about religious affiliation. By establishing the apparatus to count themselves, Jews attempted to wrest power from the state and exercise control over themselves and their future. In 1845, a *Wissenschaft* scholar explained, "The extension of equality to the Jews in society will follow from the extension of equality to the academic study of Judaism."[35]

Scientific inquiry, if nothing else, was to provide an answer to the "Jewish problem." By the mid- to late nineteenth century, however, it became clear that the answers were many, and that even a scientific study of Judaism and Jewry would yield diverse solutions about how best to reconcile Jewishness and modernity. It was also clear that research about Jewish life, while it could not provide a singular answer to the Jewish problem, itself served as a method of persuasion.[36] Beginning in the late nineteenth century, Jewish defense organizations in Germany and the United States employed statisticians and social scientists to generate detailed reports about the nature of Jewish life, all in the hopes of demystifying Jewishness and fitting it into general and familiar social categories.[37] Numbers were assumed to be powerful indicators of reality, a positivist insight held by both Jewish and non-Jewish statisticians.

When Cohen turned to social science in the 1930s, he saw it as a tool for harnessing and redirecting the realities of his world. Born in Minsk in the early 1880s, Cohen immigrated to New York in 1892. In his autobiography, he described his journey to the United States as coinciding with a rejection of his parents' Orthodoxy for agnosticism.[38] In place of religion, he put his faith in rationalism and philosophical inquiry, subjects he explored as an undergraduate at City College and a philosophy graduate student at Columbia and Harvard. Like Wirth, Cohen spent many years searching for a university that would hire a Jew. Finally, six years after earning his doctorate, he joined City College's philosophy department. There, he became a formidable presence. In his classes, no student could lurk in the shadows of the lecture hall. Using the Socratic method, Cohen drew his students into heated exchanges. A generation of City College–educated American Jewish men, many of whom went on to prominent academic and professional careers, have recounted the anxious hours they spent both fearing and idolizing Cohen.[39]

Cohen gained the reputation of an iconoclast as he systematically dismantled his students' religious faith through his own brand of reason.[40] Yet in the last years of his life, he became devoted to Jewish group survival. Though still not concerned with piety or divinity, Cohen saw social science as a source of Jewish redemption and a tool for Jewish group survival. He never expressed an ideological opposition to Jewish assimilation; he simply saw it as unlikely. "It takes a long time," he once reflected, "for a people who have lived together as a group with common tradition and common suffering to dissolve."[41] Wirth had argued just this in *The Ghetto* even as he maintained faith in the possibility of eventual assimilation.

Doubtful that assimilation would solve the problems of antisemitism anytime soon, Cohen suggested that scientific reason stood alone as a protector of the Jews. In June 1933, he gathered a diverse group of Jewish scholars and professionals—including Albert Einstein, Harry Wolfson, Felix Frankfurter, and Salo Baron—to create a new presence and stimulus for Jewish social-scientific research. Named the Conference on Jewish Relations, the organization embodied the faith that an array of Jewish scholars, whom Cohen described as "Zionists and Assimilationists, Orthodox, Reformed and non-religious Jews," placed in empirical research.[42] Although according to his biographer, David Hollinger, Cohen believed that science "sought truth of a sort that would command assent from persons of any national, religious, or ethnic background," it bears mentioning that he gathered primarily Jewish men to join in his quest.[43] Eventually a few women made their way into the inner circle: both Hannah Arendt and Sophia Robison, a demographer, criminologist, occasional lecturer at the New School, and author of several articles about Jews in the United States, were involved in conference affairs.[44] Men, however, guided the agenda of the research body. Furthermore, almost no non-Jews participated in the conference. Perhaps Cohen doubted that they would be interested in its activities, but he also at least tacitly acknowledged that scientific research about Jews was a Jewish answer to the ubiquitous Jewish problem.

Cohen, not a social scientist, relied on Salo Baron to position Jewish social research as a critical field of academic inquiry. A Columbia professor who held the first chair of Jewish history in the United States, Baron was younger than Cohen and assumed many of the daily tasks of the conference, while Cohen mainly focused on raising funds.[45] When poor finances threatened to sink the conference, Albert Einstein lent his stature to the conference to keep it afloat. In a solicitation letter sent to a select group of wealthy Jews, he told them, "We owe it to our children as well as ourselves not to wait until insuperable difficulties develop, but rather to take thought and be intellectually prepared for what the coming years may bring us."[46]

The conference developed international and domestic agendas in its first years of existence. By the late 1930s, it had dispatched a small research team to Germany to gather facts about the legal situation of minorities, and had funded a number of surveys of the American Jewish population that, among other things, catalogued Jewish interactions with non-Jews. Although the study of antisemitism loomed over the conference's agenda, Cohen did not want the group to function merely

FIGURE 4. Morris Raphael Cohen (far left) and Albert Einstein (under umbrella) leaving City College's Shepard Hall during Einstein's first visit to the United States, April 1921. Courtesy of Archives, The City College of New York, CUNY.

as a watchdog or defense agency. At a meeting in 1937, he explained, "It is of utmost importance, if we are going to be good neighbors to our non-Jewish fellow citizens, that we should not be too suspicious."[47] Better, he recommended, to "study problems most carefully, trying to obtain first of all accuracy rather than any immediate practical effects."[48]

The task of legitimating Jewish social research in the scholarly world was crucial to Cohen's vision. Only if Jewish scholarship were taken seriously by the non-Jewish world could it upend fallacious stereotypes and centuries-old prejudices against Jews. The conference members determined that a scholarly journal devoted to publishing Jewish research, aptly titled *Jewish Social Studies,* would be a perfect vehicle for establishing the significance and respectability of Jewish social research. These were not the first Jews to broker a journal as a sign of their cosmopolitanism and scholarly legitimacy. Jewish Enlightenment thinkers feverishly edited and published journals, believing that they could use the modern methods of publication to anchor their ideas in the modern world. Intellectual American Jews were struck by a similar insight. In 1915, when a handful of Harvard students brought the first issue of the *Menorah Journal* to press, they clearly believed that the printed word would lend them intellectual weight and bring more worldliness to Jewish intellectual debates.[49] Similarly, in solicitation letters, Baron and Cohen told prospective contributors that "an attempt will be made not only to get the journal into non-Jewish hands, but also to enlist the cooperation of non-Jewish scholars."[50]

Just as Wirth emphasized the universal dimensions of his research on the Jewish ghetto, Baron and Cohen maintained that social research about Jews illuminated larger social patterns. The method of studying the specific and interpreting it as indicative of universal patterns would anchor Jewishness to normal and familiar social patterns. A non-Jew, then, could become knowledgeable about the Jews simply by understanding certain essential social principles; he or she would learn that there was nothing exotic, abstruse, or threatening about Jewish life. Baron took the lead in organizing the journal, since Cohen had gone into semiretirement by the mid-1930s.[51] Nonetheless, Cohen, more senior and a larger presence in the scholarly and nonscholarly worlds, wrote the foreword for the inaugural issue of *Jewish Social Studies,* which appeared in January 1939. "Fifteen million people," he explained, "living under most diverse conditions in all the different parts of the world and yet maintaining common traditions that have a history of over three thousand years . . . certainly deserve close and attentive study on the part of the various social sciences. Moreover, the problems that face the Jews today are fateful not only for their own continued existence as a group but also for the future of progressive civilization."[52] With a mournful nod to the bygone days of Jewish European scholarship, Cohen asserted that Americans now shouldered the responsibility of creating a scientific record of Jewish life, an ultimate act of self-preservation.[53]

An article by anthropologist Franz Boas, titled "Heredity and Environment," immediately followed Cohen's introductory statement. In it, Boas concluded, "The existence of a cultural personality embracing a whole 'race' is at best a poetic and dangerous fiction."[54] Aside from a reference to Jewish head size, the article made almost no mention of Jews, yet the editors had undoubtedly chosen it carefully.

They hoped to align the journal with a Boasian conception of culture—a view that held environment, not biology, as essential to human understanding—and to publish articles that proved Jews were susceptible to the same environmental conditions as any other group of people. In doing so, the editors repudiated the framework of race science that often was employed to study Jews and that had been appropriated to justify antisemitic policies, whether immigration restriction legislation or Nazism. Clearly, Boas's emphasis on the adaptability of people to their environment favored an assimilationist view of the Jewish future.

Whether or not the final goal of empirical explanations of Jewishness was in fact for Jews to become so well understood that their distinctiveness faded remained a point of tension in Cohen's thinking, the journal's goals, and much of interwar Jewish social research. Some critics feared that empirical studies of Jewish life—like those generated by the conference and its journal—could be used not simply to assimilationist ends but for far more pernicious purposes. They cautioned that, in the wrong hands, scientific surveys might be manipulated into a justification for antisemitic policies—not an unfounded fear given Hitler's persistent attempts to create, as one scholar has written, "an antisemitism of reason."[55] A Jewish-American statistician after World War II recalled having nightmares that his data about Jews would fall into the wrong hands.[56] Cohen considered such anxieties "silly," but he also realized that his fund-raising efforts would be hampered if he rashly dismissed them.[57] Instead, in countless letters, speeches, and publicity materials, he reiterated his belief that nothing other than scientific research—done deliberately and unconcerned with immediate or practical action—could safeguard the world from evil and Jews from destruction. To a potential donor, he wrote, "In the search for truth, scholarly and scientific methods must be supreme."[58] And in a 1936 speech to the National Council of Jewish Women, he told the audience, "If we really want to deal honestly and adequately with any question, we must do what scientific medicine does[:] study the facts and not be afraid of looking at the unpleasant ones."[59]

Jewish Social Studies was quickly recognized as a leading scholarly source about Jewish life, although its small circulation numbers belied that fact. (In its first year, it sent out approximately seven hundred copies of each issue.) The truth of the matter was that few other journals were interested in publishing articles on Jewish topics. For example, during the first two decades of *Jewish Social Studies'* existence, the premier American sociology journals—the *American Journal of Sociology* and the *American Sociological Review*—published no more than thirty substantive articles about Jewish topics. Although other scholarly journals periodically published social-scientific studies of the Jews, *Jewish Social Studies* unequivocally broadened the field of Jewish social research and encouraged new scholarship about Jewish life.[60] Because few scholars at the time devoted their energies to Jewish topics, the editors of the journal often offered honoraria to contributors as a means of incentive. They also financed entire studies, bankrolling scholars who otherwise might not have found it feasible to turn their attention to Jewish matters or, perhaps, to pursue academic careers at all.

Demographic studies held a place of singular importance in the journal. Surveys of Jewish patterns, from birthrates, to marriages and intermarriage, to rates of Jewish criminality, filled the journal's pages. Other articles detailed the characteristics of Jewish populations in various locales, including postwar Europe, Afghanistan, Saint Thomas, and Shanghai.[61] All of these demographic studies offered empirical evaluations of Jewish life and reflected Cohen's desire to create a corpus of facts about Jews that would demystify Jews and prove them no different from other population groups.

It would have been a feat of deception to claim that Jewish life was entirely similar to that of other groups; numerous articles about antisemitism proved as much. As the situation for European Jews deteriorated, the editors of *Jewish Social Studies* recognized themselves as serving an immediate need: to help relocate the center of Jewish scholarship to the United States. After the war, Baron devoted himself to documenting the remnants of Jewish culture and scholarship scattered throughout Europe. In the pages of *Jewish Social Studies,* he published a catalogue of what remained, but more than anything else it revealed how much was gone.[62] In the war years and after, a number of new American institutions, and journals such as the *YIVO Annual of Jewish Social Science, Judaism,* and the *Jewish Journal of Sociology,* emerged that were devoted to safeguarding the tradition of scientific Jewish scholarship.[63] A desire to continue the now devastated European tradition of scientifically studying Jewry, and an effort to assert that Jewish life would outlive Hitler, compelled the surge in American scholarship about the Jewish experience. Yet the two goals—a commitment to scientifically objective studies of Jewish life and an investment in Jewish survival—threatened to undermine one another.

Existential Scholarship

In 1940, Cohen wrote, "Ultimately the fate of the Jews, as of other people, will be determined by such factors as the difference between their birth rates and death rates, their economic position, and their general relations with their fellow citizens."[64] Cohen never learned just how irrelevant scientific research into these factors became in the face of Nazism; as the war started, he suffered from debilitating and eventually fatal brain damage. Yet his conviction that to study Jewish life was to safeguard and confirm its existence endured in others after his death. The genocide of World War II could have caused a crisis of faith in science and social science among Jews. Not only had social-scientific pronouncements been unable to save European Jewry, but also Hitler himself had appropriated science, especially social science, to sanction his annihilation of Jews.[65] Jews in the postwar era, however, grew increasingly enchanted with social science, devoting more and more dollars to social research and placing greater faith in the fruits of scientific studies of Jewish life.

Social science provided the most effective terms for making Jews knowable and sustainable in the modern world. If, as Wirth had attempted to prove, Jews followed the same social patterns and behaviors as other groups of people, then it made little sense to direct special hatred against them. Yet similar logic challenged Jewish distinctiveness and, ultimately, the collective existence of the Jewish people as a separate social group. In 1945, when Louis Wirth attended a conference sponsored by the American Jewish Committee to discuss postwar Jewish life, he made just this point. His sociological training had taught him to be "skeptical about whether we as Jews have any distinctive values . . . that we should and could preserve or develop."[66]

When Wirth died of a heart attack in 1952, he left a legacy that challenged the survival of Jewish distinctiveness.[67] Obituaries published in all of the important sociological journals remarked on Wirth's commitment to democracy and sociology as the bases for meaningful social policy, especially concerning race relations.[68] Although each one listed *The Ghetto* as his most important publication, none mentioned that he was a Jew or that his scholarship had served as a crucial foundation for American Jewish social research. Three days after his death, a Reform rabbi eulogized the deceased professor at a memorial service held in University of Chicago's Mendel Hall. In seeking to come to terms with "Louis Wirth the Jew," the rabbi offered this: "[Wirth] was frankly impatient with chauvinists who made a virtue of difference and mistook the quirks of history for the special choice of Providence. . . . He felt that Jews spent too much energy in building preservative forces."[69] And yet throughout his own life and beyond, the Jewish world claimed Wirth as its own, inviting him to Jewish conferences and citing and reprinting *The Ghetto* until the present day.[70] Social scientists lent stature and power to the Jewish communal world, even when their conclusions dismissed it.

Before his death, Wirth had predicted that sociologists could not stand aloof from the communities that cared about their research: "Sociologists will . . . be using their sociological knowledge as research workers, as analysts and as policy makers in the various fields of social life. . . . There they will have to win their way by what they can contribute to the understanding and solutions of problems of human social life."[71] In the interwar era, one of the most pressing "problems of human social life" in the United States had to do with how America's diverse citizenry would get along. Social researchers, drawn to the question, turned to studying the patterns of intimate contact and marriage among American groups. They argued that intimacy could be seen as a gauge for how the vastly different populations in the United States could form a single nation. While social researchers may have viewed Jewish marital patterns as an interesting topic of academic inquiry, most Jews viewed endogamy (or inmarriage) as central to Jewish survival and thus had more than a fleeting interest in how this distinctive behavior might be explained in American terms. Jewish marital patterns offered just the challenge that social researchers seemed to relish: how to explain a very particular form of behavior by means of large and universal social categories? No question brought social researchers and Jewish leaders, especially rabbis, into closer contact, extending the reaches and meaning of social-scientific explanations of Jewishness.

CHAPTER 3

The Sacred and Sociological Dilemma of Jewish Intermarriage

Rabbis and Sociology

On a Friday evening in late 1939, a Reform rabbi spoke to his Chicago congregation about intermarriage. "All observers of Jewish life in this country," he informed them, "know very well that in recent years there has been a decided increase in the number of intermarriages."[1] The reason, according to the rabbi, was simple: Jews fled into the arms of non-Jews to escape potential antisemitism and to assimilate. When it came to explaining why these marriages were a problem, the rabbi had a clear answer as well. Intermarriage, he explained, was a "sociological problem," an act that went against the grain of vital sociological rules governing American and Jewish life.[2] In the interwar era, the chances that a Jew would marry a non-Jew were slim, despite the Chicago rabbi's pronouncement otherwise. In reality, the true problem that Jews faced was explaining why they persisted in marrying only one another in a country that granted them the freedom to do otherwise. Jews sought an explanation of endogamy that could balance their Jewish values with their American aspirations. Sociological language, more than any vocabulary, offered an attractive way of discerning universal, or at least American, patterns in seemingly distinctive group behaviors—like Jewish endogamy.

The struggle to explain Jewish marital behavior was nothing new. Throughout Jewish history, Jews often rearticulated the rules governing their marriages with non-Jews. These pronouncements served particular ends, sometimes helping to expand or, alternately, enclose the

Jewish people, other times fostering a belief in the purity of Jews or reaffirming the community's obedience to God. Asserting the terms of a prohibition against marriages between Jews and non-Jews also enabled Jews, at various moments, to feel a sense of control over their relationship to the non-Jewish world.[3] In the modern period, Jewish endogamy rarely rested easily with the ideals of equality, citizenship, and national identity. In countries that considered—or enacted—Jewish emancipation, Jews were often pressed to explain their attitudes toward marriage.[4] How could Jews expect entrance into a modern liberal society if they insisted on erecting impermeable boundaries, at least when it came to marriage and procreation, between themselves and others? With whom—the nation-state or the transnational Jewish people—did their loyalty rest? American Jews' patterns of endogamy similarly posed a challenge to the very American ideals that promised them acceptance, protection, and comfort.

By the early twentieth century, intermarriage occupied a vaunted symbolic place in American progressive thought. Interpreted as a birthing force, a union that could create an American out of a newcomer, intermarriage was the consummate American act. Some of the most popular theatrical productions of the early twentieth century, including *The Melting Pot* (first staged in 1908) and *Abie's Irish Rose* (performed on Broadway from 1922 to 1927), dramatized the national significance of intermarriage.[5] Both plays used the conceit of intermarriage, and specifically the love between a Christian woman and a Jewish man, as the animating force of American civilization. Treacly plots and all, the dramas suggested that people's intimate relationships had national implications.

Off the stage, intermarriage indeed presented a way to build a nation out of diversity, yet it also threatened religious codes, racial mores, and social lines on which Americans built their self-understanding.[6] In the first place, most Christian movements in the United States contained some form of censure against intermarriage. Furthermore, the pervasive cultural belief that marriage between blacks and whites—so called miscegenation—was unnatural and dangerous loomed against panegyric portraits of marital mixing. Finally, the influx of immigrant populations, especially those from eastern and southern Europe, heightened many Americans' anxiety about whether such seemingly un-American groups should be given full entrance into American life. Its paeans to American assimilation and even intermarriage aside, the progressive era was awash with fear about national contamination. Progressive ideals provided only a flimsy defense against a growing national obsession with maintaining American purity defined by presumed scientific, biological, and religious boundaries.

In the face of deep ambivalence about the meaning and efficacy of assimilation, American sociologists delved into the topic of intermarriage. Whom a person married interested sociologists not as a record of individual passion but as an indication of the social worlds that shaped people. What they concluded was that all people tended to marry within identifiable social groups. And many argued that this fact was constitutive of national harmony. Spun as a universal feature of American life and also a stabilizing one, endogamy would not mark Americans as different from one another so much as it would attest to their similar social behavior. Although progressive sociologists still predicted a future when group boundaries would dissolve and full assimilation would be possible, in truth they were mounting a sociological defense of endogamy. Their conclusions, though not matters of law, bore similarities to Hitler's decree forbidding Jews from marrying Aryans, and many southern states' so-called antimiscegenation legislation. Yet their assertion that cultural and social forces—not racial rules—functionally mandated endogamy distinguished sociologists' pronouncements from near-contemporary Nazi and Jim Crow policies.[7]

Jewish leaders, confounded by how to explain Jewish behaviors like endogamy as being properly American without sacrificing what many assumed to be the life force of Jewishness, were drawn to sociologists' conclusions. While Jewish leaders and sociologists generally did not travel in the same circles, increasingly in the interwar years their paths crossed. In part, this reflected the popularization of expert culture and the social sciences throughout American life. That Jews were among some of the most significant American sociologists, and that sociology offered an attractive language for talking about group life, also served to heighten Jewish leaders' awareness of sociology. The fact of the matter was that social scientists and Jewish leaders shared an interest in marriage, both believing that it offered a key to explaining how social life worked—or should work.

Marriage and the Measure of Man

In the mid-nineteenth century, early social scientists had begun to explore what accounted for human variations. Some posited that sexual intimacy and fertility rates could illuminate natural divisions among human beings. If a group tended not to marry another group—and if sexual intimacy between the two groups was rare and nonproductive (at least comparatively so)—then this suggested that natural boundaries existed. Sexual boundaries, so the theory went, signified biological boundaries. Many Jewish social scientists subscribed to this logic. For example, Joseph Jacobs, a late-nineteenth-century Anglo-Jewish social scientist, claimed to discover that Jewish endogamy was a natural outcome of "racial differences" by noticing that endogamous unions had higher fertility rates than exogamous ones.[8] The apparently stunted reproductive capacity of intermarried Jews proved to him that Jews were a distinct racial group, a conclusion with which other contemporary social scientists agreed. Of course, scientific pronouncements of this sort were not without ideological dimensions. Some social scientists (though not Jacobs) anchored their race-based explanation of Jewish endogamy in Zionism, a separatist ideology well served by the belief that Jewish assimilation through intermarriage was biologically impossible. Others attempted to correlate Jewish racial purity with Jewish strength and genius, and thus to prove Jews' value to non-Jewish societies.[9] In other hands, however, the belief in impenetrable racial divisions naturalized social hierarchies and turned these divisions into legal facts; proponents of antimiscegenation and anti-immigration legislation in the United States, for example, argued that they were working to avert unnatural racial mixing, or contamination.[10]

In the United States, the study of intermarriage took on a new significance for social scientists, many of them Jewish, invested in dismantling certain social hierarchies and proving that new immigrants were not inherently impervious to assimilation and Americanization. Maurice Fishberg, a Russian-Jewish immigrant trained in medicine in the United States, wrote in 1911 that the very fact that "Jews do intermarry with people of other faiths in every country where the law permits such unions" sharply refuted the existence of "an inherent racial antipathy . . . between Aryan and Semite."[11] His conclusions were consistent with the work of one of his contemporaries and fellow Jews, anthropologist Franz Boas. Both men emphasized the influence of environment on human experience and contributed to a radical assimilationist view of social progress. After all, if almost every aspect of the human form and behavior were determined by the environment, then individuals had an incredible capacity to change, and the majority culture would not be able to justify exclusionary policies as simply a fact of nature.

In the years after the First World War, a commitment to proving that Jews, like most human beings, were assimilable continued to drive Jewish social scientists to study intermarriage. Increasingly, however, social scientists started to think about whether there was a middle ground between theories that posited Jewish unassimilability and those that predicted full-scale absorption into the host society.[12] In 1921, a Jewish graduate student at Columbia, Julius Drachsler, published a comprehensive study of intermarriage in New York City. His interest in intermarriage, like Fishberg's, stemmed from a desire to unseat racial language's hold on American views of assimilation. Yet Drachsler was more ambivalent about assimilation than Fishberg. While he believed that intermarriage was a sure sign of assimilation, he also interpreted his data on intermarriage to show that, even when endogamy maintained a stronghold on a group's social patterns, that group could nonetheless fit into and enrich the United States. Not coincidentally, he argued that Jews were the best example of this dynamic.

A Jewish man born in 1889 in the town of Bella, then part of Austria-Hungary and, after World War I, Czechoslovakia, Drachsler emigrated to the United States at the age of fourteen. He arrived in New York City in the same decade that roughly one million other Jews, and a total of nine million immigrants, came to the United States.[13] Receiving his high school and college education in New York City's public schools alongside other newcomers to the United States, Drachsler came to believe that empirical research—specifically sociology—could improve society and thus had a responsibility to reach audiences outside of academia.[14] When he wrote about assimilation, he wrote as both a sociologist and a social activist.

Drachsler grounded his study on the premise that there was a correlation—though not necessarily a direct correspondence—between intermarriage and assimilation: "A study of the facts of intermarriage offers a reasonably secure base from which to begin a scientific study of assimilation."[15] Although Drachsler did his graduate work at Columbia, his dissertation bore the imprint of the University of Chicago's Robert Park. Drachsler, like Park and his students, accepted assimilation as the inevitable endpoint for all American groups, but by studying intermarriage patterns he hoped to prove that the more gradual the assimilative process, the better. To accumulate data about intermarriage, he surveyed 170,000 Bronx and Manhattan marriage licenses issued between 1908 and 1912. Drachsler categorized any marriage that crossed lines of nationality as an "amalgamation." Thus, he tallied marriage between a person of Norwegian descent and someone of Irish descent as an inter-marriage, while he characterized marriage between a Protestant and a Catholic of the same national background as an inmarriage.[16]

There were two groups, however, that defied Drachsler's nationality-based scheme: the Jews and the "coloreds." Although Drachsler noted the national origins of the members of these groups, he calculated their intermarriage rates transnationally. When he did, he discovered that they had almost identically low intermarriage rates—1.17 percent for Jews and 1.08 percent for "coloreds."[17] Yet he saw little in common between them. In the introduction to *Democracy and Assimilation,* a more popular revision of his dissertation, Drachsler asserted that there were two distinctive categories of amalgamation: marriages made within "the white race, particularly the European types," and marriages between whites and "other races in America, such as the negro, the Indian and the yellow races."[18] Drachsler apparently had few qualms about equating a low intermarriage rate with a low level of assimilation for his "colored" subjects; after all, he admitted that there remained serious questions in the minds of sociologists and biologists "as to the desirability of miscegenation among peoples of divergent races, such as the white and the black."[19]

When it came to Jews, however, whose intermarriage rates were almost as negligible statistically as those of the "coloreds" in his sample, he refused to characterize their marital patterns as proof of their unas-similability. Instead he suggested that "a low proportion of intermar-riage may coexist with a high degree of mental and social assimilation," and he added in a footnote that the Jews were an excellent example of this phenomenon, which he termed gradual amalgamation.[20] Drachsler's confidence that Jews had already assimilated into American life to a great extent enabled him to conclude that endogamy, when it acted to slow the inevitable path of assimilation, benefited all Americans.

While much of Drachsler's data showed that national groups were fairly rapidly intermarrying with one another, he nonetheless believed that those groups that exhibited more gradual patterns—like the Jews—would better safeguard American strength and harmony. He argued, "Ultimately amalgamation will take place, and with a younger genera-tion, inheriting something of the cultural past of its group, the process will go ahead on a progressively higher cultural plane. America will thus gain far more in the long run than she loses."[21] Gradual amalgamation, Drachsler continued, was also in the best interest of social stability, since it prevented the clashes that occurred when groups tried too quickly to shed their distinctiveness. Eventually, a unified American identity—what Drachsler termed a "harmonious composite"—would emerge, but only if the United States permitted groups to maintain their differences, through strategies like endogamy, into the foreseeable future.[22]

Drachsler hoped to create an alternative to the melting pot idea without replicating the xenophobia that was running rampant in many streams of American life during the 1920s.[23] Immigration restrictionists and nativists also protested the melting pot idea, but Drachsler intended to replace it with a model that protected group difference in the United States by deeming distinctiveness as essential, if only temporarily, to American strength. Horace Kallen, a contemporary Jewish thinker, although not a sociologist, had similarly argued that group distinctiveness should have a vaunted place in American society. But instead of suggesting the gradual demise of group distinctiveness, Kallen proposed cultural pluralism as an everlasting social ideal. The problem with cultural pluralism, however, was that it appeared inaccurate: it assumed that groups would maintain their differences in perpetuity, and it did not face the reality, pointed out by sociologists like Drachsler, that the lines dividing groups were already shifting, through the marriages members made across nationality and even religion.[24] Unlike Kallen, Drachsler maintained that in due time exogamy and assimilation would be the American rule.

In the world of sociology, Drachsler's study of intermarriage was formative. Few studies of marriage that followed it were without a reference to his hypothesis that assimilation and intermarriage went hand in hand. His theory of gradual amalgamation, however, had a much shorter legacy; were it not for Drachsler's death in 1927, only six years after he published his dissertation, perhaps he would have extended it. Nonetheless, in method and scope, Drachsler laid the groundwork for many decades of intermarriage studies and attempted to suggest an American justification for endogamy. He contended that members of disparate groups—like Jews and non-Jews—had the ability to forge sexual and marital unions, but that this did not mean they should.

Sameness and Happiness

In the late 1920s and the 1930s, Americans likely would have heard or read about an impending marriage crisis, evidenced by rising divorce rates and bemoaned by clergy and public officials alike. At the same time, the companionate marriage ideal, which characterized marriage as an arrangement intended for personal and sexual fulfillment, gained cultural clout.[25] Taken together, both the perceived marriage crisis and the new marriage ideal led sociologists, who, along with psychologists, comprised a growing group of so-called marriage experts, to focus their studies on what factors made successful marriages. The stakes were higher, however, than simply finding the perfect recipe for a happy marriage; rather, sociologists argued that the very stability of society depended on properly made marriages. With this goal in mind, they prescribed homogeneity, not diversity, when it came to family composition.

Throughout the 1930s, sociologist Ernest Burgess of the University of Chicago performed exhaustive studies to generate rules for predicting when a marriage would fail and when it would succeed. From his survey of over five hundred couples, he concluded that the greater the level of shared culture between two people—defined as family background, religious affiliation, social activities, courtship behavior, and conceptions of marriage—the more likely they were to become engaged and have what he termed a well-adjusted marriage.[26] In short, like should marry like.

Extending Drachsler's contention that endogamy was good for the United States, sociologists in the 1930s offered empirical evidence that the happiest marriages—and thus a stronger society—were achieved when people married their own kind, a conclusion that rabbis and other Jewish experts came to rely on in their explanations of Jewish marital patterns. In a 1933 article, Reuben Resnik, a Jewish social worker influenced by some of Burgess's early marriage studies, argued, "A study of intermarriage sociologically then is an examination of what goes on when two people of diverse cultural backgrounds marry. . . . The larger external group—the circle of friends . . . and the community—must be viewed in the light of social interaction and response."[27] Like Burgess, he argued that individuals were a sum of their social interactions, and marriages that attempted to meld together two people from markedly different backgrounds were likely to be ill fated.[28]

Of course, marriage partners could not share every facet of each other's background. It was assumed, for example, that they were not the same gender. What, then, were the most important things two people contemplating marriage should share? In the late 1930s and the 1940s, the most overwhelming answer was religion. Indeed, when they talked about intermarriage, sociologists really came to mean interfaith marriage. In part, this reflected the fact that many religious groups in the United States proscribed marriage with members of other faiths and designated intermarriage as a problem. Furthermore, other lines of social division, like nationality, were clearly losing importance, whereas religious diversity appeared to be an ongoing feature of American social difference, second only to race. In very few cases, however, did sociologists study interfaith marriages alongside interracial ones.[29] Instead, they tended to deal with interracial marriages as separate sociological phenomena, mirroring the broader culture's belief that race was irreducible and, thus, incomparable to other identity markers.

Still, sociologists understood religion, like race, as a single variable capable of illuminating a complex of sociological facts. Resnik, for example, wrote that religion was "exceedingly important . . . in developing the background of the person," and that simply knowing whether two people shared a religion could help predict the success of a marriage.[30] A few years later, in 1937, a New York University sociologist who studied intermarriage contended that it was wrong to assume that "two young people of different faiths are *different only in their religious beliefs.*"[31] Sociologists assumed that knowledge of a subject's religious affiliation offered a rich store of otherwise difficult-to-measure information—like values, educational attainment, class status, and aspirations—only tenuously related to matters of faith. Yet because religious affiliation carried such broad sociological import, it could serve as a fairly reliable measure of two people's level of similarity and, ultimately, their compatibility. Such a functional approach to religion paid little heed to the feelings of awe or mystery religion may have inspired in some. Indeed, for rabbis searching to locate Jewish difference in an American context, functionalism trounced mystery.

The Creed of Functionalism

For many years rabbis had relied on a mix of religious and racial language to explain endogamy, yet those rabbis who felt most pressed to justify it, generally Reform rabbis, found neither vocabulary particularly persuasive. In the mid-nineteenth century, alienated from religious law and in protest of racial views of Jewishness, some radical German Reform rabbis suggested doing away with the traditional prohibition against intermarriage. These rabbis resolved that a marriage should be considered a properly Jewish one as long as any children born were raised as Jews. Absent a system of civil marriage, however, this solution meant more in theory than practice.[32] While most American Reform rabbis did not endorse such a radical solution (which could have worked, at least in law, given that the United States maintained a system of civil marriage), they realized that their commitment to modernity, liberalism, and universalism did not rest easily with Jewish endogamy. In 1907, a rabbi explained, "After liberalism and tolerance have drawn the races closer together, [after] Jew and non-Jew have come to study and understand each other better, after the natural repulsion and inherited bias and bigotry have, to a large extent, been overcome[,] . . . intermarriage . . . must be considered a burning question."[33] A burning question, indeed, not because intermarriages happened often—they did not—but rather because the core ideals of liberalism and modernity issued a direct challenge to endogamy. The fact that Jews predominantly married other Jews, would, unless explained carefully, foreclose Jewish efforts to prove themselves modern Americans.

In 1909, the Reform movement considered issuing an authoritative statement banning rabbis from officiating at intermarriages. At root, the rabbis were searching for an appropriately American language in which to explain endogamy. One rabbi argued that, if the movement could not pass such a basic resolution, "then I declare once and for all, let us go over to Unitarianism and have done with it."[34] Nonetheless, the language of religious compulsion—that the Reform movement could compel its rabbis and their congregants to do or not to do something—was met by an outcry of protest. "If a resolution of this kind is passed," one rabbi predicted, "it is the beginning of religious tyranny."[35] Likely aware of the suspicion with which groups like American Catholics were regarded because of their obeisance to hierarchical religious authorities, and aware of their own powerlessness to enforce a blanket condemnation of Jewish behavior, the rabbis agreed only that intermarriage was "contrary to the tradition of the Jewish religion and should, therefore, be discouraged by the American rabbinate."[36]

Had the rabbis possessed a more concise vocabulary for explaining their attitude toward intermarriage, then perhaps they would have passed a firmer resolution. Particularly for early-twentieth-century Reform rabbis, the fact that a practice was contrary to Jewish tradition was rarely reason to avoid that practice. Yet discussions among rabbis revealed that most hoped that intermarriage rates would remain low. They simply did not have an effective language—one that would not undermine their liberalism or force them to subscribe to racial or religious teachings contrary to their beliefs—with which to communicate their opposition to intermarriage.

By the 1930s, however, with a mounting body of sociological scholarship defending and defining religious homogeneity as the norm in marriage, rabbis crafted new explanations of Jewish endogamy. In 1937, Rabbi Louis Mann delivered a lecture titled "Intermarriage as a Practical Problem in the Ministry" to Reform rabbis who met for a conference in Columbus, Ohio. Because a new generation of men had entered the rabbinate, the leaders of the conference had asked Mann to prepare a discussion about intermarriage so the body could decide if the 1909 resolution still made sense. The rabbi started his lecture with little fanfare: "No new discoveries in the realm of history, biology, sociology or theology have thrown any new light on the age old problem."[37]

The very vocabulary Mann used to talk about intermarriage, however, reflected the beginnings of a monumental change in how Jews thought about intermarriage. In crisp language, Rabbi Mann pointed out that it was hypocritical for rabbis to offer religion as their excuse for not officiating at intermarriages. He gestured toward the same conclusion that sociologists were reaching: the problem with intermarriage was sociological not theological. If "religion *is all important,* why should we not welcome a devout religious liberal more than a scoffing atheistic Jew?"[38] The fact of the matter was that two Jews, no matter their level of observance or belief, could easily receive a rabbi's blessing in marriage.

Religion, as defined by religious law, was irrelevant when it came to understanding or explaining why Jews persisted in their endogamy—and even why they should continue to do so. The real reason was much more practical and, therefore, more persuasive: religion was a measure of identity. Those who held a religion in common would find a whole world of similarity unfold before them. It may happen, Rabbi Mann allowed, that young people "in moments of romantic idealism" lose sight of the importance of their "background" and fall in love with a person from another faith. Under the spell of love, they become blind to "the added difficulties they are placing on their offspring; they cannot believe that such a marriage will have greater obstacles to their happiness."[39] With a rhetorical flourish, Rabbi Mann asked, "Is one's cultural heritage or one's religious birthright something like a glove or a hat, that one can put on, take off, or change with ease?"[40] Rabbis, armed with a sociological understanding of religion and marriage, could explain to starry-eyed lovers that love could not conquer all.

A sociological defense of endogamy would not demand any particular rabbinic resolution, since basic social truths, not religious rules, mandated against intermarriage. Mann probably had not read Burgess's fairly academic study of marriage, but he was undoubtedly aware of the growing number of marriage experts and counselors who relied on Burgess to suggest that marriage across religious lines produced unhappy families and, in turn, an unstable society.[41]

In the late 1930s, rabbis also would have encountered several recently published articles about Jewish intermarriage that made their way into the popular press. In each case, the authors drew on their personal experiences to make larger points about the obstacles that mixed-faith couples faced. In 1933, for example, George Sokolsky, a Jew and a well-known columnist, wrote about his intermarriage in the *Atlantic Monthly*. "Mixed marriages," he admonished, "should not be entered by individuals who are not certain that they have transcended racial, national, and religious affiliations."[42] Although his marriage had weathered ten years, he advised his readers that the stark differences between him and his wife—"she, Chinese, Christian, British; I, Polish, Jewish, American"—would put many marriages on a course for failure.[43] At the end of the decade, in 1939, the *Atlantic Monthly* published companion pieces about Jewish intermarriage, again personal narratives, documenting the significant challenges faced by intermarried couples. The two articles were penned anonymously, one written by a woman— "I Married a Jew"—and another by a man—"I Married a Gentile." Together the articles warned against intermarriage, not because either of the authors was particularly religious, but because their religions bespoke larger traits, values, and behavioral patterns.[44] That same year an Episcopalian man married to a Jewish woman wrote in the *American Magazine,* "Whatever system of worship we may choose, the world regards me as a Christian and my wife as a Jewess."[45]

Popular voices seemed to mesh with expert ones: religion was less a designation of belief and more a remarkably inelastic marker of identity. Rabbis, like other Americans, found their way to an expanding body of sociological literature about marriage and religion. Jacob Weinstein, rabbi at Chicago's oldest Reform temple, was armed with social-scientific and anecdotal evidence when it came to explaining why he would not perform a marriage between a Jew and a non-Jew. In 1941, he described meeting a distraught mother whose son was planning on marrying a non-Jewish woman. Her own reaction to her son's impending marriage was as disturbing to her as the marriage itself; after all, she told the rabbi, she was not religious. "It is always difficult for us, brought up in the individualistic tradition of the American environment," the rabbi explained, "to realize how strong are the dictates of the group."[46] Yet as much as American liberalism empowered the individual over the group, when it came to marriage an individual's group identity mattered incredibly. Although Weinstein acknowledged that the interdiction against intermarriage stemmed from traditional Jewish sources, he was certain there was a more modern sociological rationale: "Other things being equal, those who come from a similar background have a better chance of successfully living together than those whose backgrounds are dissimilar."[47] He quoted directly from "I Married a Jew," concluding that his prediction for that marriage, like most intermarriages, was "not very rosy."[48]

Jewishness, far from a discrete piece of a person's background was, in Rabbi Weinstein's words, "a way of life, deeply and subtly imbedded in the emotions and value judgments, something which one does not slough off or put on like a new garment."[49] Recall that Rabbi Mann, speaking to the convention of Reform rabbis had employed almost the same apparel simile to make his point. In calling attention to a person's inability to clothe himself or herself in a new identity, the rabbis suggested that religion was lodged deeply and was as intrinsic as a part of one's body. Yet they communicated the presumption that Jewishness was organic and unchanging through the terminology not of race but of social forces.

"Marriage," Rabbi Weinstein explained, "is a social as well as a personal act." Although some individuals could strike out on their own and marry with no regard for the background from which they came, most could not. Marriages happened in the context of families and communities. Weinstein, like other rabbis of his day, believed that women more than men bore the responsibility for creating families that were hardy enough to maintain Jewish marital norms. He wrote, "Unless we train our daughters to be willing to help their husbands in the first hard years . . . to run a house without paid help, many fine young Jewish men will continue to find their mates among non-Jewish girls."[50] No mention was made of Jewish sons' responsibility for choosing to pursue non-Jewish women. Instead he suggested that materialistic daughters reared by negligent mothers drove Jewish men into the arms of non-Jewish women.[51]

In the mid-1940s, a sociologist who studied intermarriage patterns in Derby, Connecticut, explained that Jewish parents held very different expectations for their sons and daughters. For their daughters, the adage "No *chuppe* [wedding canopy], no *shtuppe* [sex]" was enforced. Boys, however were encouraged to "sow their wild oats" with non-Jews.[52] Girls were expected to wait for those boys and, in marriage, to put in whatever work was necessary to create stable domesticity.[53] Far from an exclusively Jewish goal, domestic stability was, sociologists and rabbis agreed, a requirement of a strong nation.

The Triple Melting Pot: Religion, Marriage, and American Stability

For communicating putatively similar American values (so-called Judeo-Christian ones) while limiting potentially disruptive intimacy among different American groups, religion served wartime and postwar national goals ably.[54] The proof of religion's significance was not in its theological prescriptions or ritual demands but in the fact that religion was a reliable index of other social patterns. Sociologists helped endow religion with an American purpose by describing it as an instrument of social—and, notably, marital—organization. In the midst of wartime, many sociologists, politicians, and religious leaders shared the goal of reconciling the fact of American diversity with the aspiration for national unity. By designating certain forms of diversity as embodying the essence of American identity, leaders attempted to mold American diversity to fit national goals. Identifying religion as the quality that most differentiated Americans from one another, but that also gave them a set of shared values, sociologists, politicians, and clergy pronounced religion to be central to American life. Racial divisions remained largely outside of this understanding of American national identity, which was premised on a white American public. As interpreted by sociologists, Americans' marital patterns offered the soundest indication that religious divisions remained sharp in American life.[55]

In the early 1940s, new language for thinking about American diversity and national identity arose directly from an instrumental approach to religion. The triple melting pot, a coinage of the non-Jewish sociologist Ruby Jo Reeves Kennedy, was intended to reflect the fact that religious divisions alone (she relegated race to the sidelines) persisted in the midst of cultural, political, and economic transformation. How did Kennedy ascertain that religious divisions endured in American social organization? She had studied whom Americans married. By looking at marriage licenses filed in New Haven between 1870 and 1940, she had discovered that with remarkably high frequency Protestants married Protestants, Catholics married Catholics, and Jews married Jews. As Drachsler had predicted, nationality had become decreasingly important to Americans' marital patterns. Religion, however, remained vital—as long as one understood religion according to the distinctions, which ignored denominational variations, drawn by wartime agencies.[56] Despite some rather serious methodological flaws (critics wondered how she determined religion in the case of civil marriages and whether her findings would hold true outside of New Haven), her theory built on 1930s sociology, reflected wartime sensibilities, and created a vocabulary for talking about religion as a fixed social boundary.[57]

Kennedy's triple melting pot idea gained many adherents. For example, Milton Barron, a Jewish man who received his doctorate from Yale, concluded in his 1946 study of intermarriage in Derby, Connecticut, "Ethnic intermarriage . . . is preponderantly within the framework of religious endogamy, clarifying the religious stratification of the population as Roman Catholics, Protestants and Jews."[58] Kennedy revisited her theory in a 1952 article that took into account New Haven marriage data from the preceding decade. She concluded that religious endogamy had become "considerably more pronounced."[59] Her earlier hypothesis, that "cultural lines may fade, but religious barriers are holding fast," appeared enduring.[60]

The triple melting pot theory suggested that what was often seen as minority or ethnic behavior—endogamy—was actually an American act. Although Jews had the highest rate of inmarriage compared to Catholics and Protestants, their patterns were categorized as typical, not anomalous, and certainly not threatening. Kennedy was not Jewish, and there is no evidence that her theory grew out of any particular concern with Jews in the United States. She did, however, intimate that she had decided to study intermarriage because she was skeptical about the sociological soundness of the melting pot idea.[61] Additionally, shortly after Kennedy's death in 1970, she was remembered as a "social sociologist" who believed that a clear connection existed between her scholarship and her social ideals.[62] Much of her social activism was connected to her later research about mental retardation, but she may have viewed the triple melting pot model as a contribution to a postwar order that would upend the intolerance ingrained in a single-melting-pot vision.

Even if Kennedy did not intentionally address Jewish concerns, Jews took note of the sociologist who defended endogamy with statistics. In

1960, she served as an expert at a symposium about intermarriage sponsored by the Theodor Herzl Foundation and attended by rabbis, Jewish educators, and Jewish social scientists. Kennedy was the only non-Jew and, it so happened, the only woman on the program. In her talk titled "What Has Social Science to Say about Intermarriage?" she credited Jewish endogamy with maintaining the "cohesiveness" of the Jewish family and Jewish subgroup.[63] In the next few years, she occasionally lectured about intermarriage at synagogues near her home in New London, Connecticut.[64]

By the 1940s, however, Jews did not have to travel far to learn about sociologists' views on intermarriage. True, most sociologists published their studies about intermarriage in scholarly journals, but increasingly they ventured into more popular media, agreeing to be quoted in articles about intermarriage or, in some cases, writing the articles themselves. These articles extended the authority of sociology to prescribe proper behavior, and they also helped professionalize the role of marriage expert. In 1941, for example, sociologist Ernest Groves wrote an article titled "The Problem of Mixed Marriage" for the *Ladies' Home Journal*. Groves, who held a degree from Yale Divinity School, had made a name for himself by offering the first college-level course on marriage in 1927.[65] He explained that "all religious leaders" tried to discourage intermarriage, but rather than citing the theological or creedal reasons for doing so, he insisted that "religion is more than a belief: it is a way of life."[66] He continued: "One can be indifferent to religious matters without realizing how one's emotional attitudes are bound up with little childhood happenings and family habits that are of the essence of the particular religious culture."[67] In other words, the functional realities of religion made religious exogamy an unwise choice for individual and, more broadly, American stability.

Articles appearing in *Time, Cosmopolitan, Seventeen, Good Housekeeping*, the *Christian Century*, and the *New York Times* similarly built a case for religious endogamy by assuming a sociological understanding of religion.[68] Taken together, the articles defined intermarriage as deviant, and almost all cited statistics correlating marriages across religions with high divorce rates and offered evidence showing the overwhelming frequency of religious endogamy.[69] Still, they also implicitly suggested that intermarriages were occurring often enough to merit media attention. That many of these magazines were geared toward female readers was no accident. Most of the authors shared Rabbi Weinstein's assumption that women were responsible for regulating marriage, upholding religion, and socializing their children. When any of these things went awry—as readers learned they would if people married outside their religious worlds—women were taught to blame their own misconduct. For Jews, this was even more the case because, according to Jewish law, women singularly conferred Jewish identity on their children. While this fact granted women a level of power, it also held them uniquely responsible for their families' religious composition.[70]

Rabbis were quick to learn the power of numbers, often citing the same statistics about divorce and religious endogamy that were used in popular magazines.[71] Attempting, it seemed, to tie their own normative authority to the new cultural authority carried by sociology, surveys, and statistics, postwar rabbis learned to explain Jewish endogamy in a new language. Few of them lingered long in the language of religious prescription. Instead, many appropriated the increasingly popular and persuasive sociological framework that predicated marital success on a couple's shared background. Whether speaking to Jews or non-Jews, they explained Jewish endogamy as being mandated by distinctly American sociological facts.

Jewish Survival and Sociological Jewishness

In June 1947, the CCAR once again debated whether to amend its 1909 resolution about intermarriage. Aware of the weight of history on the group, one rabbi reflected, "I have the feeling that the desire to strengthen that resolution is an expression of a mood of despair and reaction in Judaism today."[72] The destruction of European Jewry had placed the issue of Jewish intermarriage, imagined as being coterminous with Jewish survival, front and center for many rabbis. Finally, however, they had access to a vocabulary for explaining Jewish endogamy as simultaneously good for the Jews and good for America.

Among the rabbis debating intermarriage that day were many World War II chaplains.[73] Gunther Plaut, for example, had served as chaplain for the 104th Infantry Division in Germany, his birthplace. In the spring of 1945, his unit had helped liberate the Dora-Nordhausen concentration camp. His days were spent giving proper burials to the corpses that littered the ground.[74] At the rabbis' meeting in 1947, Plaut admitted to his colleagues that, before the war, he had performed the occasional intermarriage, "but ever since I came back from the war, I have come to look at our people in a different light. . . . We are in an age which calls for the strengthening of those forces which make for a policy of survival for our people."[75] Others were stirred to the same conviction. Expressing sentiments that would have shocked many of their predecessors, one rabbi criticized the 1909 resolution for lacking "enough punch," and another added, "We ought to set standards for our people."[76]

Disturbed by these authoritative-sounding pronouncements, Rabbi Julian Morgenstern, a respected leader among the rabbis, warned them that their emotions could set into motion "a renewed tendency towards particularism in Judaism."[77] Although he had never officiated at an intermarriage and assumed he never would, he frankly reflected, "Were I starting in the rabbinate today as a young rabbi facing the problem of intermarriage realistically and seeking to do that which I think is best for the Jewish people[,] . . . I think I would officiate at intermarriages under certain conditions."[78] The lesson from the war, he believed, was one that fostered openness not insularity. Another rabbi agreed and admitted that he had recently started to officiate at intermarriages because it was impossible to "legislate love" or dismiss the "human side" of marriage.[79] Better to draw more people toward Judaism than to drive them away. "I do not think Jewish survival can be achieved by compulsion," a rabbi concluded, dismissing the suggestion that a reinvigorated resolution could make a difference.[80]

Few of the rabbis, in fact, believed that changing the resolution one way or the other would make much of a difference. Rabbinic decrees against intermarriage paled in comparison to sociologists' expert testimony that intermarriage was a sociological rarity and a sociological mistake. This balance of authority made sense to the majority of the rabbis, who realized the persuasive power of sociological language. No new resolution needed to be passed if Jews—like other Americans—were coming to understand that, in one rabbi's words, "marriage between people when there is a fundamental difference in the ways of life" was a bad idea.[81] "As Americans," this same rabbi continued, "we believe in the home as units of democracy," and any force that destabilized the home would weaken the nation as well.[82]

According to a new logic of sociological Jewishness, rabbis, alongside sociologists, recast Jewish endogamy as indispensable to American life. By the 1940s, religion in the United States was shorthand for understanding who a person was. The triple melting pot theory and general pronouncements in favor of religious endogamy put Jews on equal footing with non-Jews, describing their distinctive behaviors as iterations of sociological rules followed by all American religious groups. Social division, far from being contrary to the goals of American unity and national strength, was reenvisioned as a bulwark of social order. The question of why those divisions existed in certain places and not in others took a backseat to the functional value of social divisions. Intimacy across them was difficult and disruptive. In the eyes of sociologists, the fact of an individual's Jewishness was enough information to conclude that his or her interests, values, and behaviors would resemble those of other Jews more than those of non-Jews. The strength of sociological Jewishness was in its inevitability. In this respect, it resembled a biological identity. But unlike a race-based definition of Jewishness, it located identity in the realm of the social group. Groups could adjust to new norms even if their boundaries remained fixed. Sociological Jewishness was simultaneously flexible and unyielding, able to change in content without ceasing to exist.

Still, the shortcomings of sociological Jewishness were unavoidable. In the 1950s, as Jews moved to the suburbs in droves, attended American universities in unprecedented numbers, and felt more comfortable in the United States than ever before, rabbis and sociologists had to wonder whether new sociological realities were undermining the staying power of sociological Jewishness. Even before that, the narrative of immigrant success, told fondly by many mid-twentieth-century Jews, maintained that individuals, no matter their background, all had the capacity to flourish in the United States by virtue of their own pluck. Sociological theories that designated one's background as destiny, at least romantically speaking, chafed against long-held Jewish goals of inclusion and called into question the terms of Jewish success in America.

Yet rabbis were unmistakably drawn to sociological Jewishness for its ability to endow distinctiveness with national purpose. In their efforts to explain Jewishness to the United States, rabbis had come to believe that Jewish survival depended on Jews' ability to articulate their contributions to American life. When understood as a sociological designation, Jewishness could serve as a public good without running into the age-old problem of how to balance claims about the universal importance of Jews and Judaism with a commitment to specific and distinctive Jewish survival. Now through sociological vocabulary, Jews could explain their group survival in universal terms and could redefine their group survival as serving a public American purpose.

In 1934, Mordecai Kaplan had observed that intermarriage "is the one sentiment which may be said to form the common denominator of all Jews who have not definitely made up their minds to break with the Jewish people. Even those who have abandoned all Jewish religious beliefs and observances think twice before they give their sanction to intermarriage."[83] Marriage was the most elemental way a Jew expressed his or her Jewishness; it was also the starkest way of renouncing one's Jewishness. The elision of intermarriage with apostasy reflected centuries of Jewish experience in places that made no allowance for civil marriage. If marriage, by definition, occurred within a religious framework, then for a Jew to marry a non-Jew (unless the non-Jew converted to Judaism, a rare event) meant that the Jew also left Judaism. Even in the United States, where civil marriage was an option, Jewish intermarriage, at least until the latter part of the twentieth century, tended to be understood as a clear rejection of Jewishness.[84] Increasingly, Jewish leaders recognized that, more than religious doctrine, sociological pronouncements offered a key for explaining and maintaining Jewishness: why Jews did (and should) marry other Jews, and why, far from magnifying the difference between Jews and other Americans, Jewish endogamy was just one of multiple ways that Jews served the American good.

CHAPTER 4

Serving the Public Good and Serving God in 1940s America

Useful Jews and Model Minorities

In 1943, with war raging across the oceans, President Roosevelt wrote a letter of praise marking the fiftieth anniversary of the Jewish Chautauqua Society: "Even during these trying days of national emergency, through your academic program of spreading knowledge about the Jew and his background, your society will continue to give due weight to the need for enlightenment on the best that every minority people may have to offer toward our unified American ideal."[1] The ease with which FDR categorized Jews as a "minority people," not a religious people or a separate race, indicated the growing sway of sociological definitions of Jewishness and American group identity. He suggested that Jews could serve the United States by assuming the role of a proper minority group, one committed to strengthening—not diminishing—American unity.

Whereas earlier Reform rabbis, from those who lectured to non-Jews for the JCS to those who proposed enacting a missionary program, had used religious language to explain how Jews contributed to the United States, by the 1940s sociological language had proved itself more powerful. Fitting Jews into emerging models of the American minority group, Jewish leaders were able to explain Jewishness in terms familiar to Americans and indispensable to the functioning of democracy. The notion that the minority group served and enacted American ideals prompted the JCS to focus new attention on black schools. By 1945, black colleges and universities comprised nearly 10 percent of the campuses reached by JCS rabbis.[2] One rabbi, after lecturing at a number of black schools in the South, observed that African American students "recognize that the Jewish and the negro peoples are both minority groups. . . . From us they [want] guidance in the conduct of their internal affairs."[3] Energized by his experiences, this rabbi, along with others, found a new Jewish purpose and a new way of explaining Jewishness through the role of model minority.

In the 1940s, Jewish Chautauqua rabbis were hardly the most prominent voices when it came to asserting that Jews, in their collective existence, served the public good. Indeed, Conservative rabbis were the most vocal leaders to stake out a public purpose for the enactment of Jewishness in the United States. In these years, the rapid growth of the Conservative movement, especially in the ever-expanding suburbs, brought Conservative rabbis into greater contact with the non-Jewish world. Often finding themselves amid non-Jews and serving congregations filled with Jews who had recently left their urban childhood neighborhoods, Conservative rabbis felt compelled to craft new explanations of Jewishness.[4]

Conservative rabbis, who had played a much more minor role in explaining Jewishness to the United States in previous decades, now saw it as their task to convince Americans that Jewishness was both good for America and a good, or commodity, for public consumption. Although Reform rabbis participated in the effort to present Jewishness in the service of the American public good, Conservative leaders in the 1940s were most active in these efforts. Influenced by Mordecai Kaplan's functionalism and the political climate of the 1940s, these leaders worked to define Jewishness through its service to the American public sphere. In proclamations, often addressed to a broad audience, rabbis described Jewishness as indispensable to American public life. As a distinctive people and the inheritors of a particular worldview, Jews were intimately bound to the fate of America's democratic experiment. Their survival, rabbis argued, would guarantee the strength of democracy just as much as American democracy would guarantee their own existence.

In the 1940s, new modes of nationalist discourse provided Jews with opportunities to equate their distinctive existence with the maintenance of democracy. Wartime inspired greater efforts to generate unity among America's diverse, though predominantly white, citizens, even as it also circumscribed a smaller sphere of acceptable behavior. Groups deemed acceptable in their diversity were given the

chance to constitute themselves as being united with American concerns and values.[5] The novel notion that the United States was a Judeo-
Christian nation, and that democracy sprung from Judeo-Christian
values, was in many ways hatched at the conferences that Conservative
leaders came to organize in the 1940s.[6] While the term *Judeo-Christian*
itself seemed to indicate shared spiritual foundations, its originators
envisioned its function as political and sociological. The widespread
acceptance that the United States was—and had always been—a Judeo-
Christian nation connected American political stability to the ongoing
survival of Jewishness, a product of the living and breathing Jews who
inhabited American space.

A decade marked by a fierce assertion of American power and the
incomprehensible destruction of Jewish life, the 1940s was a time when
to be an American Jew was to feel a kind of unevenness. As Americans,
many participated in the rising sense of power and prosperity that came
on the heels of the Second World War. As Jews, they experienced exis-
tential despair. The sociological conception of Jewishness, emerging
from university campuses, rabbis' studies, and the pages of Jewish and
non-Jewish periodicals, grounded Jews in American patterns—and
thus, American successes. But it begged the question of a Jewish purpose: Was Jewishness merely a conduit to Americanness? Or did it contain some larger purpose, a purpose that could justify and ensure Jews'
continued existence even after the horrors of Nazism?

Conservative rabbis hoped to persuade American audiences that
Jewishness was instrumental—indeed indispensable—to American success. These rabbis maintained that Jewish survival was imperative for
the good of the United States, even if it was left to Jews to prove that
this was the case. By showing Americans that Jewishness served the
public good, and by teaching each Jew to see the goal of Jewish group
survival as a personal duty, rabbis crafted a durable modern form of
Jewishness that would survive the annihilation of European Jewry and
help establish the United States as the center of diasporic life. In this
achievement, some rabbis and Jewish intellectuals saw deeper failure,
charging their colleagues with surrendering the sacred to the social, or
as Christian theologians would have put it, choosing culture over
Christ. If Jewishness existed only to serve the public good, and if Jews
occupied a distinctive sociological space only because man-made social
rules seemed to demand it, then Jewishness itself held no ultimate
meaning. Some Jews interpreted this as the worst kind of nihilism:
emptiness clothed with a facade of purpose. Yet in daily life, the case for

Jewish survival seemed best served by Jews who could prove their utility to the public good.

Defining the Public

Louis Finkelstein, the leader of the Conservative movement in the 1940s, once told a story about baseball. As a young rabbinical student, he had bumped into Solomon Schechter on the streets of Manhattan. Schechter, an eminent scholar and the chancellor of the Jewish Theological Seminary, looked over the student and asked, "Can you play baseball?" Shyly Finkelstein shook his head no. "Remember this," Schechter told Finkelstein: "unless you can play baseball you'll never get to be a rabbi in America."[7]

What baseball had to do with being a rabbi was perfectly clear to countless American rabbis who found themselves straddling the Jewish and non-Jewish worlds. Rabbis devoted their careers to serving the Jewish people, but they often did so in places and contexts that demanded they make Jewishness familiar to non-Jews. Schechter's instruction, apocryphal or not, that Finkelstein learn to play baseball was a prescient statement about the new public that rabbis would be expected to serve. This public, Jewish and non-Jewish, would have to be trained to see the connections between Jewishness and Americanness and, even more, would have to be convinced that Jewish group survival was more beneficial to the United States than assimilation or, worse, removal. Conservative rabbis, greater in number and serving a larger sector of the American Jewish population than ever before, recognized that a sociological understanding of Jewishness, which valued the group dimensions of Jewish life and focused on the functional purpose of Jewish survival, had the best chances of making sense to the broadest American public.

In 1942, just as Americans received the first reports of Hitler's final solution, a group of Conservative rabbis met in Chicago to discuss the role of Judaism in the modern world. Although none predicted the devastation Hitler's plan would wreak, the rabbis who gathered that spring believed that world events demanded that Jews reformulate their identities and their purposes for the larger world. Albert Gordon, a rabbi in Minneapolis at the time, who would later conduct sociological studies about Jewish life in the United States, called for rabbis to serve the American public in its broadest sense. "If we are working for anything that resembles a Kingdom of God," said Gordon, "that Kingdom of God is going to be created here on this earth, and it depends upon . . . the way in which we translate and interpret religion to the people round about us."[8] Other rabbis agreed. Jews needed to reach out beyond themselves and show the world—or at least the United States—that their Jewishness was essential in the effort to strengthen the forces of good.

"The gist of our discussion lies," one rabbi summarized, "in the word 'interpreter'—the Seminary as *interpreter* of Judaism to the world."[9] The "Seminary," shorthand for the Jewish Theological Seminary, stood at the center of wartime discussions about a new Jewish purpose. Founded in 1886 and substantially reconstituted in 1902, the Seminary was the training ground for traditional rabbis, and only over the course of the first decades of the twentieth century did it become the defining institution of a new American Jewish movement. Like Columbia University, the Seminary moved from midtown Manhattan to the uptown neighborhood of Morningside Heights. In 1930 a small but stately campus was established on the corner of Broadway and 123rd Street. Columbia stood only a few blocks to the south, and the Union Theological Seminary, home to Protestant theologians like Reinhold Niebuhr and Paul Tillich, was the Seminary's across-the-street neighbor.[10] The rabbis who gathered in 1942 imagined that the Seminary, more than any other Jewish institution, could prove Judaism's centrality to all of humankind. One of the rabbis explained, "We won't be an institution merely to serve three or four million citizens of America, important and all-significant as that may be, but we recognize that Judaism plays a part in the thinking of the whole of the world."[11]

Louis Finkelstein, who attended the Chicago conference in 1942 and offered a closing benediction, must have felt a deep sense of satisfaction as he listened to the rabbis. As leader of the Conservative movement, he dedicated himself to broadening the Jewish role in the United States and insuring, as he told outgoing chancellor Cyrus Adler in 1939, that Judaism "has its place in the modern world order."[12] Finkelstein perceived what many Reform rabbis—like those who supported missionary work or JCS activities—had already realized: for Judaism to survive in America, it would have to explain and market itself to non-Jews as a public good. But even more forcefully and vocally than Reform rabbis, Finkelstein created a new logic for Jewish survival in the United States that defined Jewishness through its function.

Finkelstein's conviction that Judaism would not survive if it detached itself from the broader world emerged from a central premise of Conservative Judaism.[13] The Conservative movement worked to conserve the laws and beliefs of Judaism by infusing them with social relevance. The Rabbinical Assembly, the professional organization for Conservative rabbis, articulated this functional approach toward Jewishness when it stated in 1934, "We who profess to dedicate ourselves to the advancement of Jewish religion must bring it into the arena of social life as a force for reconstruction and rebirth."[14] That same year, Mordecai Kaplan, who trained at the Seminary, published *Judaism as a Civilization*. Reflecting his own immersion in the literature of sociology, Kaplan proposed that Judaism in the modern world would be best apprehended as a distinctive civilization marked by social practices and behaviors. The practices of Judaism mattered insofar as they fostered in Jews a sense of "otherness," which defined them as members of a unique civilization. Yet, as he argued, one could be a member of multiple civilizations. For Jews in the United States, membership in multiple social worlds was a necessity of survival, and for this reason, exhibiting loyalty to the United States was as essential to being Jewish as practicing certain Jewish customs was. Although Kaplan would become disgruntled with Conservative Judaism, his formulation of Jewishness became integral to the movement and to Jewish life more broadly.[15]

A 1955 study of the Conservative movement suggested that "social utility" and not theological or ideological commitments drove the development of Conservative Judaism in the United States.[16] For Finkelstein and other midcentury Conservative leaders, the social utility of Jewishness reigned supreme. Jews enacted their Jewishness not by sequestering themselves in a purely Jewish civilization but by offering the fruits of their civilization to the rest of the world. A ghetto existence would do neither Jews nor the world any good; rather, the more Jews could prove themselves useful and indispensable to the public good, the more they would insure their own survival.[17]

Many Jewish leaders found it attractive to equate the maintenance of American democracy with the survival of Judaism, but Finkelstein, more than any other World-War-II-era Jewish leader, proclaimed the equation to be the crux of the Jewish public purpose. Throughout those years, he worked to turn the Seminary into an intellectual center, inviting scholars and religious leaders to convene there for a series of conferences about the interdependence of democracy and religion.

By hosting these conferences, Finkelstein implicitly argued that Judaism was as essential to the ethical and moral core of democracy as any other religion. More than this, however, he believed that Jews were uniquely positioned to foster unity even among the many religions in the United States and to help harness the strength generated from religious unity to American democracy. A 1938 statement from the Seminary, likely penned by Finkelstein, affirmed that Jews "exemplif[ied] another special role of a minority religion in the Western World: the linking together of followers of other traditions."[18] Similarly, in 1945, Finkelstein emphasized, "Jews have a job to do in this world—and the job is to act as bridgers and conciliators."[19]

In late 1942, as the Seminary celebrated its fifty-fifth anniversary, the *New York Times* editorial page observed enthusiastically: "As long as the doors of the Jewish Theological Seminary of America and like institutions speaking for the brotherhood of man remain open, our democratic traditions and ideals cannot be destroyed."[20] The newspaper of record praised Judaism for its service to democracy and, much as FDR had written in his letter to the Jewish Chautauqua Society, implied that Jews' secure place in the United States hinged on their fulfillment of national goals. Thus, disagreements about theology were trivial. Whether Jesus was a divine manifestation or not mattered little as long as Jews joined the pursuit of strengthening democracy. Their distinctive patterns and behaviors—which constituted, in Kaplan's terms, a Jewish civilization—could be mobilized to illustrate just how effectively American democracy united all Americans together in a common purpose.

Starting in the early 1940s, Finkelstein hoped to define the terms for a new American civil religion. In his view, religion was the moral center of democracy, but only if religion was understood as having multiple forms of expression.[21] He established the Institute for Religious and Social Studies and an annual Conference on Science, Philosophy, and Religion, as well as a number of smaller conferences and working groups, all with the goal of creating a religious arm of democracy located well outside a purely Christian context. Finkelstein had faith that democracy, in its true state, was inherently respectful of religion because it depended on religion for its moral basis. Furthermore, he believed that Judaism, embodied by a set of moral ideals and the ongoing survival of the Jewish people, was particularly fit for the work of democracy.

Ira Eisenstein, one of Finkelstein's protégés, declared at a Rabbinical Assembly meeting in 1949, "The affinity of democracy and Judaism is a happy one for both. In the free atmosphere of a democratic society,

Jews can survive to practice their Judaism; and Judaism, with its deep-seated penchant for democratic ideals, can reciprocate with ardent aid in defense of those ideals."[22] With the zeal of a postwar patriot, he explained that if Judaism and democracy ever came into conflict, "I would rather remake Judaism in the image of democracy than otherwise."[23] Far from being a heretic, Eisenstein shared Finkelstein's faith in democracy. Kept in check by the presence of multiple religious groups, democracy would never demand atheism or religious uniformity—the price of communism and totalitarianism—from those who subscribed to it. Epitomizing its confidence in the religion of democracy, the United Synagogue of America, a coordinating body for Conservative congregations, recommended in 1950 that the government-sponsored radio program *Voice of America* include "biblical readings, daily, in order that the religious basis of our democracy may be carried to the world, and that all men everywhere may benefit by the inspiration and strength that the Bible affords."[24]

By lending their support to a putatively generic form of religious expression—as religiously generic as the Bible (presumably the Hebrew Bible) could be—Conservative rabbis believed they were promoting Jewish survival. After all, if they helped define the qualities of public American religion, then they could de-Christianize the public sphere by making Jews and Judaism an essential part of it. The dangers, however, of supporting a greater religious presence in the American public sphere were plenty.[25] For one, try as Jews might to define the nature of the public sphere, the Christian majority was likely to continue to possess greater authority to define it. And even if Jews managed to gain a significant voice, they would have to do so by emphasizing the similarities among American religions, and, thus, diminishing Jewish distinctiveness. Activities concerned with brotherhood and interfaith relations almost always emphasized religious synthesis and humanity as a whole, not particularistic beliefs or group distinctions.

Finkelstein, much like those rabbis working to explain Jewish endogamy or entertaining missionary possibilities, confronted the perennial conflict that Jews since the Enlightenment had faced: how to reconcile the uniqueness of Judaism with its universal message. The sociological distinctiveness of Jews, Finkelstein maintained, was essential to the universal—or at least American—good that Judaism could do. For example, in the preface to the proceedings of the 1944 Conference on Science, Philosophy, and Religion, Finkelstein and his coeditors explained, "Judaism is a religion which seeks to serve the world. But in order to serve the world, it must exist. If it is to exist, its institutions and forms must be directed to an emphasis on their own value."[26]

For Jews to serve the world, as Finkelstein believed was their ultimate purpose, they first had to be Jews. According to mainstream Conservative and sociological thought, one was foremost a Jew because of his or her particular social location. Yet even as Jews remained the reflection of a distinctive collective entity, they also adhered to larger patterns exhibited by all social groups. Thus, according to Finkelstein, they could rise above their particularities to serve a greater whole.

Finkelstein hoped to balance his attraction to universalism with his commitment to Jewish survival by turning Judaism into a commodity with public utility for Jews and non-Jews. He was, however, too certain that Judaism had to prove itself as a public good in order to survive to let this insight be contained. The conferences that Finkelstein organized, although important in the eyes of some intellectuals and even the *New York Times,* had a limited audience.[27] To reach the public that he dreamed Jewishness could serve, he and other Conservative leaders found a new voice that could speak their truth to the masses.

Jews on the Air

Starting in 1944, millions of Americans in their own homes were able to hear Finkelstein's message by tuning their radios to *The Eternal Light.* Taking its name from one of the Temple rituals mentioned in the Book of Exodus, the program fashioned itself as a *ner tamid,* or eternal light, for all of America.[28] In introducing a book that reprinted the scripts from the show's first few years, Finkelstein characterized *The Eternal Light* as bringing together scholars and dramatic artists to "translate ancient, abstract ideas into modern dramatics."[29] Elsewhere he emphasized that the radio program's goal was "to interpret Jewish religion in terms that will reach as wide a group as possible, both within and without Jewish groups."[30]

By the time of the Second World War, radio was the best medium for reaching the American public. Although radio was soon to be replaced by the television, radios could be found in 83 percent of American homes in 1940.[31] Finkelstein was hardly the only religious leader to exploit the possibilities of radio. In fact, the National Broadcasting Company, the station that aired *The Eternal Light,* was required by the Federal Communications Commission to dedicate a certain portion of

FIGURE 5. NBC president David Sarnoff (left) and Louis Finkelstein in NBC's broadcast studio in the 1950s. Courtesy of the Ratner Center for the Study of Conservative Judaism, Jewish Theological Seminary.

its airtime to public and noncommercial programs, like those produced by religious groups. By World War II, broadcasting ecumenism was the prevailing norm, echoing a broader national trend; Jews would get their share of airtime alongside Protestants and Catholics.[32] NBC's decision to award the Conservative movement, and not the more established Reform movement, a portion of the available public broadcasting time was partially a function of geography (the Seminary was located in New York City, not Cincinnati) and partially a function of who knew whom (a board member of the Seminary organized an initial meeting between Finkelstein and the president of NBC). More than anything else, though, it was an indication of the ascension of Conservative Judaism in the United States and the fact that Conservative rabbis were becoming the chief spokespeople of Jewishness in the United States.

In 1946, the Hooper Rating Company estimated that five million listeners tuned in to each episode of *The Eternal Light*.[33] Jews and non-Jews across the country wrote letters praising the show and often requested scripts from episodes they had particularly enjoyed. Some Jews remarked that the program made them feel proud to be Jewish and gave them a deeper understanding of who they were. To the delight of the producers, others characterized it as an embodiment of democracy. A listener from Denver, for example, wrote that the show brought "new meaning to democracy when we hear our Jewish ideals drama-tized in a Jewish way as freely as other people's." Jewish and non-Jewish soldiers stationed in training camps throughout the United States wrote that they tuned into the show regularly and found that it helped fuel their patriotism and desire to defend American democracy. Small-town Jews emphasized that the program was one of the few ways they could connect with the larger Jewish world. A listener from Lyndonville, Vermont, compared the show to "manna from heaven." Both Jews and non-Jews commended the program for fostering better interfaith relationships, using terms like *goodwill* and *tolerance*. A woman from North Charleston, South Carolina, wrote, "I am a Gentile who is finding it easier to admire and like the Jewish people thru *[sic]* your broadcast."[34]

No matter the specific topic addressed—an episode in Jewish history, a story from Jewish literature, the life of an important Jew—modern American values were central to the message of *The Eternal Light*. Unlike other religious radio programming, *The Eternal Light* never broadcast sermons or religious services, instead opting to focus on how Jews and Judaism contributed to modern life.[35] An episode titled "The Microscope and the Prayer Shawl," for example, told the story of a Jewish doctor named Waldemar Mordecai Haffkine, who discovered a vaccine for cholera in the late nineteenth century. His scientific prowess was praised along with his loyalty to Judaism. In one scene, a professor interrogates him:

> *Professor:* Haffkine, doesn't your science get in the way of your religion?
>
> *Haffkine:* I don't think so. Both teach me to try to live decently. I haven't found any conflict. Should I?
>
> *Professor:* I should think you'd be satisfied with the scientific method.
>
> *Haffkine:* I don't know. Science tells me how . . . religion tells me why.[36]

Later, Dr. Haffkine lauds the scientific foresight of Judaism, explain-ing that the rituals of Kashruth are "now confirmed and blessed by the modern microscope."[37] Far from presenting Judaism as a challenge to modern science, the program illustrated Judaism's modernity, even sug-gesting that Judaism prefigured modern scientific discoveries.

Listeners learned that Jews had steadfastly contributed to the world during every historical era in which they lived, a lesson that Finkelstein and the writers hoped would convince Americans to view the Jews of their day in a favorable light. The details of Jewish ritual or cadences of Jewish prayer, though perhaps bespeaking a Jewish ethos of serving the world, were far less helpful in illustrating Jewish contributions than were historical anecdotes and biographical sketches about Jewish heroes. For example, an episode about the Warsaw ghetto uprising focused on Jewish heroics, not on the tragic fate that most Jews in Europe met.[38] The fight against totalitarianism was one with which most Americans would sympathize, and one that the program's producers hoped to prove Jews had uniquely contributed to.

As the leader of the Conservative movement during its most striking period of growth, Finkelstein attempted to draw Americans' attention to the ways Jews served the United States and contributed to the public sphere of American life. Through the conferences he organized and his support of *The Eternal Light,* he created a functional case for Jewish survival. For some Jews, however, this functional approach to Jewishness rang hollow. Ultimately, it offered no sui generis explanation of Jewish existence, no way of thinking about Jewishness apart from the social goals its served. At any moment, Jews may have served the public good, but who were they when they were not doing that?

"A Footnote to Democracy"

As was the norm in most synagogues, Milton Steinberg spent part of every Yom Kippur trying to persuade his congregants to dig deeper into their pockets and offer financial support to Jewish causes. In 1944, however, his Yom Kippur appeal took the form of protest. Off the rabbi's list of worthy organizations for the first time since he had started his rabbinical career was the Jewish Theological Seminary.[39] In justifying his decision to boycott the Seminary, Steinberg took aim at Finkelstein for turning Conservative Judaism into an apprentice to American values and neglecting its distinctive spiritual ideals. All the energy Finkelstein spent on his conferences and the radio program, Steinberg suggested, would be better spent focusing on Jews and their spiritual needs. When Finkelstein requested a meeting with a group of his detractors, Steinberg sent him a memo enumerating his offenses, including his "penchant toward (a) cultivating Goyim (b) . . . cultivating assimilationists

(c) involving Conservative Judaism in all sorts of enterprises except those most necessary for Jewish life."[40] Another Conservative rabbi once complained that Finkelstein treated Judaism as "a footnote to democracy," a criticism with which Steinberg would have agreed.[41]

In the aftermath of World War II, Milton Steinberg emerged as one of the most outspoken critics of Finkelstein's brand of functional and sociological Jewishness, in part because he could also see the wisdom in it. As he told his New York City congregation, "What I voice is the especial bitterness of one disappointed in his own, of one failed by that which he has counted on."[42] Throughout his life, Steinberg had been torn between his attraction to rationalism and functionalism on the one hand, and to faith and divinity on the other. On the side of rationalism, he believed that Jewishness had to be situated in society in order to thrive, and that its function—in the world and in individuals' lives—was its true meaning. By emphasizing the contributions that Jews as a sociologically distinctive group could make to modern life, Jewish leaders had honed what they hoped would be a foolproof mechanism for Jewish survival. Yet the wisdom that Steinberg saw in this rational approach to Jewishness was undermined by the awe he felt for unadulterated faith. In working so hard to situate Jews in modern life, he believed, Jewish leaders had lost the ultimate meaning of being Jewish, replacing it with a soulless kind of functionalism. His disillusionment with Finkelstein reflected his disappointment with himself and his inability to resolve the tension between faith and reason.

Born and raised in Rochester, New York, in the early twentieth century, Milton Steinberg was drawn to the rationalism of ancient Greek literature and philosophy from a young age. He had little formal Jewish education, and neither of his parents—not his father, a yeshiva student turned socialist, nor his apparently aloof mother—made much of an effort to instruct their son in Jewish topics. Only his maternal grandparents, with whom the family lived, cultivated in him an appreciation for Judaism. In later years, he would recall hearing Mordecai Kaplan speak at a 1914 Zionist conference in Rochester, though it is likely that this fact gained significance only in retrospect. When his family relocated to New York City, he met Ira Eisenstein, a future leader of the Conservative movement, and joined the youth group at Eisenstein's synagogue. There, Steinberg met Rabbi Jacob Kohn, whose faith pierced a hole in Steinberg's rationalism.[43]

Like many of the American-born sons of Jewish immigrants, Steinberg attended City College.[44] And, like many other motivated

Jewish young men, he found himself in philosopher Morris Raphael Cohen's classroom, where rationalism and empiricism were worshiped like gods. Steinberg would often come home from class and tell his friend Rabbi Kohn about Cohen's latest denunciation of religion. Kohn would then ask Steinberg pointed questions about the limits of a rationalist approach to the world, questions that a few days later Steinberg would lob back at his professor. Whether faith could be squared with reason, or whether only one or the other adequately explained the world, was the perplexity that came to define Steinberg's intellectual life—a rabbi on one side, a philosophy professor on the other. After Steinberg's death, a friend described him as combining the "rationalism of modern philosophic thinking with deep Hasidic piety."[45] Yet more often than not, the two ideals were at war in his mind.

In 1924, Steinberg entered the Jewish Theological Seminary because he wanted to learn how the American Jewish luminaries of his day had resolved the strife between faith and reason. He, like countless other Conservative-trained rabbis, almost immediately came under the sway of Kaplan, who taught at the Seminary from the early to the mid-twentieth century.[46] Kaplan's sociologically inflected model of Judaism allayed Steinberg's angst for the next two decades.[47] Years later Kaplan recalled, "He responded with all the ardor of his soul and the brilliance of his mind to my plea for a new approach to the inner problem of American Jewish life."[48] Speculations about God's true nature were far less important than the way that Judaism was woven into people's daily lives and the kinds of actions Judaism compelled Jews to take. With his model of civilization, Kaplan offered his students a program for synthesizing a distinctive Jewish life with a full commitment to the United States. After all, as Kaplan himself made clear and as Steinberg echoed for many years, one could live with "two heritages."[49]

Immediately after completing his rabbinical training, Steinberg assumed a pulpit for a congregation in Indianapolis. A year later, in 1929, his new wife, the former Edith Alpert, joined him. He had wooed her since she was a fourteen-year-old student in a synagogue course he taught. His love for her was intense, but his other passion—understanding the meaning of faith in a modern and rational world—left her cold. The life of a *rebbetzin*, a rabbi's wife, wore on her, and twice during their first year of marriage, she fled Indianapolis for her parents' home in New York City.[50] It may have been during those lonely and difficult months in Indianapolis that Steinberg started to think about the vastness of the United States and his hope that Jews and Judaism could survive in it. In 1933, just as he left Indianapolis to become the rabbi at the Park Avenue Synagogue in Manhattan, his first articles about Jews appeared in the *Atlantic Monthly*. These formed the basis of his first book, *The Making of the Modern Jew*, also published in 1933.

The Making of the Modern Jew, Steinberg explained in its preface, was intended for Jews and non-Jews who "have been fascinated by the strange confusion of the Jew. To them this book offers an interpretation which is also a rational explanation."[51] Although in part the book addressed itself to the history of Jewish survival, its true focus was on the modern problem of Jewish survival. More than anything else, the book offered a proposal, based on Kaplan's philosophy and the insights of sociology, for how Jews could maintain their identities in the modern world. Echoing Louis Wirth's conclusions, Steinberg wrote that even Jews who wished to shed their Jewish identity could never shake lingering traces of it. These traces, which he eventually termed "social identity," were inescapable.[52] Thus, for Jews to survive in the United States, they had to prove that all Americans benefited from Jewishness. His attempt to create a proof of Jewish utility revolved around his belief that America could only be strengthened by the "fructifying stimulation" generated by the Jews in its midst. As members of a distinctive civilization with its own literature, language, and folkways, Jews possessed "unique and irreplaceable" qualities.[53]

In words that Finkelstein, Kaplan, or any number of Reform rabbis just as easily could have written, Steinberg further explained in a 1941 article that "America is best served by its Jews when they strive to exploit the special resources of their group."[54] While he averred that the Jewish *Weltanschauung*, or "worldview," would always be "secondary to the general American environment" when it came to Jews' political loyalties, he also argued that it was an invaluable part of the United States.[55] Were it possible for Jews to cast off their "organic ethical code, and patterns of ritual," something Steinberg doubted they could do fully, the United States would be sapped of some of its strength.[56] Using himself as an example of the kind of synthesis he had in mind, he wrote, "Lincoln and Jefferson are my heroes together with Rabbi Akiba and Moses Maimonides. The four get along in my imagination quite companionably. . . . I sing Negro spirituals, American ballads, and Hasidic or Palestinian folksongs with equal vigor and tonelessness."[57] (One wonders if "Negro spirituals" were as American in his mind as Lincoln and Jefferson, or if he was suggesting broadening what constituted American civilization.) In the next decade, Jewish social researchers, like Oscar Handlin and Nathan Glazer, would make strikingly similar assertions and argue that every individual needed a group identity, which would complement and enhance his or her American identity.

Steinberg's uncompromising political loyalty to the United States, and his equally fervent commitment to Jewish survival, found expression in his involvement in America's war effort. In addition to joining protestors at a 1942 Stop Hitler Now rally held in Madison Square Garden, Steinberg enlisted in the army. He wanted to be a chaplain and administer to the needs of soldiers overseas, but he failed the army physical and instead was assigned a position as inspector of chaplaincy programs at home-front training camps.[58] In January 1944 his duties were cut short when he suffered a heart attack in Dallas. Heart problems would plague him for the rest of his life, ultimately leading to his untimely death in 1950 at the age of forty-six. In the six years between his first heart attack and his final one, a new variable—his own mortality—was introduced into his lifelong struggle between faith and reason. The answer that a sociological and functional model of Judaism had temporarily offered him, crumpled under the weight of his illness. Reason, it seemed, was a lesser guide than faith when it came to leading him through the loneliness of death.

The Complications of *Basic Judaism*

Steinberg wrote *Basic Judaism* after his first heart attack and during a period of renewed theological introspection. Published in 1947 by Harcourt, Brace, and World, the book did not entirely disavow a sociological definition of Jewishness, but its focus was "those beliefs, ideals, and practices which make up the historic Jewish faith."[59] Steinberg had assured his editor that "this . . . kind of book . . . should sell forever," and, indeed, it remained required reading in introductory courses (especially for converts) to Judaism for many decades.[60] He explained in his preface that he was writing for multiple audiences: for believing Jews, for indifferent Jews "groping to establish rapport with the Jewish Tradition," and for "those many non-Jews who happen to be curious about Judaism."[61]

In writing a book that non-Jews could understand, Steinberg focused his explanation of Jewishness on religious categories—like God and belief—that would have been familiar to non-Jews. Yet his emphasis on religion, far from leading him to make statements about the essential similarities between Judaism and Christianity, led him to a bold rejection of Christianity. In a section that Steinberg fought with his editor to retain, he systematically refuted Jesus's divinity and criticized him for being ill-tempered and possessing an egocentric preoccupation with his own salvation. Justifying his desire to keep the section, Steinberg explained to a friend, "I think that gentiles who are interested in getting the Jewish view of Jesus . . . ought to get it fairly straight and not in . . . garbled, saccharined misrepresentations."[62] He also wished to disabuse Jews of any romantic feelings they may have harbored toward the "Jesus myth."[63] Newsweek's review of the book highlighted this section as its downfall, warning that many readers would find the chapter on Jesus "offensive."[64]

It clearly took audacity to write in such searing terms about Jesus at a time when many Jewish leaders, whether out of conviction or pragmatism, were agreeing with the equivalency that the Judeo-Christian idea suggested existed between the two faiths. In Steinberg's mind, however, his bigger gamble was to break with the sociological Jewishness of his teacher Mordecai Kaplan and to reject Finkelstein's conviction that Jewishness was the sum of its ability to function as a public good. The same year that he published *Basic Judaism,* Steinberg wrote a religious manifesto in the *Reconstructionist,* an intellectual journal established to disseminate Kaplan's ideas.[65] There he made his case for putting belief and God at the center of Jewish life. He averred that "the Jew without religious belief . . . is in a sorry case—as a human being, in the first instance, but more specifically as a Jew."[66] Steinberg's statement was so out of line with the spirit of the journal that the editors issued a disclaimer saying that they did not endorse any particular conception of God.

Steinberg had become disenchanted with the prevailing form of Jewishness that, in his estimation, subordinated the sacred to social purposes. Under the sway of Finkelstein and Kaplan, the Conservative movement was home to a functional approach to Judaism, where Jewishness was defined as a collective identity that served a larger public good. Yet Steinberg desired something entirely different from Jewishness; it must "inform us concerning the nature of things in a manner which we could not derive from any other science or human discipline."[67] Jewishness, he believed, must be irreducible, not a manifestation of a larger sociological rule or a reigning political ideology.

Much to his dismay, then, Steinberg found himself targeted for endorsing just the kind of functional and democracy-serving Jewishness he had come to despise. In the eyes of some intellectuals, *Basic Judaism* breezily popularized an undemanding conception of Jewishness that equated religion with function and the collective. In a biting review published in *Commentary*, Irving Kristol lambasted Steinberg for writing so basic a guide to Judaism that "no one's religious sentiments are excluded from participation."[68] Kristol accused Steinberg of turning Jewishness into a mere reflection of liberal American social ideals, an accusation that Steinberg himself had made against Finkelstein. The end result of such an accommodation, according to Kristol, was a conception of Judaism as a feel-good social doctrine bereft of theological complexity. The truths of human suffering and evil were excised, turning Judaism into an ineffectual confirmation of the essential goodness of the world and the status quo. Theologian Reinhold Niebuhr's voice wove throughout Kristol's review. Niebuhr, too, was dismayed by religion that mirrored society and did not press individuals to reckon with the limits of the human capacity to understand or imitate God.[69]

Those who knew Steinberg well were more confident in his rejection of sociological Jewishness. For example, Will Herberg, who had become Steinberg's study partner in the 1940s, was convinced that Steinberg had rejected the reigning sociological and functional Jewishness because he realized it did not offer a "compelling motive" for Jewish survival.[70] After Steinberg's death, Herberg remembered him as possessing a deep appreciation for the "mystery of Israel" and rejecting efforts to substitute "society for God as an object of worship."[71] Herberg could just as well have been describing himself.

Steinberg's personal struggle between faith and reason—not incidentally, the two words etched onto his gravestone—was replicated in a larger communal debate about sociological definitions of Jewishness and theological ones. Nonetheless, for many years the debate was dominated by Kaplan's philosophy, or at least his sociologically inflected suggestion that Judaism be viewed as a civilization, and by Finkelstein's commitment to Jewishness as a public good. At root, these modes of explaining Jewishness corresponded well to the contours of American Jewish life. Moreover, they turned Jewish survival into an American good.

Survival

In the 1940s, as Jewish life in Europe crumbled, Reform and Conservative rabbis joined together in their desire to plant Jewish life firmly in the United States. Particularly before the establishment of a

Jewish state, there simply did not seem to be another place that Jews could thrive. The case that rabbis made for Jewish survival in America was, however, often articulated as a litany of contributions that Jews made to the nation. While the fact of the matter was that Jews could not imagine their survival without the United States, many rabbis emphasized that it was the United States that could not survive—or at least would not thrive—without Jews.

Finkelstein, as the leader of the Conservative movement, established intellectual institutions devoted to showing the indispensability of religion, including Judaism, to American democracy and morality. He placed himself and Jewishness front and center in the redefinition of the American public sphere. Instead of disavowing an American civil religion, he tried to expand and de-Christianize it. At the same time that intellectuals gathered to discuss religion, democracy, and morality, average Americans could tune into a weekly radio program sponsored by the Conservative movement that similarly defined Jews by the contributions they made to modern life and not by the rituals they practiced or beliefs they maintained.

The equation between Jewish usefulness and Jewish survival reflected American rabbis' need to feel a sense of control over Jewish fate, felt all the more urgently as the European tragedy unfolded. Conservative rabbis, like many of their Reform colleagues, gravitated toward a definition of Jewishness premised on Jewish social utility. They hoped to prove that Jews could use their Jewishness to serve the United States, and that, by doing so, Jews would guarantee their own survival. Yet the closer the rabbis tried to tie Jewishness to Americanness, the more they struggled to explain why Jews should not—or could not—simply fade into America. Steinberg's disgruntlement with Finkelstein, with Kaplan, and with reason grew from his fear that a Jewishness based on social function was a Jewishness of society, not God, and that it would eventually become as irrelevant as any other social philosophy. To be eternal, Jewishness could not subordinate itself to the society or the sociological position that Jews happened to occupy at one particular moment in time. Still, in beseeching Jews to tie themselves to God, not society, Steinberg may have drawn a distinction that pitted modernity against religion, as if a person had to choose one or the other.

Postwar Jewish social researchers, hardly convinced that Jewishness was a matter of faith, continued the work their predecessors had started in the 1920s and 1930s. Many realized that Jewish leaders had come to rely on a sociological vocabulary to lend authority and meaning to their explanations of Jewishness. Few social researchers could remain aloof from communal politics. Even those who were agnostic about the question of Jewish survival often relied on Jewish funding to support their research, and found their audiences at conferences sponsored by Jewish agencies. Most social researchers, however, were not indifferent to the question of Jewish existence in the United States. A cadre of academically trained Jewish intellectuals who emerged in the postwar era helped fashion an American vocabulary of Jewishness more durable than any that had ever before been elaborated. While the language they used— that of the ethnic group—was a clear product of the postwar context, its derivation was not. What postwar social researchers were able to do was create an intellectual and semineutral academic infrastructure for the social-scientific turn that had already started to take shape among rabbis and earlier Jewish intellectuals. In their hands, sociological Jewishness became almost irrefutable, as a description of what Jews were like and how they fit into the United States, and as a brilliant, yet flawed, self-sustaining logic of Jewish survival.

CHAPTER 5

Constructing an Ethnic America

Oscar Handlin, Nathan Glazer, and
Post–World War II Social Research

Tercentenary Mandates

In 1954, as Jews attended dinner parties, parades, and museum exhibits to commemorate three hundred years of Jewish life in the United States, a group of Jewish intellectuals marked the tercentenary the way they knew best: with a conference.[1] Sociologist Seymour Martin Lipset convened the proceedings by asking a simple question: "Why [are] there so many Jewish sociologists and so few sociologists of the Jews?"[2] Even the late Louis Wirth, whom Lipset noted was "unique among leading American sociologists in writing a book about the Jews," never seriously returned to the subject after publishing *The Ghetto*.[3] Answering his own question, Lipset suggested that many Jews entered the social sciences as a "way of escaping from their Jewishness."[4] He believed that in the postwar world, however, this could change. The Conference on Jewish Relations, Morris Raphael Cohen's brainchild, had sponsored this tercentenary event specifically to persuade Jewish intellectuals that it was meaningful—personally and intellectually—and necessary for them to study Jewish life.[5] "We call on social scientists," the attendees, among whom were several social scientists, proclaimed at the end of the conference, "to interest themselves more than heretofore in research projects which deal with problems of Jewish social relations in America and in other countries of Jewish settlement."[6]

That same year, Oscar Handlin and Nathan Glazer—a social historian and a sociologist, both of whom were invited to the conference—wrote studies of Jewish life in the United States.[7] Handlin in his book

Adventure in Freedom, and Glazer in a lengthy article published in the *American Jewish Year Book* that he then revised into his 1957 book, *American Judaism,* set out to explain Jewishness to their colleagues and the American public. Not so unlike Wirth and his colleagues at the University of Chicago, and Cohen and his interwar cohort of social researchers, Handlin and Glazer believed that the particular elements of Jewish life carried with them universal significance. And similar to rabbis in the 1940s, they maintained that Jewishness served the public good.

In the era after World War II, Jewish social research achieved unprecedented prominence in the scholarly and nonscholarly world. More than ever before, it shaped the way Jews talked about being Jewish. The seeds for this social-scientific turn in Jewish discourse had already been planted in earlier decades, but they fully blossomed only after the Second World War. While they certainly drew on a host of predecessors and contemporaries, Handlin and Glazer were instrumental in sculpting a sociological language of Jewishness that fit into postwar nationalistic aims and answered prevailing Jewish concerns. Their lives, experiences, and aspirations were intimately connected to the social theories they proposed, and serve to illustrate the thin line that separated Jews and Jewish scholarship in this era.

Handlin and Glazer were born only eight years apart—Handlin in 1915 and Glazer in 1923—to immigrant parents in New York City. Both attended New York City public colleges, and neither served in World War II.[8] In 2002, when I had the opportunity to meet them, they occupied offices on opposite sides of Harvard's campus. Though they were secular intellectuals throughout their careers, their Jewishness was nonetheless central to their vision of how social difference could best be organized and understood in the United States. Both proposed the existence of a universal American ethnic pattern.

While the language of the "ethnic group" predated their work, Handlin and Glazer were two of the most important theorists of a new, white ethnic norm, where ethnic affiliation was a requirement of Americanness.[9] They built on the theories that Jewish intellectuals, like Louis Wirth, Mordecai Kaplan, and Horace Kallen, as well as non-Jewish researchers such as Robert Park, W. Lloyd Warner, and Ruby Jo Reeves Kennedy, had proposed about group identity. Yet they extended the reaches of ethnic theory in the academic and Jewish communal world by enmeshing it with the sensibility of postwar America and the particular exigencies of postwar Jewish life. The meaning of Jewishness, they explained, rested not primarily on external social pressures and prejudices—as Wirth and earlier sociologists had suggested—but on the assumption that all Americans were members of subgroups, and that these subgroups, no matter how inconsequential their differences, defined American social structure. It is worth emphasizing that Handlin was not a sociologist—he was a social historian—but that his scholarship was still in constant conversation with sociology, especially the theoretical models of assimilation and immigrant identity suggested by Chicago school sociologists. He, like Glazer, worked to define the United States as an ethnic nation and helped convince Jews and non-Jews that Jewishness was best understood as a sociological certainty.

Americans in the postwar years learned to see themselves anew through social-scientific studies of their lives. The Kinsey reports, Gallup polls, and best-selling books like *The Lonely Crowd* became the new arbiters of normalcy and deviance.[10] Studies like these drew attention to Americans' social behaviors—explaining to them, for example, their sexual habits or the way they responded to small- and large-group situations. In the wake of World War II, social-scientific investigations of hatred, prejudice, and minority experience in particular proliferated. Many were funded by federal grants, but some of the most significant ones received financial backing from Jewish organizations, most importantly the American Jewish Committee.[11] Through these studies, new models to describe minority life emerged that shaped the way Americans understood group difference and the relationship between social diversity and national identity.

In a more sustained fashion than their predecessors had, postwar Jewish social researchers wrote Jews into American social structure via the language of sociology. At the same time, they revised the very models that described American social structure according to their perceptions of Jewish trends. The ethnic model was extraordinarily persuasive; it seemed to conform to the realities of American life, and it offered a cure for the loneliness and conformity that postwar critics had warned would erode the nation's strength.[12]

The ethnic model also had serious limitations. First, in trying to create a totalizing social theory, social researchers like Handlin and Glazer tended to overlook inconsistencies. When they observed deviations from the so-called normal pattern of social life, they blamed individuals, not a larger social system that in fact did not operate as uniformly as they imagined. Additionally, while naming ethnic identity as an American norm, they neglected its content, a shortcoming that Milton Steinberg had already perceived in the 1940s and that would continue to plague rabbis and other Jewish devotees of sociological Jewishness. Still, the language of sociology and ethnic identity brilliantly drew Jewishness into the center of American social theory and American life without exacting Jewish survival as its price.

The Jewish Investment in Postwar Social Research

Well before and well after the Second World War, the Jewish communal world offered far more professional opportunities for Jewish social researchers than the American university. For many Jewish social researchers, the places they published, the salaries they drew, and the scholars with whom they collaborated were connected to Jewish organizations. By the postwar era, the American Jewish Committee (AJC), founded as a reaction to a wave of pogroms that coursed through czarist Russia in 1906, had become the most important supporter and sculptor of Jewish social research. Reflecting the rising importance of the social sciences and echoing the faith that interwar researchers like Cohen had placed in empiricism, the AJC established a Department of Scientific Research in 1944.[13] Max Horkheimer, a German Jewish refugee who had been a member of the Frankfurt Institut für Sozialforschung (Institute for Social Research) before fleeing Nazi Germany, was appointed the first director of the department.[14] Under his tutelage, the research wing was given the charge "to investigate the extent and the causes of antisemitism in the United States, to develop testing methods by which the effectiveness of current techniques of combating antisemitism may be evaluated and to integrate eventually its theoretical research with a practical program of the American Jewish Committee."[15] The importance of these tasks grew as Americans tried to come to terms with Nazism.

In December 1945, the AJC gathered a group of Jewish intellectuals to discuss how they could harness their talents and expertise to the job of helping American Jews adjust to postwar realities. The participants, including Louis Wirth, Salo Baron, Horace Kallen, and Mordecai Kaplan, concluded—much as the participants at the tercentenary conference would a decade later—that social-scientific research was essential to any effort to organize and sustain American Jewish life. One participant recommended that the AJC fund "a study of the Jews in America that will achieve the reputation that a study like Myrdal's did."[16] He was referring to Gunnar Myrdal's 1944 book *An American Dilemma,* an analysis of the "Negro Problem" sponsored by the Carnegie Foundation, which had gained wide public notice. Myrdal, a Swedish economist, had suggested that, despite material evidence of persistent racism in the United States, an "American Creed" existed that would prevail over racism and ensure equality and the steady improvement of life for black Americans.[17] While Myrdal's conclusions appealed to the group, the Jewish intellectuals and social scientists in attendance at the conference were even more enthusiastic about the possibility that a similar Jewish study could affect "not only . . . ourselves, but . . . the people of the country that one would hope such a study would influence."[18] Horkheimer, as director of the Department of Scientific Research, was immediately put on the task.

With an almost giddy faith in social research, the leaders of the AJC proclaimed that a broad study of prejudice and Jewish life would first "[present] the Jews to the world . . . with a right to dignity and to the respect of the other cultures and civilizations. And secondly, it would give fiber and strength and vitality to Jews."[19] Sweeping studies of anti-semitism had been published before—most recently Isacque Graeber and Steuart Henderson Britt's 1942 *Jews in a Gentile World: The Problem of Anti-Semitism*—but the group envisioned something more widely read and publicized.[20] Some conference participants were skeptical about the extent to which academic research could substantially alter American attitudes, but most were optimistic and supported the research that culminated in the publication of the Studies in Prejudice series.[21]

By comprehensively examining the mechanisms of hatred and prejudice, AJC leaders believed they could learn to recognize and squelch the trends they imagined had ended in the tragic destruction of European Jewry. Far from concluding that prejudice grew from structural flaws in a society—like unequal class or race hierarchies—the studies published in the series located hatred and prejudice in individual pathology. The individual could be cured of his or her prejudice through education, a far less disruptive path than radically restructuring an entire society.[22] Although German Jewish refugee scholars researched and wrote most of the volumes in the series, their Marxism was quieted in favor of American empiricism, patriotism, and optimism. Nathan Glazer, who had been employed by the AJC as Horkheimer's research assistant, recalled that the researchers "were always very frightened of being, in some sense, unveiled for what they thought of the Jewish bourgeoisie and the American Jewish Committee."[23] Yet by emphasizing its commitment to America and disavowing potentially subversive critiques of society, the

AJC positioned itself well to conduct and disseminate research to help secure Jewish life in the United States.

The leaders of the AJC, much like earlier leaders of the Conference on Jewish Relations, also believed that the creation of a journal would aid in their pursuit to harness intellectual energies to the project of Jewish survival. The journal, called *Commentary* (the successor of a brief and far less popular AJC journal called the *Contemporary Jewish Record*), was launched while Americans were still reeling from V-day celebrations. Elliot Cohen, its editor, predicted in a foreword to the first issue that the celebrations would end soberly for Jews and Americans alike. Jews would be left haunted by the European genocide; Americans haunted by a weapon massive enough to destroy civilization in one blow.[24] No, a journal could not solve the world's problems, but, he suggested, it could encourage "fresh and free-ranging thinking, by bringing to bear upon our problems the resources of science, philosophy, religion."[25]

Like *Jewish Social Studies, Commentary* was conceived in a moment of transition, at a time when one could imagine that knowledge and free thought might make a difference in the course of events. Born into the immediate postwar world and financed by the deep-pocketed AJC, *Commentary* could, however, speak with a louder and often more tendentious voice than *Jewish Social Studies* had in the late 1930s. As such, it became a forum where predominantly Jewish intellectuals could experiment with studying themselves and explaining themselves to an imagined American audience.

Here, in the growing sphere of professional Jewish social research, Oscar Handlin's and Nathan Glazer's lives intersected, as did the lives of most postwar social researchers. For Glazer, the AJC and *Commentary* magazine acted as conduits to secular scholarship and learning. For Handlin, the vector moved in the opposite direction; his professorship at Harvard and his stature in academic circles acted as passageways to the Jewish world, a world he had left as a young graduate student.

Between the Yard and the Charles: Oscar Handlin

If not from the age of eight, as legend has it, then certainly by the time he entered college, Handlin knew he wanted to be a historian.[26] In 1936, he attended his first American Historical Association meeting. To this third-year Harvard graduate student, the conference represented the most impressive face of the academic world. Scholars gathered that year in Providence, Rhode Island, and as Handlin roamed the ballroom, the lounges, and the halls of the Biltmore Hotel, he rubbed shoulders with men whose books he revered, and listened attentively to their conversations. "I had one foot in . . . Harvard, but most of me was still in Brooklyn which perhaps accounted for the excitement of the sessions."[27] Perhaps timidly, or maybe ushered in by one of his advisors, Handlin approached the circles of men and felt immediately drawn into a group of "shared values and interests."[28]

Handlin believed—or it may be that his hope became belief—that one's background meant nothing in the intellectual world. In Handlin's recollection, that young man from Brooklyn, one shoe still covered with the dirt of the city street, was generously welcomed into the academic elite. How could it not have been difficult to be a Jew at Harvard in the 1930s and 1940s? Handlin raised one foot and rested it on an open desk drawer when I asked him about this. "I never thought about it," he answered.[29] Historians would have, and have, predicted a far different answer. The story is familiar: under President Abbott Lawrence Lowell, Harvard identified and dealt with its "Jewish Problem" in the 1920s by enacting admissions quotas limiting the number of Jewish students.[30] Handlin's Jewishness was not inconsequential. In a letter of recommendation, he was described as having "none of the offensive traits some people associate with his race."[31] Still, when pressed again, Handlin told me, "Everybody here knew that I was Jewish, but it didn't seem to make any difference."[32] Is it possible that he never faced obstacles—or at least prejudice—as a Jew at Harvard? Perhaps or perhaps not. What is significant, however, is his testimony that he did not, an effort to reconcile his past with his assumptions about how the world should work.[33]

When I met Handlin in December of 2002, he was eighty-seven. He spoke quietly, his Brooklyn-inflected voice often reaching no louder than a whisper. His office was dusty, overflowing with books, littered with scraps of yellow legal pad paper, and certainly not imposed upon by a computer. Ask him how long he has been at Harvard, and he will answer, "I've never left."[34] For decades, he has sat near the top of Widener Library with a window facing the Charles, not Harvard Yard. Few of the immigrants he chose to study—those who traveled to the United States in the nineteenth and early twentieth centuries—ever set foot in the Yard (after all, Harvard was loath to let them on its soil for many years). Most lived in crowded, urban neighborhoods, like those across the Charles.

FIGURE 6. Oscar Handlin in his office at Harvard, December 2002.
Photograph by the author, used with permission.

To Handlin, it is a matter of little speculation why he studied immigration, first in *Boston's Immigrants* and then in his Pulitzer-winning *The Uprooted*. Yes, his parents, Joseph and Ida, were immigrants, among those Jews who came to the United States at the turn of the century from what was then czarist Russia, and yes, he attended Brooklyn College, a hub for children of immigrants, particularly Jewish ones.[35] In his mind, his biography, however, offers few clues to his decision; rather, his intellectual pedigree and, in particular, his relationship with Arthur Schlesinger Sr., a professor of history at Harvard, provide the explanation. The way Handlin tells it, he had wandered into Schlesinger's office one day, and Schlesinger, who had become a mentor to the young Handlin, asked him if he had found a dissertation topic yet. Handlin replied no. "So [Schlesinger] said, 'I have a good subject that someone else was just beginning.'"[36] And so began Handlin's dissertation on Boston's Irish immigrants.

Arthur Schlesinger, like Handlin, was the son of immigrants. He was raised by a Catholic Austrian mother and a Jewish Prussian father in turn-of-the-century Xenia, Ohio. In his later years, Schlesinger reflected,

"I accepted as a matter of course the diversified make-up of the American people, for it formed part of my daily experience."[37] Handlin too grew up surrounded by people who had traveled to the United States from foreign lands. Although it is difficult to accept his claim that his childhood circumstances were insignificant to his scholarly decisions, Handlin's own disavowal of a connection is consistent with the narrative he tells about his life and career.

What America meant to Handlin, both as a student succeeding in the New York public school system and as a fledgling historian making it at Harvard, was opportunity. Clearly, he was aware that there were certain limits to his opportunities. For example, I asked if he ever advised students in his early career at Harvard to study ethnic history. He reflected, "They didn't come to Harvard in order to reimmerse your—," he paused and corrected himself, "themselves in their community. They knew they would probably wind up in a middle-class, Yankee town, and what good was it to be known as an expert in Irish-American or Italian-American history if you were going out to Northampton?"[38] Yet as it happened, Handlin was instrumental in legitimating precisely those fields, among others, of ethnic specialization. For the most part, however, he resisted explaining his Jewishness as fettering or shaping his professional success.

Handlin maintained that the intellectual world of which he was a part had no use for group distinctions or prejudices based on them. In his well-known 1964 study of assimilation, Milton Gordon similarly argued that American intellectuals "interact in such patterned ways as to form at least the elementary structure of a subsociety of their own, and that this subsociety is the only one in American life in which people of different ethnic backgrounds interact in primary group relations with considerable frequency and with relative comfort and ease."[39] Contextless and free from communal bonds, the intellectual, like Robert Park's marginal man, was aloof from social structure. According to Gordon, a Jewish sociologist, this was an ideal position for a putatively unbiased commentator on society. In the mid-1960s, Christopher Lasch similarly described the intellectual as "a person whose relationship to society is defined, both in his eyes and in the eyes of the society, principally by his presumed capacity to comment upon it with greater detachment than those more directly caught up in the practical business of production and power."[40] Yet in the decades since Gordon and Lasch characterized intellectuals as hovering outside the strata of society, new trends in literature and history have challenged the assumption that intellectuals are immune to the everyday pressures and biases of living in this world.[41] Nonetheless, Jews, who already occupied an outsider status in the predominantly Christian American environment, may have found, ironically, a measure of acceptance—at least among intellectuals—by emphasizing the unique perspective that their outsiderhood afforded them.[42]

Born a Socialist, Reborn a Sociologist: Nathan Glazer

The day before I spoke with Oscar Handlin, I had trekked clear across Harvard's campus to William James Hall—a building as minimalist and modern as Widener is sumptuous and neoclassical. There, on the sixth floor, I met with Nathan Glazer. His office was modest, and when I walked in, he was addressing an envelope and affixing a Chanukah postage stamp to it. Glazer at eight, or for that matter at twenty, was not set on an academic profession. But as he tells it, at nine he did discover socialism. The Depression took its toll on his family, and Glazer, the youngest of seven children, remembered watching his older sisters leave for work every day. Only they, employable as secretaries, were able to eke some sustenance out of the withering economy. Glazer was too young to try and find work, so he was sent off to school. In 1932, at the age of nine, he learned that his father, a struggling garment worker, had voted for socialist Norman Thomas for president.[43] His father's modest involvement in socialism that was, according to Glazer, "socialist, but not too socialist," allowed Glazer in later years to describe himself as socialist by descent, not only by choice.[44] In 1940, after attending James Monroe High School in the Bronx, Glazer entered City College, planning to be, like Handlin, a history major.

Glazer graduated deeply immersed in the rising social sciences and a moderate Zionist form of socialism. The once-intended history major became an ardent sociology student. Far from being a mere academic pursuit, the study of social structure seeped into Glazer's extracurricular life. He recalled, "I was active in a Zionist organization when I was at City College. . . . It thought itself part of the general socialist, non-Stalinist left. . . . One of the characteristics of this group—Avukah [American Student Zionist Federation], it was called—was [that it was] very high on the promise of the social sciences."[45] There was, no doubt, an element of radicalism in learning about the social sciences for those who came to them through socialism. "It is almost embarrassing to say we believed in revolution," Glazer has remarked.[46] While talk of revolution may have fueled Glazer's passions, the meetings he attended were more like study sessions, tutoring him in the classic texts of socialism and social science and introducing him to the most cutting-edge political theories (*Partisan Review* and the *New International* were required reading). By the time Glazer graduated in 1944, his involvement in Avukah had both schooled him in social theory and opened the door to the New York intellectual scene. He became part of the circle of City College–educated, mainly Jewish, New York–based, socialist talent.[47] Heady with ideological fervor, he expected that he would not have to abandon his socialist stance to play a vital role in American life and shape a meaningful career.[48]

One of the most important differences between Handlin and Glazer is that Handlin never was a socialist. Those who did identify with socialism (to recall Lasch's words, a critique of the "business of production and power") saw it as a badge of their outsider status. Much like other intellectuals, American socialists imagined themselves removed from mainstream society, a position they saw as essential to their ability to perceive its flaws. Socialism, akin to Gordon's intellectual subsociety, promised to create a society where one's ethnic background was inconsequential. Socialist politics and intellectual pursuits were appealing to immigrants and their children who felt marginalized by mainstream society.[49]

For Glazer and many within his Jewish intellectual circle, the allure of socialism faded quickly as the Second World War ended. Their socially critical ideology was remade into an ideology that explained and defended existing social arrangements. Despite early pronouncements to the contrary, most of Glazer's circle chose to, or felt compelled to, abandon their socialism as they entered the professionalized, and often government-sponsored, sphere of American social research.[50] After all, it was difficult to call for revolution when one's government-funded think tank or research project would suffer from the fallout.[51] Histories of American politics and radicalism also note more generally that after World War II the possibility of a socialist revolution had largely faded in the United States, hastened by the expanded opportunity for upward mobility and the growing clout of anticommunism.[52]

In Glazer's recollection, by the mid-1940s he felt disgruntled with the totalizing nature of socialist theory, so totalizing that it simply started to feel untrue. "It always seemed to me," he explained, "that

·FIGURE 7. Nathan Glazer in his office at Harvard, December 2002.
Photograph by the author, used with permission.

whatever the large generalization, one would always have to comment,
'It all depends.'"[53] As the United States emerged victorious from World
War II, Glazer ceded his socialism to sociology. Much like socialism,
sociology offered him a tool for understanding society without, in his
estimation, demanding blind "fealty to any theory or methodology."[54]
Whereas socialism explained the way the world should work and suggested toppling America's social and political structure to achieve that
new world order, postwar sociology tended to explain that the nation's
liberal democracy worked just fine, operating according to fair and
knowable social rules. As a sociologist, Glazer contended that he still
pursued politics, only "through academic means."[55] Glazer's ideological fervor had not died, but he replaced his critical stance against
American capitalism and liberalism with a far more optimistic assessment, cultivated in part through a faith in the nation's unique ability to
ensure Jewish survival.

In 1945, Elliot Cohen, the editor of *Commentary*, hired twenty-two-year-old Glazer. At the time, Glazer was a graduate student in sociology at Columbia, but he had already been a staff writer for *Commentary*'s short-lived predecessor, the *Contemporary Jewish Record*. *Commentary*, in Glazer's assessment, attempted to "present Jews to the American public world" and relied on those "who did not speak to the Jews from within the Jews" to do so.[56] Recalling his early years as a writer and editor at *Commentary*, he smiled sheepishly and explained that most of the Jews who staffed it in the 1940s and 1950s "had little sympathy for the Jewish institutions and leaders who had the most influence on American Jewish life."[57] In the late 1940s, Rabbi Milton Steinberg accused *Commentary* of being "deficient in that ultimate love of Judaism without which no Jewish enterprise can be other than morally bankrupt."[58] He pilloried the editors of the journal for slavishly seeking respect from the non-Jewish world and sacrificing Jewish interests to the cause. Why, Steinberg wondered, did Jewish ideas have to be "dejudaized" in order to translate them to the non-Jewish world?[59]

Rabbi Steinberg failed to notice, however, that the reverse was also true: to explain Jews and Judaism to the world, Jewish intellectuals and especially social scientists often attempted to Judaize the world, or at least social theory. From the very first issue of *Commentary*, Glazer was responsible for the "Study of Man" column, a regular feature that focused on recent social-scientific scholarship. The existence of the column was a sign of the cultural authority—in Glazer's words "the weight"—of the social sciences.[60] In his first column, Glazer explained to readers that, as editor of the section, he was committed to publishing general studies about society because "whatever affects mankind affects us [Jews]."[61] Morris Cohen's 1939 foreword to the first issue of *Jewish Social Studies* reverberated in Glazer's statement; both men intended to prove that Jews were subject to the same pressures and social forces that all other groups faced. Glazer, however, took the argument one more step: "As a group, we [Jews] seem to be particularly exposed to the social climate of our times, its changing winds and weather."[62] Thus, he parlayed the universal appeal of social science into a very specific Jewish necessity and consciousness. Jews needed social science to help them understand themselves, and the world needed Jews and their social research to better understand itself.

Jews and the American Ethnic Pattern

In the pages of *Commentary,* Handlin and Glazer found a forum in which to suggest a resolution—for Jews and for Americans—to the long-standing tension between the dictates of assimilation and the tenacity of group identity. Each had received his scholarly training at a time when historians and sociologists were influenced by Chicago's prominent and prolific sociology faculty. Although neither had attended the University of Chicago, both learned that assimilation was a linear social process experienced similarly, if not simultaneously, by all American immigrant and minority groups.[63] Yet the events of World War II eroded many Jewish social researchers' faith in an assimilationist model of American Jewish identity. In the years after the war, these scholars were forced to come to terms with the fact that assimilation, no matter how complete, had not spared Jews from Hitler. Irving Howe, a Jewish intellectual from Handlin and Glazer's generation, later reflected, "We were living directly after the holocaust of the European Jews. We might scorn our origins; we might crush America with discoveries of ardor; we might change our names. But we knew that but for an accident of geography we might also now be bars of soap. . . . Our Jewishness might have no clear religious or national content, it might be helpless before the criticism of believers; but Jews we were, like it or not, and liked or not."[64]

It would have been difficult to overstate the difference that an "accident of geography" made. Even as American Jews in the 1950s confronted the immensity of the violence that had destroyed European Jewry, they also created comfortable and secure lives in the United States.[65] In the midst of their upward social and economic mobility, however, few American Jews shed their Jewish identities or their affiliations with Jewish social networks. This was a conundrum for social observers wed to an assimilationist model, and it was the starting point from which Handlin and Glazer theorized an American ethnic pattern.

In their scholarship, Handlin and Glazer both argued that the fact that Jews continued identifying as Jews, even in a time and place that seemed to offer them the possibility not to do so, was neither strange nor distinctive. Rather, they claimed, the ongoing Jewishness of Jews reflected the steadfast significance of group—or ethnic—affiliation to American social patterns and, more important, to the success of liberalism. America's "ethnic pattern," a phrase Glazer coined in a 1953 *Commentary* article, relied on a social structure that blocked neither assimilation nor group cohesion but rather treated individuals as full-fledged Americans without demanding that they cede their group allegiances. Whereas once politicians and immigrants had worried about assimilation, in recent decades almost every group of Americans felt, according to Glazer, a "complete identification" with the United States, evidence of the nation's openness to new and different kinds of people. Yet alongside the broad patterns of Americanization, he also observed a "heightening of ethnic consciousness," particularly among immigrants' grandchildren.[66] The simultaneous high level of acceptance that the United States granted its diverse citizenry, and ongoing group consciousness that continued to demarcate one group from another, characterized the nation's ethnic pattern.

Such a rise in ethnic identification, according to Glazer's model—and Handlin agreed—did not in turn compromise anyone's ability to achieve success and security in the United States. In the articles he wrote for *Commentary* in the 1940s and 1950s, Handlin proposed that the United States could not be what it most wanted to be—liberal and democratic—absent the existence of diverse social groups. National efforts to smother people's "diverse loyalties," he wrote in a 1950 article, undermined the very promise of American liberalism.[67] The United States depended on the diversity of its inhabitants as proof of liberal democracy's superiority over other governing systems, especially communism.[68] The nation's ethnic pattern, therefore, was the foundation and enactment of American strength.

Ethnic groups mattered less because of the content of their difference and more because of the way they structured American life. In a 1949 symposium sponsored by the Yiddish Scientific Institute (YIVO), Handlin had contended that Jews were "at the heart of the American experience, and that to learn about the Jews is to learn about all America."[69] Using strikingly similar language, he averred in the first pages of his 1951 study of immigration, *The Uprooted*, that "immigrants *were* American history."[70] Near the end of the book, he described an Old World father and a New World son in terms that resonated with his own biography. "Looking at the old man's bent head in the chair, who came so far at such cost," Handlin wrote, "the son knows at once he must not lose sight of the meaning of that immigrant journey. We are come to rest and push our roots more deeply by the year. But we cannot push away the heritage of having been once all strangers in the land."[71] The son symbolized progress, and he was not bound to his father's traditions, but he could not deny them or their place within

him. The first-person plural—"we"—brought the weight of the universal and the depth of the personal to Handlin's final observations about
immigrant life and the United States. Both Handlin and Glazer rested
their ethnic theories on idealized visions of American social structure.
They believed that the United States evenly extended its opportunities
to all people, no matter what their group affiliations.

Although Handlin and Glazer each defined the individual as being
tied to a particular social group, neither acknowledged that the individual could be hindered in the broader public arena by his or her group
affiliation, whether ethnic or otherwise. For example, their assertion
that all Americans were given the same opportunities to succeed bla-
tantly discounted the obstacles that half of all Americans—women—
faced at that time. Take Handlin's own wife, Mary Flug Handlin. She
was a trained social scientist with a master's degree from Columbia and
worked as a research historian at the Social Science Research Council in
the 1940s.[72] One of Handlin's earliest doctoral students recalled noticing her sitting in the back row at Handlin's lectures feverishly taking
notes. He later learned that she used those notes to write some of her
husband's books, filling in and revising where necessary.[73] Occasionally
listed as coauthor, Mary Handlin never received the public recognition
or respect that her husband did. This was not in the least unique to
their situation.[74] The generic terms in which Handlin and Glazer rendered the American ethnic pattern belied the gendered assumptions
within it; the individual who achieved public success while still retaining some connection to an ethnic past was male. Few social scientists at
the time, however, were particularly interested in producing or testing
broad social theories from the standpoint of women's experiences and
gender disparities.[75]

Even if the gender assumptions ingrained in Handlin and Glazer's
ethnic theory would have gone unnoticed at the time, one suspects that
incidents of antisemitism in the United States would have issued an
immediate challenge to their contention that the maintenance of group
identity had few public consequences. To the contrary, Handlin and
Glazer had faith, much like Myrdal did in his 1944 *An American
Dilemma,* that these episodes of discrimination were anomalous and
incapable of puncturing America's essential fairness. In 1948, Handlin
and his wife had written a pamphlet for the Anti-Defamation League
titled *Danger in Discord: Origins of Anti-Semitism in the United States.*
Despite the pamphlet's stated goal of illuminating the history of antisemitism in the United States, the Handlins introduced the topic by

disputing its relevance to American history. They wrote, "Most important of all, the prejudiced here have had to struggle against an important article in the American creed, the faith that the individual was to be judged, and to be treated, on the basis of his own worth, and not in terms of his status, class, race, or religion."[76] Whatever anti-Jewish behavior cropped up in the United States would quickly wither in the "inhospitable soil" of American liberalism.[77]

Five years later, in his article about the nation's ethnic pattern, Glazer would agree that the coexistence of ethnic attachments with an American tradition of individualism and tolerance accounted for the success of American liberalism. In his youth he had flirted with a political ideology that promised to eradicate all modes of distinctiveness, but by the end of the Second World War, he pledged his love to an idealized American democracy that promised to ignore distinctiveness when it came to individuals, and protect it when it came to groups. Glazer and Handlin believed that the United States treated all individuals as assimilable equals and did not, aside from a few isolated historical instances, interfere with individuals' group identity. Likewise, ethnic life made certain claims on individuals, but it did not, aside from a few unfortunate cases of ethnic nationalism, interfere with national life. According to both men, nowhere could this balance between ethnic loyalty and American individualism be seen more clearly than among themselves—that is, among Jews.

The Jewishness of America's Ethnic Pattern

Shortly after Handlin published *The Uprooted* and Glazer wrote "America's Ethnic Pattern" for *Commentary,* both men produced book-length studies of Jews in the United States. Handlin's 1954 *Adventure in Freedom* and Glazer's 1957 *American Judaism* explained the history and persistence of Jewish identification in the United States less as a function of a providential Jewish character and more as an illustration of the nation's ethnic character. The books shared an almost identical structure, first recounting the waves of Jewish immigration and then examining the effects of American culture and society on the Jews. Glazer's title referenced Judaism, while the subtitle of Handlin's book claimed "Jewish Life" as his topic. They both, however, classified the Jews as an ethnic group, although neither offered a particularly concise definition of the term.[78]

In the preface to *Adventure in Freedom*, Handlin explained that the book represented his "individual hope. . . . By enlightening the present, it may thus aid all those who seek such meaning to shape their visions of the future."[79] Later he recalled that he wrote it as a way of marking the tercentenary of Jewish life in the United States. According to Handlin, he had suggested to some important Jewish leaders in New York City that they stage a celebration. "They thought it would be a good idea," Handlin recollected, "but in effect, nothing came of it because the Jews in New York were too fragmented to come together."[80] History, of course, documents multiple well-planned tercentenary celebrations. Handlin's revisionism stemmed, it seems, from his unhappiness that his own book was not adopted as a central feature of the celebrations.[81]

Glazer similarly hoped to write a book that could explain the present and suggest the future of Jewish and American life. In the spring of 1955, Daniel Boorstin had invited him to speak in a series at the University of Chicago about Protestants, Catholics, and Jews in the United States. From these lectures as well as an article Glazer wrote in the tercentenary edition of the *American Jewish Year Book*, he generated his book *American Judaism*.[82] Glazer recalled self-consciously writing *American Judaism* "from almost a non-Jewish perspective," so that "if you want to learn about American Judaism, and if you are in a religious studies department, you would pick it up."[83] Echoing Handlin's equation of immigration history and American history, Boorstin's preface to Glazer's book proclaimed, "In telling the story of a people with a vivid tradition who have had to come to terms with the New World, Glazer is retelling the story of all Americans."[84] Half a century later, the book remains in print, after three reprints.

What the books accomplished was to set out Jewishness in sociological terms that made its existence appear both inevitable and comparable to that of other groups in the United States. In the final pages of their books, Handlin and Glazer assessed Jewishness in their own times and characterized it as best apprehended through sociological categories. They acknowledged that Jews, like other Americans, were increasingly asserting their religion as an expression of their Americanness. Yet they believed that, far from a true revivification of Judaism, this was a pragmatic Jewish response to cold war pressures to disavow atheistic communism.[85]

In 1955, after Handlin's book was published and before Glazer's went to press, another Jewish intellectual, Will Herberg, explained in his book, *Protestant-Catholic-Jew,* that religion served as a surrogate for ethnic and cultural identity: instead of demanding theological rigor and daily devotion, the three predominant American faiths were simply expressions of American belonging.[86] Like Herberg, Glazer and Handlin doubted that current Jewish enthusiasm for Judaism—or at least for synagogue membership—was an accurate indicator of the future. Glazer regarded Jews' recent upsurge in religious affiliation an act of "instrumental efficacy" that helped them fit into the regnant patterns of American social life.[87] Handlin similarly wrote, "It was not theory or theological speculation that led the Jews in the United States more often than formerly to order their communal life around religion, but rather the terms of the society in which they lived."[88] Handlin and Glazer concluded that Jewish life would survive in the United States as a result of external inducements—in Handlin's words, "diversity, voluntarism, equality, freedom, and democracy"—and internal impulses.[89] They expressed a faith less in the enduring qualities of Judaism or the Jews and more in American liberalism's tolerance for and expectation of group affiliation.

If sociological patterns—or "the terms of the society"—and not theology or biology defined Jewishness, as Glazer and Handlin, along with a number of other postwar commentators, explained, then Jewishness was a manifestation of American values. In one of the most biting reviews his book received, Handlin was upbraided for his unwillingness to see Jews beyond generic terms. "The Jews are supposed to be the central characters in this book," Charles Bezalel Sherman, a Jewish sociologist, wrote, "but with very little change it could just as well pass as the story of the Greeks in America or the Italians or the Swedes."[90] Sherman, of course, intended to disparage Handlin's efforts, yet for Handlin the reviewer precisely hit on the strength of the book: its universal implications. Handlin explained to me that he often placed Jews alongside other immigrant groups when he wrote and lectured about them, "to convey . . . that we're not that unique."[91] Likewise, a *Christian Century* reviewer praised Glazer's book for dissolving the "popular image of American Jews" and showing that Jews and Christians shared common struggles.[92]

Handlin and Glazer's attempts to prove the existence of an American ethnic pattern paralleled their desire to categorize Jewish experience in universal and American terms. Both wrote Jewish survival into a broad theory of American social structure, arguing that all American groups felt the same tension between group cohesion and

American integration. Although Glazer described a "bond of feeling among almost all Jews . . . that makes most Jews feel part of the same group," there was nothing distinctly Jewish about this bond.[93] Rather all Americans searched for a sense of belonging, and according to Handlin and Glazer, more often than not they found it in their ethnic group—even if they had to invent an ethnic heritage to fit the bill. Americans who lacked an ethnic identity were, in actuality, the most marginal Americans, bereft of the kinds of associations that defined American identity.

Handlin preached just this universalized ethnic vision to a contingent of New York Jews, to whom it appealed because it did not appear distinctly Jewish. "I remember," he told me, "I'd gone down to [New York City] to talk to some people who were of a slightly younger generation."[94] These were wealthy Jews who knew him through *Commentary* and the AJC and were impressed by his Harvard degree and faculty position. They congregated at the posh Harmonie Club on East Sixtieth Street (where Einstein had thrown a fund-raiser for the Conference on Jewish Relations in 1936 and where eastern European Jews had been barred from membership for many years). Handlin gravitated toward these Jews who lived a long train ride from Boston. "I knew that there were Jews in East Cambridge and Mattapan and Dorchester," he explained, "but that was a different world."[95] Indeed, Boston was a different world, and he worked hard to keep his academic life in Boston separate from his involvement with the Jewish community in New York. At Harvard he saw himself as a historian, but in New York he could be a Jew.

The elite New York Jews were not the Jews of Handlin's youth; while he attended Brooklyn College, they went off to the Ivy League; his parents were eastern Europeans, theirs (or perhaps their grandparents) were central Europeans. Yet they found in Handlin's worldview a reassuring and compelling way to think about their Jewishness. According to Handlin, a number of them felt alienated from their Jewish identities. The only way they were connected to anything Jewish—"they had no religious commitments"—was through their wealth and the Jewish philanthropic responsibilities they had inherited from their parents.[96] Their anxiety, in Handlin's recollection, "was all about the future." He elaborated, "A number of these people had non-Jewish spouses, you know. . . . So they were really troubled about how they would explain themselves to themselves, and then, of course, when they had children, how to explain that to their children."[97]

"I would ask them questions," Handlin remembered. "What else would you be if you weren't, you know? The whole institutional life was organized around . . . these lines. It's all right if you wanted to become a Catholic, then you can fit into a different niche. But you couldn't be a just [sic] nothing."[98] Handlin told them that their Jewish identities were not going to vanish unless they made a conscious decision to assume a new identity. After all, it was impossible to be "just nothing." Certainly, it was their decision if they wanted to assume a new identity. But he counseled them against doing so, because all of their history was "entrenched in enterprises that were Jewish or quasi-Jewish. You couldn't stop."[99] And because the historical ball was rolling, and it was not simple or beneficial to leave one's identity behind, especially when society expected each person to have a group identity, it was best to stay Jewish.

Handlin was not an alarmist. His contact with these Jews did not cause him to worry about the survival of the Jewish people; he believed that the forces of history and sociology would preserve the Jewish group. His own life proved as much. He had worked to distance himself from being Jewish, especially as a student and young faculty member at Harvard, yet he still had ties to his Jewishness. Handlin saw nothing particularly unique in his experience. Rather he defined himself as part of a broad (and apparently male) sociological phenomenon: the son's generation.

According to Handlin, the son, alienated and seeking success, freed himself from his father's world perhaps through education or by moving to a new place. But along the way, the son recognized that true freedom did not have to exact one's past as its price. For Handlin, of course, father and son were not simply faceless metaphors. In the second edition of *The Uprooted,* published in 1973, Handlin extended his familial imagery and concluded with a strikingly intimate description of the loss of his own father: "Drops of dextrose now sustained his life, and draining tubes. In weekly drives of futile piety, we crossed to Whitestone, hit the parkway and approached."[100] Perhaps his family background had not compelled him to study immigration, but in the pages of his scholarship Handlin paid homage to his ancestors and identified himself as the son of an immigrant father. In his ailing father—"that wasting frame"—Handlin searched for a way to balance the past and the future. He eulogized him stirringly: "I will . . . not turn away from the hope that there will be no forgetting the meaning of the America he and the millions more expended their lives in making."[101]

Ancestral devotion seemed to be an intrinsic piece of the ethnic feeling: Glazer dedicated *American Judaism* to his father, Louis Glazer. He wrote that, even as successive generations moved away from being entirely enmeshed in a Jewish worldview, they still could sense their Jewishness in a "voice or the echo, perhaps not even the echo of the echo. But something is still left."[102] In the years after he completed *American Judaism,* Glazer teamed up with Daniel Patrick Moynihan to show that this ethnic echo, a stirring that tied people to ethnic communities, existed among all Americans. In the book they coauthored in 1963, *Beyond the Melting Pot,* they proposed that ethnic groups, "continually recreated by new experiences in America," were the building blocks of American social structure.[103] They argued that the ethnic group was a "new social form" through which Americans organized themselves and their interests. So prevalent was this social form that few Americans, even white Protestants, existed outside of an ethnic group: "the 'majority' group . . . has taken on the color of an ethnic group, too."[104] As the book's title made clear, Glazer and Moynihan saw no indication that these ethnic groups were fading into a uniform American melting pot; instead they predicted the ongoing centrality of ethnic life to American social structure. When it came to defining the content of ethnic life, however, Glazer and Moynihan, like Handlin, had far less to say.

Ethnic Content

In the 1950s, a young Jewish sociologist averred that a new kind of Jewishness was developing in the rapidly growing suburbs: "symbolic Judaism." Herbert Gans, who had been trained by some of the luminaries in the sociology department at the University of Chicago, had spent months observing Jewish life in Park Forest, Illinois.[105] What he saw convinced him that, although few Jews were interested in arranging their lives according to Jewish practices and behaviors, most remained connected to those few activities, objects, or places that enabled them to "feel and express their Jewishness."[106] A Jewishness that was symbolic—arranged, according to Gans, around a few token experiences or objects that gestured toward a larger Jewish system—fit remarkably well into Handlin and Glazer's American ethnic pattern: one could be connected to an ethnic group without feeling many particular demands on one's life.

Although Handlin and Glazer believed that Jewishness would be sustained in the United States through the American ethnic pattern, they also perceived a potential vapidity to it. In 1957, Handlin was asked to prognosticate about the state of American Jewry in the year 2000. As quoted in the *New York Times*, Handlin predicted, "The danger is not so much that the community will disappear, but that its culture will become a museum piece, preserved out of a sense of curiosity and ancestral piety, but devoid of meaning."[107] That same year, in *American Judaism*, Glazer predicted that Jews were on the road to becoming "custodians of a museum."[108] Still, as eviscerated and rarified as Jewish identity might become, Glazer, like Handlin, did not expect Jewish life to end. Jews, Glazer wrote, possessed "a stubborn insistence on remaining Jewish."[109]

Handlin and Glazer, after all, had remained (perhaps stubbornly in the face of quiet whispers and muffled remarks) Jewish. They had constructed a social model—the American ethnic pattern—premised on the survival, not dissolution, of Jewishness, identifying it as essential to American social organization. They likely recognized the potential shortcomings of translating ethnic distinctiveness into a generic American norm. Yet the strength of the model was twofold: it marked Jewish experience as paradigmatic of American minority experience, and it guaranteed Jewish survival. On both these counts, however, critics found reason to question whether an American ethnic pattern truly existed.

Starting in the 1960s, a group of sociologists influenced by the civil rights movement challenged the assumption that Jews were a typical minority group from whom one could generalize minority experience. In 1960, leftist Zionist and Yiddishist Charles Bezalel Sherman, who in 1954 had scathingly reviewed Handlin's book, wrote *The Jew within American Society: A Study in Ethnic Individuality*. "The Jews," he averred, "are the single white group whose ethnic solidarity is not disappearing in America."[110] Despite one reviewer's misgivings that Sherman was reverting to an unscholarly "chosen people" approach, Sherman's work augured a brand of ethnic particularism and pride that flowered in the late 1960s and 1970s.[111] While Sherman worked to undermine the notion of a universal pattern of ethnic difference, other critics took aim at American social structure to argue that some ethnic groups were treated less equally than others.

For Handlin and Glazer, to abandon a universal American ethnic pattern was to ravage American liberalism. If each ethnic group maintained a different relationship with the American state—in legal, historical, or social terms—then each individual would not be guaranteed the same access to American opportunity, an idea jarring to many 1950s liberals. Handlin and Glazer grew particularly frustrated with trends in scholarship and public policy that drew a line of distinction between so-called white ethnics and people of color.[112]

In a 1958 article about Puerto Ricans in New York City, Glazer predicted that this new group of immigrants would eventually be perceived, like all other ethnic groups, "as an assimilating ethnic group, rather than a special racial group," and he characterized New Yorkers as "quiescent" toward and tolerant of the new immigrant in their midst.[113] The next year, Handlin published a study about New York City's growing African American and Puerto Rican populations. His approach was slightly more nuanced than Glazer's, and he allowed for the fact that the color line produced material and psychological obstacles unlike any experienced by European immigrants. He explained, "The mobility of the low-income Negro Family in the region is not now nor will it be in the near future a matter of personal choice."[114] And yet, by the end of his study, Handlin recommended that individuals, whether white New Yorkers or Puerto Ricans and African Americans, cultivate proper attitudes in order to repair social disparities. He instructed Puerto Ricans and African Americans to invest the "will and energy" to fight against difficult circumstances and advised white New Yorkers to develop greater tolerance and free themselves of prejudice.[115] In other words, Handlin still had faith that, if people on all sides tried hard enough, the American ethnic pattern would prevail.

Neither Glazer nor Handlin believed that the group determined an individual's capacity or opportunity to succeed. For many social scientists, it took the explosiveness of the civil rights movement to see just how varied group experience in the United States could be—Jewish American experience was not Italian American experience was not African American experience.[116] Handlin and Glazer refused to accept that ethnic variation resulted, in some measure, from state policy, and therefore, that what an individual achieved was inseparable from his or her group background. Furthermore, neither of them could swallow the growing body of scholarship and cultural criticism that drew attention to the structural inequalities of American society. In 1970, Handlin acerbically wrote, "In the 1960s, victimization explained everything; deprivation, failures to achieve, cultural inadequacies, and personal maladjustments, past as well as present—all ultimately originated in the society that corrupted its members."[117] Handlin and Glazer had both invested their professional and personal lives in the belief that group life in the United States was a generic phenomenon that could be explained by a single pattern.[118] To see that pattern undermined was tantamount to seeing their world crumble.

Mountains and Bridges

The American ethnic pattern—a simultaneously vacuous and profound insight that everyone had to have some group identity in the United States, and that group identity did not hinder individual success— emerged in Glazer and Handlin's work as a way to embed Jewish survival in American social structure. In theorizing an American ethnic pattern, Handlin and Glazer envisioned the United States as achieving a perfect balance between ethnic survival and integration, a balance that mirrored their hopes for Jewish life in the United States. Clearly, they were motivated by their ideological beliefs about Jewish survival, American liberalism, and individual meritocracy. In fact, it was in the process of studying—or explaining—Jews that they clarified many of their beliefs about what it meant to be Jewish and American.

Scholars speak from the ground on which they stand. In an essay in 1977, Handlin wrote, "I came to the mountains after having spent my childhood on the plains."[119] From the peak of a mountain, a place perhaps like the sixth floor of the Widener Library at Harvard, he could survey the world from which he had come. And when I spoke to Glazer, he described himself as a bridge, part of "a crossover generation" that spanned the Jewish world and the predominantly non-Jewish academic world, yet never rested firmly in either.[120] Scaling mountaintops and bridging worlds, each reflected and created the world around him.

The sociological, ethnic-based definition of Jewishness helped create a uniquely American vocabulary of difference. Religion remained a piece of what distinguished Jews from non-Jews—or one ethnic group from another—but not because social researchers thought belief mattered. Religion, instead, was just another way that American social groups defined themselves, as were foodways and patterns of residence. For Jewish leaders in the 1950s and 1960s, however, the ascendance of ethnic or sociological vocabulary made it both easier and more complicated to explain Jewishness to non-Jews. Although it offered a familiar and distinctly American framework in which to place Jewishness, sociological

Jewishness also challenged the extent to which non-Jews could fully understand—and, even more so, join—the Jewish people. How could Jews serve the public good—as some Conservative and Reform leaders in the 1940s had suggested was their central purpose—if they simply adhered to an ethnic pattern shared by all Americans? Particularly for rabbis invested in showing Americans that Jewishness carried universal value, that it could be a gift to the United States, the notion that Jewishness was the sum of one's background and ran parallel to other group identities threatened to undermine their efforts. Even those rabbis not bent on proving the universal significance of Jewishness confronted the limitations of defining Jewishness through sociological terms. As early as the 1950s, some rabbis noticed that the kinds of patterns that had once seemed to fix Jewish identity as sociologically distinctive and an inevitable outgrowth of American social life were, in fact, changing.

CHAPTER 6

What Is a Jew?

Missionaries, Outreach, and the
Cold War Ethnic Challenge

Beyond Sociology

In March 1958, the Kertzer family sat down for a Passover seder. A couple of inquisitive guests joined them, but every American with a television was invited to celebrate the spring holiday with the family. For loyal viewers, this may have even been their second seder with the Kertzers, who the year before had opened their Long Island home to *The Tonight Show* crew. And the most devoted viewers would have already known some of the family members, especially the father, Rabbi Morris Kertzer, quite well. Starting in the early 1950s, he had appeared periodically on television, sometimes with his daughter or his two young sons in tow, to share Jewish ideas, beliefs, and practices with Americans. Television was an ideal medium for his task; between 1948 and 1955, two-thirds of all American homes had televisions installed, and by 1960 the average person watched five hours of television a day.[1] Rabbi Kertzer saw no higher calling than to extend the reaches of Judaism throughout the world, and saw no better way to do this than through the mass media. He once marveled that, in a single day, he could reach more people than Saint Francis of Assisi had in a lifetime.[2] Reflecting on his television appearances, he explained, "All of this is not likely to stimulate a mass flight toward Judaism, but it has normalized the *fact* of Judaism."[3]

Kertzer, like many Jewish leaders and intellectuals in the middle of the twentieth century, hoped to convince Americans that Jewishness was simply part of the United States. His case for Jewish acceptance hinged on the language of sociological and ethnic Jewishness, a language that enabled him to translate Jewish values and practices into American idioms. With it, he could assert that Jewish difference was analogous to other forms of American difference. By bringing the rituals of a seder—the special foods, the Hebrew blessings, the songs—into Americans' living rooms, Kertzer attempted to show that Jews' practices were unique, but that their purpose and values were not so different from other Americans'. Yet insofar as Kertzer also worked to prove that Jewishness was open and accessible—a tradition and identity that anyone could learn—the framework of sociological Jewishness was much less useful.

By defining themselves as a sociological group, like other American ethnic groups, Jews made themselves comprehensible to non-Jews. But the logic of sociological Jewishness presupposed an indissoluble boundary between Jews and non-Jews that guarded Jewish distinctiveness and maintained the moral force of the group in American democracy. Sociologists like Glazer and Handlin tended to depict the boundary as social, not biological, but they also characterized it as natural—not consciously learned but born into or inherited. For rabbis who believed in the universal dimensions of Jewishness and, furthermore, believed that the survival of the Jews depended on their ability to highlight their universal messages and wisdom, sociological Jewishness raised serious problems. If non-Jews came to see Jewishness as a social identity that was natural not intellectual, inherited not learned, then what precisely could Jews offer the non-Jewish world? Sociological Jewishness, although conceived as an ideology that would carve out a sustainable position for Jews in the United States, contained the seeds of a new brand of insularity.

Particularly those rabbis who wished not only to educate non-Jews— as Rabbi Kertzer did—but also to transform the willing into Jews found sociological or ethnic Jewishness a serious impediment. After all, theirs was a fantasy of incorporating actual non-Jews into the world of Jewishness. A person might convert to a new religion, but could a person assume a new sociological identity? The identity markers sociologists saw as most vital—family background, class status, educational level, friends, and residential patterns—would not necessarily change along with an individual's decision to assume a new belief system; and some of them, like family background, simply could not change. Even rabbis who were not necessarily committed to attracting converts but wished to prove to non-Jews that Jewishness issued a universal and indispensable message ran into the limitations of sociological Jewishness. If Jewishness were merely the sum of social facts, then what particular meaning might it convey? Was it enough to assert that Jews contributed to the United States simply by being Jews, or did their Jewishness have to carry a larger purpose?

By the middle of the 1950s, cracks were appearing in the sociological conception of Jewishness, even as it also grew in force and informed how Jews and non-Jews thought about Jewishness. Historians and sociologists have noted a contradiction in the public status of American religion in the 1950s. On the one hand, in public discourse, religion became exceedingly important, especially as a way of differentiating communism (described as atheistic) from democracy (described as God-believing). On the other hand, the meaning of religious categories—like God, faith, sin, and ritual—communicated by particular religions appeared to weaken, at least in the estimation of social critics of the day and many historians since.[4] This tension in the public display of religion—between a generic valorization of religion and a disregard for the content of any specific religion—manifested itself in Jewish leaders' uncertainty about which terms for explaining Jewishness would best resonate with non-Jewish Americans. Americans seemed interested in religion as a public category, yet countless critics of American life were certain that Americans cared very little about the intricacies of particular religious practices and rituals. Similarly, the postwar liberal creed offered more tolerance for ethnic distinctiveness than ever before, yet the acceptable range of ethnic difference appeared to be narrowing, to the point that some critics wondered if ethnic markers held any true meaning.

In the 1950s as in earlier decades, rabbis sought to prove that Jewishness had a public purpose. But they lived in confusing times for religion and for minority life in the United States. In attempting to revitalize missionary Judaism, a movement that had receded since the late 1920s, and in crafting new modes of Jewish outreach, rabbis became ensnared in the confusions and contradictions embedded in postwar Judaism and Jewish life. They possessed a growing arsenal of sociological and ethnic terms with which to explain who Jews were, but as much as this language helped secure a place for Jews in the United States, it also fundamentally challenged the value of Jewishness. Already in the 1940s, Milton Steinberg had asked where God or any fundamental meaning could possibly be in a system that defined itself solely by collective patterns and mundane functions. Yet there was no getting around the tight grasp of sociological conceptions of Jewishness, even for rabbis who wanted to talk about God, belief, or meaning.

Searching for American Jewish Theology, Missionary Style

When in 1950 Ferdinand Isserman, a Saint Louis Reform rabbi, organized an institute on Jewish theology, he was certain that nothing less than Jewish survival was at stake. In the conference's opening statement, he explained, "We have learned from men and women who experience[d] the brutality of the concentration camps, that nothing was as powerful in sustaining their morale, maintaining their courage, lifting them above despair and cleansing their souls of bitterness than an abiding faith. . . . Those in their midst who had no religious faith could not survive."[5] Many of his colleagues, however, were far from persuaded that the topic of Jewish survival merited attention. On a questionnaire he circulated prior to the meeting, one rabbi wrote, "Incidentally, I am not too happy about the term 'theology' as applied to Judaism. No formulation of it has succeeded in the past and, frankly, I hope the one you have in mind will have no greater success."[6] Perhaps these same naysayers would have pointed out that faith had little to do with who did and did not survive the Nazi concentration camps. Isserman, however, like many other Jewish thinkers, was scrambling to find order amid destruction.

Hoping to draw attention to the gravity of Jewish theology, Rabbi Isserman asked Arthur Hays Sulzberger at the *New York Times* to make sure "that this institute . . . will receive good press coverage."[7] Although the *New York Times* printed a brief article about the conference, regional Jewish newspapers drew readers' attention to the sexiest angle of an otherwise staid conference: its missionary proposal. Bold-faced headlines printed in newspapers (mainly regional Jewish ones from across the country, but also the local Cincinnati dailies) summarized it: "Parley of Reform Rabbis Hear Bold Proposal: That Jewry Readopt Pre-Christian Proselytism"; "Jewish Missionary Effort Proposed at Rabbis' Meet *[sic]*"; and "Urge Judaism Be Missionary Religion."[8] Almost every article about the institute used near-identical copy. Cribbed from a dispatch by a Jewish press service, each reported that rabbis had considered "suggestions that Judaism return to its pre-Christian-era role of an active missionary religion."[9]

In truth, the rabbis who participated in the conference's sessions about missionary Judaism had mainly discussed ways to draw unaffiliated Jews back into the fold of religious affiliation, but they had indeed used the term *missionary,* a word that harked back to proposals in the 1920s and indicated new energy to extend the reaches of Judaism.[10] The articles reported that Rabbi Isserman affirmed the statement made by a prominent liberal English rabbi that "Judaism may well make converts and it should accept readily any proselyte who comes to it with sincere desire to give it their devotion."[11] Each article concluded with a succinct endorsement by former army chaplain Rabbi Albert Goldstein: "More than all, we must propagate Judaism through active proselytism. Judaism is no mere tribal cult. It is a universal faith."[12] Unlike the 1920s discussion, which had barely made a ripple beyond the rabbinical conference's minutes, by the 1950s the Jewish missionary idea assumed a public face.

Not all publicity is good publicity, of course, and some of the rabbis may have wished the press had not been so eager to spread the racy-sounding story. Shortly after the conference, a columnist in the *California Jewish Voice,* who had read about the missionary discussions, wrote tauntingly, "Seems like the Reform rabbis feel that they have done a pretty solid job 'judaizing' their own flocks[,] . . . who know as much about Judaism as a fox-terrier does about Kiddush [the blessing said over wine]."[13] Indeed, the attention the missionary idea received forced the rabbis to decide just how serious they were about creating a missionary movement. Their discussions in the past had always been more academic than anything else, but the new decade—a time when Jews felt more accepted than before, and a time when religion served as a clear expression of American patriotism—seemed to offer an opportunity for rabbis to move their missionary ideas from the abstract to the concrete.

Since its brief efflorescence in the 1920s, the missionary discussion had lurked in the shadows of rabbis' main concerns. The missionary idea, like many religious institutions more generally, had receded since the Depression era. The president of the Central Conference of American Rabbis in 1931 complained, "We are suffering not only from financial depression: the depreciation in spiritual and religious values is evident at every hand."[14] If spiritual and religious values could be measured by synagogue membership and capital gains, the president was correct. One of the largest Reform synagogues, Temple Emanu-El of New York City, saw its membership drop by 44 percent in the decade

after the Depression. Congregations were forced to downsize, elimi-
nating staff and programming that had been essential to their growth in
the 1920s.[15] The wilting of Jewish institutions did not, however, indicate a complete neglect of religion. Jeremiads at the time and certain
historical assessments aside, neither American religious life nor questions about the meaning of being Jewish withered away during the
Great Depression.[16]

The mission idea was hardly irrelevant in the 1930s and early 1940s.
In fact, the ideology of a permeable Judaism, accessible to all who
chose to educate themselves in its ways, had enabled the Reform movement to broker a middle-ground position on the Zionist question.
Since 1897 the Reform movement had officially opposed the creation
of a Jewish state, but in the 1930s, as political conditions in Europe and
the United States made that position less tenable, the movement
announced public support for Zionism.[17] At the same time, Reform
rabbis expressed continued allegiance to the mission idea. Whereas
Zionism attempted to secure Jewish survival by creating a physical land
devoted to Jewish life, a Jewish mission implied that Judaism knew no
borders. If a Jewish missionary commitment could coexist with
Zionism, then Jews could escape the narrowness of a national identity,
and more tangibly, American Jews could justify their continued diasporic existence while, at the same time, defending the Jewish state's
right to exist.[18] To say that Jews had a purpose in the United States, a
mission, was to say that Zionism would not contain or constrict the
Jewish role in the world.

Rabbis' interest in invigorating missionary Judaism after World War
II was linked to their desire to prove that Jews had an inextinguishable
purpose in the world. A few months after the institute on theology, in
May 1950, Rabbi Louis Wolsey invited a small group of rabbis to
Philadelphia to strategize about how to gain support for a Jewish missionary movement. Some of the most important men in the Reform
movement attended the meeting: Wolsey was a past president of the
Central Conference of American Rabbis (CCAR), another would
become president in the late 1950s, and others were rabbis at some of
the largest temples in the United States. In a letter, Wolsey wrote, "In
my judgment [the lack of missionary activity] has been almost fatal, for
in my poor opinion, it seems to me much of the sad lot of the Jew
during all of these centuries is due to the fact that our people have not
seen the vision of proclaiming their religion to the world."[19] All the
stumbling and mumbling and hemming and hawing had to end so that

a "historic result might eventuate."[20] Wolsey was clear about the results he wanted: in a Reform movement journal, he wrote, "If like the Mormons and many Christian denominations, we were to inspire gifted young men and women to undertake as their career in life to bring the message of Judaism to an unhappy world, we would have contributed much to the peace and justice of mankind."[21]

The group of rabbis proposed that the CCAR pass a resolution "to study practical means of extending the influence and acceptance of the Jewish religion," and in June 1950 the resolution was accepted after contentious debate.[22] One of the most vocal proponents later recalled, "It was a very innocuous kind of motion but everybody knew what it meant. It meant to study the possibility of going out into the non-Jewish world with some sort of a program of attracting non-Jews to Judaism."[23] By the end of the 1950 meeting, the Reform rabbis had established a Committee on the Unaffiliated. The word *unaffiliated* skirted the most controversial issue. Few rabbis had a problem with setting out on a missionary-style campaign to attract unaffiliated Jews. Many, however, were uncomfortable with extending the campaign to non-Jews, because they worried about overstepping the bounds of American tolerance, and because they could not imagine what it would mean for non-Jews, in any significant numbers, to become Jews.

Early Reformers, often called "Liberal Jews," had attached their faith to universalism because they believed it offered the best path to modern respect for both Judaism and the Jews. By the 1950s, amid America's rhetorical commitment to religious tolerance and cultural pluralism, the rabbis were no longer certain whether Jews were best served by aligning their heritage with a doctrine of universalism or by defending the right of many competing belief systems and communities to coexist. One rabbi, listening to the discussion at the 1950 CCAR meeting, argued, "We have pleaded with our non-Jewish friends not to engage in proselytizing Jews. How can we go forth and missionize the gentile?"[24] Another rabbi retorted, "I have been impressed by the timidity of this Convention. When we speak of universal qualities of Judaism, what does it mean if not to go out and give our message to the world?"[25] Still another replied, "There is no reason for proselytizing unless you believe in the redeeming features of a certain creed. This has never been part of our religious belief and practice."[26] At the crux of their debate rested anxiety about how Americans would respond to Jewish efforts to spread Judaism, and how Jews themselves might react to a campaign to gain new adherents.

Bernard Bamberger, a supporter of the missionary idea and a prominent New York City rabbi who later became president of the CCAR, suggested a way to sidestep the tension between the increasingly popular
doctrine of cultural and religious pluralism and the dictates of universalism. He agreed with one of his colleagues that the rabbis should focus on
reaching the "vast numbers of unchurched people in the United States
who have neither been baptised nor confirmed—call them secularists."[27]
Bamberger elaborated: "We cannot say to members of another faith: you
have no right to spread your teachings among us, but we can say to
them: you have a right to make propaganda for your view point and
we have a right to make propaganda for our view point."[28] According to
Bamberger's formulation, rabbis would be neither breaching religious
tolerance nor claiming that Judaism was "the exclusive avenue to salvation."[29] Yet they could still assert the universalism of Judaism and its
appropriateness for any person bereft of spiritual direction. Furthermore,
by formulating the Jewish mission as serving "secularists" and the
"unchurched," rabbis would align themselves with the anticommunist
ideology of the day, which maintained, among other things, that religious
affiliation itself was a defense against communist world domination.[30]

Bamberger, like other supporters of missionary Judaism, attempted
to emphasize the permeability of Jewishness, implicitly arguing that, as
long as a person shared the beliefs of Judaism, he or she could become
a Jew. Attempting to discredit more rigid conceptions of Jewishness,
Bamberger reminded the rabbis that Judaism "does not . . . [regard]
itself as a religion only for the Jewish race—whatever that may mean."[31]
Especially in the wake of World War II, Bamberger's disavowal of racial
conceptions of Jewishness was likely quite persuasive. Yet for many
American Jews, Jewishness was more than a religious marker. The
prospect, then, of opening their community to individuals who were
not born as Jews was an uncomfortable one. If rabbis were to prove
that Jewishness had a public purpose beyond the Jews, they had to
depict Jewishness as primarily learnable, not only inheritable.

The Mission in Practice: Non-Jews Who Become Jews

In 1950, Rabbi David Max Eichhorn, who chaired the Committee on
the Unaffiliated and became a vocal proponent of missionary Judaism,
wrote, "In this evil time, the forces of Liberal Judaism have a duty to
perform, a mission to fulfill, a mission fashioned by history and tradition

and compelled by the urgency of the present hour."[32] Eichhorn had served as a chaplain in World War II and experienced the human costs of evil. Leaving a wife and four children behind, he had joined combat troops and witnessed the liberation of Nazi concentration camps. In a letter, he reported, "We saw 39 boxcars loaded with Jewish dead in the Dachau railway yard, 39 carloads of little, shriveled mummies that had literally been starved to death. . . . And we cried not merely tears of sorrow. We cried tears of hate. Combat hardened soldiers, Gentile and Jew, black and white, cried tears of hate."[33] Eichhorn left the service convinced that those Jews who survived had a duty to improve the world and could do so only by opening themselves and their traditions to non-Jews. As chair of the Committee on the Unaffiliated, he conducted a comprehensive study of converts in hopes of finding evidence to support a missionary agenda.

While the missionary discussion was certainly not a new one in the Reform movement, the 1950s marked the first time that the rabbis showed any interest in actual converts. For a number of reasons, their earlier discussions had been marked by an almost willful neglect of those people who had, in fact, converted to Judaism. In the first place, especially in the 1920s, there were very few converts to Judaism. Perhaps more important, most of those who had converted to Judaism were women marrying Jewish men.[34] Had the mission focused on demographic realities, fears that the missionary plan would result in a "feminized" Judaism could have undermined the project and its larger aim of improving the status of Judaism.[35]

In the 1950s, to some rabbis' dismay, women continued to convert to Judaism more often than men did. At the same time, however, the rabbis who reintroduced the Jewish mission idea had far more practical goals than their predecessors had been able to imagine. As a reflection of Jews' greater sense of belonging in the United States and their attempt to make sense of the losses of World War II, the mission that emerged was attached to actual human beings, which made the question of what differentiated Jews from non-Jews all the more pressing. For the rabbis in the 1950s, there was no way of getting around the authority that sociological methods and conclusions carried in Jewish and American life.

When Rabbi Eichhorn set out to understand who converted and how effective their conversions were, he followed social-scientific procedure. Social scientists had convinced Americans that empirical data generated by surveyors was the clearest indication of reality; the Gallup Poll, for example, had become an authority on public opinion starting in the

1930s.[36] Using a method familiar from American pollsters, Eichhorn sent out surveys with yes-or-no questions, multiple-choice questions, and space for additional comments, to Reform and Conservative rabbis (Orthodox rabbis had refused to participate). He then determined which responses were normal and which were deviant, illuminating these findings with a sample of illustrative quotations.[37] The decisions he made about how to interpret and represent his data were likely overshadowed by the common belief that numbers spoke for themselves. From the 785 responses he received, Eichhorn found that roughly two thousand people had converted to Judaism between 1952 and 1953, a steady increase, he observed, from earlier years. Although the data clearly revealed that non-Jewish women comprised the majority of converts, and that almost all of them entered the Jewish fold through marriage, Eichhorn drew attention instead to the number of "non-marriage-motivated conversions," which he characterized as quite substantial given "the fact that neither Conservative nor Reform Judaism has made the slightest effort to attract non-Jews, but, on the contrary, both groups have done much to create the impression that they are not wanted."[38]

Eichhorn reported that both Reform and Conservative rabbis agreed with the statement "proselytes are more faithful to the Jewish faith than born Jews," which reinforced his own views.[39] When asked, the rabbis categorized the converts with whom they had contact (for whom they had likely performed conversion ceremonies) as being above average in their "Jewishness." Not only did converts attend synagogue more regularly than born Jews, but they also were active in Jewish clubs and associations (most prominently synagogue sisterhoods). The fact that converts integrated into synagogue life, both its religious and associational aspects, seemed ample evidence in Eichhorn's mind that Jewishness could accommodate new arrivals. He concluded that converts to Judaism "are a constant reminder of the modern Jew's neglected obligation to share [the Jewish] heritage more unselfishly with those who are dissatisfied with the faiths of their fathers and who are yearning for a more meaningful explanation of human existence and a more satisfying way of life."[40]

The survey results and Eichhorn's interpretation of them filtered beyond the CCAR. Eichhorn published his findings in *Jewish Social Studies,* and an editorial column in the *Christian Century,* a liberal Christian journal, summarized and lauded his research for its readers. "If, in the free field of American society," the editors wrote, "Judaism should frankly avow its intention to seek converts on the same terms Christians, Muslims and Buddhists do, that would clear away such misunderstandings as have grown out of a widespread belief that the purpose of many synagogues and rabbis has been to employ Judaism to block the normal assimilative processes of American life."[41] The *Christian Century*'s pronouncement that missionary Judaism would allow for Jews to participate in the "normal assimilative processes of American life" struck some rabbis as the best argument against the mission idea. If Judaism were retooled to be an agent of assimilation—allowing Jews to seem more like other Americans by bringing non-Jews into the fold—then the sociological and ethnic dimensions of Jewishness would most certainly evaporate.

For critics who believed a Jewish mission would undermine the ethnic or sociological integrity of Jewishness, a set of suggestions about targeting the Japanese through a missionary campaign may have been most disturbing. At the 1954 CCAR convention, after listening to Eichhorn's survey results, a rabbi who had served as a chaplain in Japan estimated that more than three thousand Japanese were "interested in becoming converted to Judaism."[42] In 1958, the *New York Times* reported that, in ten years' time, "Israel may have a population of 100,000 Japanese Jews."[43] Although Eichhorn publicly dismissed the predictions as fanciful, he agreed that the Japanese had a growing interest in Judaism.[44] That same year, a Conservative rabbi, considering the possibility that Reformers' missionary idea had some merit to it, similarly recommended starting a missionary movement in Japan. His suggestion made its way into *Time* magazine's "Religion" column.[45] According to these various sources, some Japanese, disillusioned with "chauvinistic nationalism, the barbarism of war and the bitterness of defeat," and recently acquainted with Judaism through the Jewish chaplains who had served in the Pacific theater, found Judaism attractive.[46] Although little came of the minor frenzy over exporting Judaism to Japan, even the suggestion that Japanese could become Jews (and that Jews should encourage this) challenged American Jews' sociological presumptions about Jewishness. For someone reared far outside the Jewish social context to become Jewish implied that anyone could do so, and that Jewishness was entirely learnable.

The Making of an Outreach Rabbi

Rabbi Morris Kertzer, for one, was committed to convincing Jewish and non-Jewish Americans that Jewishness was learnable. Whether celebrating Jewish rituals in front of television crews or writing about Jewish beliefs in popular magazines and books, he devoted his life to making Jewishness accessible. In the early 1950s, he told an interviewer that religious leaders who thumbed their noses at the mass media would lose out in the end. If they wished to keep their religious message vibrant, he suggested, they had to take a cue from journalists and learn to talk about religion in common terms for the masses. Rather defiantly, Kertzer explained he considered it a "privilege," not a compromise, to appear on television.[47] This made sense coming from a man who, early in his rabbinical career, committed himself to "interpreting my Jewish heritage to the world at large—Christian as well as Jew" and in 1953 published a bestselling book titled *What Is a Jew?*[48] In his countless efforts to explain Jewishness to Jews and non-Jews, Kertzer attempted to bridge the sociological elements of Jewishness—the fact that being a Jew encompassed an entire and not easily replicable way of life—with other, easily learnable elements. His synthesis suggested that Jewishness was both the special provenance of the Jewish people and a tradition that non-Jews could learn. Even Kertzer's synthesis, however, left unresolved the question of whether a non-Jew could enter the sociological dimensions of Jewishness through the path of study, or a gap would always remain between the non-Jew who learned Judaism and the Jew who was born into it.

From the age of fourteen, Kertzer had been intent on becoming a rabbi. He was born in Ontario in 1910, only one year after his mother had left Russia and crossed the Atlantic to reunite with her husband in Canada. With a college degree from the University of Toronto in hand, he moved to the United States when he was nineteen to attend an Orthodox rabbinical school in Chicago. Although as a child he had zealously enforced strict Jewish observance in his home, he discovered quickly that he was not interested in the life of an Orthodox rabbinical student. Kertzer transferred to the Jewish Theological Seminary, where he was ordained in 1934 as a Conservative rabbi. With his new wife, Julia (Hoffman), Kertzer moved to Champaign-Urbana to assist Abram Sachar in his efforts to establish a Jewish student organization, what became known as Hillel, at the University of Illinois. After a brief stint working to export the Hillel model to the University of Alabama, Kertzer relocated to Iowa City in 1939 and became the Hillel director at the University of Iowa.[49] There he also taught a class about religion alongside a Catholic and a Protestant, and in an article he wrote about the class—reprinted in papers in the Bronx, Montreal, Pittsburgh, Baltimore, and Bangor, Maine—he explained that his experience had taught him that it was vital for Jews to learn how to talk about themselves to non-Jews.[50]

FIGURE 8. Morris Kertzer during his tour of duty as a
United States Army chaplain, France, circa January 1945.
Courtesy of Ruth Kertzer Seidman.

World War II offered Kertzer a new opportunity to reach out to non-Jews and explain Jewishness to them. In April 1943, he left his post at Iowa to start his duties as a chaplain in the United States Army. Like countless other rabbis who served as chaplains, Kertzer became convinced during his tour of duty that Jews and Judaism had an obligation to speak to the non-Jewish world. In the army, chaplains often shared close quarters with clergy from other religions, and they witnessed soldiers cooperating and becoming friends across lines of difference.[51] When Kertzer returned from the war, he wrote *With an H on My Dog Tag*, a breezy and anecdote-filled book about his service. His overseas duty had started in 1944, at the Anzio Beachhead, where he led Jewish services for soldiers who were fighting to maintain control over this strategic foothold in Italy. While stationed in Anzio, he had his first encounter with a Nazi soldier. Leaning over the wounded soldier, a supine victim now, Kertzer told him he was a Jew. The Nazi looked up and, in Kertzer's recollection, said, "I'm a Catholic. We both worship the same God. To the devil with Hitler."[52]

If war could transform a Nazi into an interfaith idealist, then it could also transform the way Jews and non-Jews thought about Jewishness, or so Kertzer believed. In his estimation, even those Jewish GIs who came into the army certain only that to be a Jew was to be hated by non-Jews gained a new sense of pride in their Jewishness. They found succor in the prayers and rites that reminded them of home and connected them to something larger than themselves. Kertzer remarked, "Of the Jewish soldier . . . we may say that the impact of what he experienced will certainly affect his thinking and his attitudes as a Jew during the next decade."[53] Over the next several decades, Kertzer drew on his war experiences as a basis for his vision of interfaith cooperation and, just as important, to gain the credibility he needed in order to reach out to millions of Americans.

What Is a Jew?

In the summer of 1952, Kertzer published an article titled "What Is a Jew?" in *Look* magazine. More than his rabbinical appellation, the large photograph that accompanied the article was intended to command American respect. In the photo, Kertzer stood holding an open prayer book and facing a group of seated GIs, each wearing his combat helmet. The caption explained that Kertzer was leading Passover services for the Jewish soldiers who had stormed Anzio, and that it was customary among Jews to cover one's head while praying. The magazine's millions of readers would learn about Jews and Judaism from a rabbi who had put his own life in danger to protect the United States in the last world war.[54]

Kertzer's article was part of a series about religious movements in the United States that Leo Rosten, *Look*'s editor, believed would "answer the kind of questions which an ordinary man might ask of a religious body to which he did not belong, or of which he knew not much."[55] More expansive in his vision of postwar religion than many people at the time, Rosten included a broad range of religious groups, from several Protestant denominations (Episcopalians, Methodists, Baptists, Presbyterians, etc.) to Mormons, Christian Scientists, and even agnostics. All the authors in the series followed a readable question-and-answer format to give readers the nuts and bolts about each religious group. Kertzer may have been asked to write for the series because he was then the director of the interfaith division of the American Jewish Committee, and also because he had already published a book about his experience in World War II that proved his knack for writing in easily digestible prose. Later he would acknowledge Rosten for training him in the art of writing about Judaism for a "general audience."[56]

Kertzer's list of seventeen questions started with "What is a Jew?" The word *what*, instead of *who*, indicated a belief that being Jewish somehow carried with it qualities better understood by means of the impersonal *what* than a personal *who*. Kertzer outlined a religious, cultural, and "practical" definition of a Jew. The practical definition, which he attributed to his teacher Mordecai Kaplan, maintained that Jews shared history, literature, liturgy, morality, and spirituality. Implicitly favoring the practical definition, Kertzer concluded, "Judaism is really a way of life."[57] A full-length book also titled *What Is a Jew?* was soon commissioned by the head of World Publishing, who had read the *Reader's Digest* version of Kertzer's article and immediately decided the idea was saleable. In his book, Kertzer elaborated: "A Jew is one who considers himself a Jew or is so regarded by his community."[58]

Kertzer explained that, even if a Jew did not follow every Jewish tradition (like wearing "hats" during prayer), most adhered to the "principal tenets" of Judaism: a belief in God, and the belief that humans must strive to imitate God.[59] These were ideas that anyone could learn intellectually and that many non-Jews, in fact, knew already. To the question "Do Christianity and Judaism agree on anything?" Kertzer answered that the two faiths were indeed quite compatible. In addition to sharing the Bible (the "Old Testament"), monotheism, and the Ten Commandments, both faiths firmly believed in "the democratic ideal as a guide to the political and social order."[60] Grounding the similarity of the two faiths in their Americanness, Kertzer emphasized that Jews, like Christians, were loyal to the United States, "no ifs or buts." Like many before him, Kertzer also described Jews as avatars of true democracy. While the word *democracy*, he wrote in his book *What Is a Jew?*, may come from ancient Greek, "the social creed by which the Jews have lived for centuries is democracy's highest tradition."[61] Jews, therefore, were well prepared to be full American citizens, even if they did not share Christians' belief in the divinity of Jesus, original sin, and salvation through Christ. Unlike Milton Steinberg, whose 1947 *Basic Judaism* was in many ways the forerunner to *What Is a Jew?*, Kertzer made no attempt to discredit Jesus or Christianity. Instead he concluded, "Today, in the United States, we have begun to create a single community of Christians and Jews based on mutual respect and understanding."[62]

In the winter of 1953, *Reader's Digest*'s DeWitt Wallace wrote to Kertzer, "It is no news that your article 'What Is a Jew?' was read by the largest magazine audience in the United States."[63] Kertzer was well aware of this. He spent hours each day answering mail from Jews and non-Jews across the country, and even outside the United States, who had read his article—the original in *Look*, *Reader's Digest*'s abridged version, or a reprint commissioned by the AJC—heard him give a radio interview about it, or simply knew about it from their friends.[64] Of the letters that survive, women wrote the majority. They were the primary readers of *Look* and *Reader's Digest* and, furthermore, tended to be more engaged with maintaining and practicing religion.[65] A Jewish woman from Chicago wrote that Kertzer's article had "helped immeasurably to answer the questions of my Gentile friends."[66] Similarly, a woman from Levittown, New York, told Kertzer that she had lent the article to a number of her non-Jewish neighbors and felt that "through it they have a more sincere understanding of what a Jew is."[67]

Along with praise, Kertzer also received letters from Jews who were less than pleased with what he had written. (These, interestingly, tended to be written by men more than women.) A Dr. Ira Fink from New York City wrote that, although he had shared the article with a number of Christian friends who found it "helpful and easily understandable," he was dismayed that Kertzer fell into the trap of claiming that Jews could do no wrong. Pointing to Kertzer's contentions that Jews had lower rates of juvenile delinquency, alcoholism, and divorce than other groups because of their strong family life, Dr. Fink scoffed, "I don't know where you Rabbi's [sic] get your information from."[68] Another letter writer echoed Fink's ire and said he was sick of how much "apologizing" Jews did for themselves.[69] Other Jewish critics simply wrote that they would have presented Jews differently had they been asked to write the article.

By far the most impassioned letters Kertzer received were from non-Jews hoping to save his soul by turning him toward Christ. Mrs. Frost of Portland, Oregon, wrote, "Please I beseech you don't just lay this letter aside before first getting on your knees and ask [sic] God with a contrite and humble heart whether these things be so and whether the Lord Jesus Christ is the Son of the living God."[70] Kertzer, who was conscientious about responding to his mail, wrote to another woman who had similarly asked him to accept Jesus: "While it may seem incomprehensible to a believing Christian that a Jew does not accept the principle of Christianity, a believing Jew finds that it is altogether possible to accept the moral teachings of Jesus without accepting the rest of the Christian creed."[71] His diplomacy, it seemed, shaded into apologetics.

A number of letter writers, though not the Christian proselytizers, ended with a request that the rabbi send them a list of other articles or books about Jews and Judaism. To these Kertzer recommended Steinberg's *Basic Judaism* and mentioned his own forthcoming book, an expansion of his article.[72] In fact, reviewers tended to compare Kertzer's book to Steinberg's earlier *Basic Judaism,* noting that *What Is a Jew?* was more accessible to non-Jews because it was written with a little more "light" and "warmth."[73] Kertzer, who had served as Steinberg's assistant rabbi in the 1940s, recalled Steinberg's frustrations with writing *Basic Judaism:* "He desperately wanted to write 'in the language of the common man.' That was not easy for a man who was most at home in metaphysics and epistemology."[74] Kertzer, however, felt no similar struggle and saw no greater achievement than to translate Jewishness into accessible language.

Kertzer's small efforts to promote his book to those who asked for reading recommendations paled in comparison to the publisher's campaign. According to one report, the book received more advance publicity than any other "book by a Jew for both Jews and non-Jews" had before it.[75] After *What Is a Jew?* was released, the publicity did not abate. A quarter-page advertisement in *Newsday* invited the public to hear Kertzer talk about the book and buy signed copies at a New York department store. According to the ad, the book was "attracting widespread interest" for its efforts to "guide . . . Gentiles to a better understanding of the thinking of their fellow Jewish-Americans and to enable Jews themselves to rediscover forgotten roots of tradition and belief that shape their role in American thought and culture."[76] *What Is a Jew?* also received publicity from the National Conference on Christians and Jews and the Jewish Book Guild.[77] Finally, a number of newspapers—including ones in Tucson, Pittsburgh, San Francisco, and Miami—published excerpts from the book and encouraged readers to buy copies.[78] These publicity efforts were not in vain; almost eight thousand copies of the book were sold in its first year, and the most recent edition of the book, updated and revised in 1996 by Kertzer's nephew, Rabbi Lawrence Hoffman, claimed that the book had sold a total of "more than 400,000 copies."[79]

Kertzer's efforts to explain Jews to the United States did not end with the publication of his book. The piles of letters he received taught him the power of mass media and encouraged him to exploit new technologies to reach wider audiences. Even if he had to mute some of the complexities of Jewishness, Kertzer believed, the benefits of reaching out to non-Jews and teaching them about Jews and Judaism were justification enough. He appeared frequently on radio programs but quickly realized that television held far more possibilities. Here, on the screens in American's living rooms, he could help create a public face for Jews that depicted them as sociologically distinctive, yet with beliefs that were learnable and familiar.

What Does a Jew Look Like on Television?

In 1953, Kertzer brought his fifteen-year-old daughter, Ruth, into a CBS studio to tape a program called *Faith of a Teen-ager.* Viewers were invited to be flies on the wall while father and daughter discussed a recent book about Judaism. Although the two had prepared a script beforehand, Ruth wrote her own answers to her father's questions. When he asked her, for example, if she could conceive of a world without God, she answered, "I think that's almost impossible. . . . It would have no meaning."[80] This was neither the first nor the last time Ruth would appear on television with her father. Earlier, she had spun a dreidel for a Chanukah program, and in the late 1950s, she, along with the rest of her family, participated in the two televised Kertzer family seders.[81] The first was broadcast live from their home in 1957. The following year CBS fabricated a replica of the family's kitchen, living room, and dining room and taped the seder at its New York studio.

Titled *Tell Thy Son,* the 1958 seder captured Kertzer's attempt to reconcile the sociological dimensions of Jewish distinctiveness with a universal and accessible Jewish message. Couching his lesson about Jewishness in a family-centered ritual, Kertzer illustrated the centrality of family background and tradition to Jewishness. Even the youngest of his children was already steeped in Jewishness, a system he had inherited at birth. The seder itself, however, was a testimony to the universality of Jewish beliefs. The family chanted blessings in Hebrew and discussed the symbolism of the Passover rituals, but Kertzer highlighted the holiday's message as being one that any American could appreciate: the struggle to bring freedom to all people. A non-Jewish guest joined in the discussion of this message and helped, through her well-planted questions, to translate foreign sounding words into American terms. At one point, she asked rather incredulously whether Jews truly believed

FIGURE 9. Taping *Tell Thy Son* at a CBS studio in New York, 1958. Clockwise from Rabbi Morris Kertzer (standing): Cathy Pike, Marvin Silbersher, Ruth Kertzer, David Kertzer, Julia Kertzer, and Jonathan Kertzer. Courtesy of the American Jewish Committee.

that the prophet Elijah visited every home on Passover and drank from a special glass of wine poured for him. In his answer, Kertzer evaded her question—about belief in spirits and prophet—and also avoided discussing the vengeful verses generally chanted at the moment in the seder when Jews open the door for Elijah. Instead he insisted that the tradition was an expression of Jews' hospitality and openness to accepting all people.[82]

Sitting at the head of the table in his well-appointed replica dining room, Kertzer appeared to be a consummate American middle-class father. Just as he had established his American credibility in the *Look* article by letting readers know about his wartime service, Kertzer peppered his description of the seder with a few anecdotes from his war days. His wife and daughter took care of the final food preparations for the seder, and his family and guests listened attentively to his explanations and laughed enthusiastically at his jokes. Aside from a few strange food items and the sprinkling of Hebrew, the Kertzer home could have been any home in suburban America. This, however, was only part of what Kertzer wished to convey: Jews were just like other middle-class Americans, but they were also different. Communicating a message this subtle, especially over television, was no easy task.

In 1958, he wrote, "I believe that *Judaism in its essential form* has a vital message for the world. . . . I also believe that Judaism, *as it is now interpreted and practised,* has little to commend itself to the non-Jew."[83] His point was that, if Jewishness were seen as simply another form of Americanism, then it would lose its purpose and, eventually, would fade into oblivion. Yet as director of the American Jewish Committee's interfaith division for many years, and as a self-proclaimed outreach enthusiast, Kertzer was invested in breaking down the barriers that in one guise caused social discord, but that in another guarded the integrity of Jewish social existence.[84]

The ultimate measure of whether Kertzer believed Judaism was open and accessible to all or a sociologically defined identity marker—open only to those people whose backgrounds and ways of life marked them as Jewish—was his attitude toward conversion. In *What Is a Jew?*, which preserved the question-and-answer format of the *Look* series, Kertzer posed a final question to himself: "How does a non-Jew become a Jew?" He answered that in recent years most converts came to Judaism by marriage, but he also noted that some joined Judaism because they "have decided that Judaism offers to them the best medium of religious expression."[85] Kertzer, who over the course of the 1950s gravitated away from the Conservative movement and toward Reform Judaism, was clearly aware that some of his Reform colleagues advocated a missionary movement. Yet he never joined the cause. Still, after his book had gone through many reprints and new editions, he would take great pride in the fact that it was widely assigned in conversion classes. Most of the students, however, would have been women (and occasionally men) interested in conversion because they were marrying Jews.[86] From sermons he gave, it is clear that, while he encouraged non-Jewish spouses to convert to Judaism—an indication that he believed a non-Jew, if tied to a Jewish family, could become a Jew—he was ambivalent about whether a full-fledged missionary effort was in the interest or spirit of Judaism.[87]

The belief that Judaism had a message to impart to the world helped rabbis define a Jewish purpose and envision Jewish survival. Yet such a belief did not rest easily with sociological understandings of Jewishness, which located Jewish survival in the ongoing distinctiveness of a bounded collective. The accessibility or universality of Jewishness only threatened to erode its sociological fixity. For rabbis committed to portraying Jewishness as broader than the Jewish people—as learnable and not only inheritable—the sociological model was crippling, unless they could prove one of two things: that the sociological dimensions of Jewishness were secondary to the religious (and teachable) ones, or that one could learn a new social identity just as easily as one could learn a new religion.

A Sociological Conversion

Mission theology, of course, was a long-standing component of the Reform movement, but its claim—that Jews were solely members of a religious group whose aim was to improve the world—seemed far from the lives that most American Jews lived. In the postwar proposals to reinvigorate the mission idea, the rabbis tried to reconcile classical Reform ideology with regnant understandings of Jewish group life. In discussions at the 1954 Reform movement convention, one rabbi had claimed enthusiastically that the missionary idea proved that Judaism was "culturally (not somatically) acquired and can be so acquired by anyone whose heart maketh him willing."[88] The rabbi did not aver that anyone could learn the beliefs of Judaism; rather, he declared Jewishness was defined through culture, an assent to the sociological view of Jewishness, yet also an avowal that a sociological conversion was just as possible as a religious one.

Throughout the mid- to late 1950s, Reform rabbis adjusted the language they used to talk about the missionary idea to reflect a respect for the sociological dimensions of Jewishness, hoping that they could rearticulate mission theology to fit the needs and sensibilities of postwar Jewish life. They proposed, as a tool for self-definition and a tool for survival, a missionary movement that would serve American Jews and non-Jews. In 1955, an article in support of the mission idea, written by Jakob Petuchowski, a Reform rabbi, appeared in *Commentary* and then was summarized in a column about religion in *Time* magazine. While Petuchowski favored missionary work, he stressed that missionary Judaism would succeed only if non-Jews were taught to become part of the "Jewish *people*."[89] Making a clear reference to Mordecai Kaplan's sociological formulation of Jewishness, the rabbi argued that missionary efforts bereft of a cultural or sociological component would ultimately undermine Jewish survival. Similarly, Trude Weiss-Rosmarin, in an editorial in the *Jewish Spectator,* offered her support for missionary Judaism with the condition that converts be taught how to integrate into the fullness of Jewish life. She acknowledged that this was far more challenging than simply teaching potential converts a set of beliefs. In fact, Weiss-Rosmarin doubted that first-generation converts would ever feel entirely part of the Jewish community, but as long as Jews were welcoming, then converts' children would have a normalized Jewish identity that did not challenge the sociological basis of Jewishness.[90]

The Reform movement communicated its respect for the sociological basis of Jewishness through a new set of conversion requirements issued in 1957. Although Rabbi Eichhorn had pressed his colleagues to set up practical means—like pamphlets about Judaism, television and radio broadcasts, and preaching missions—to extend the influence of Judaism to the world, the rabbis instead asked the Committee on the Unaffiliated to revise the movement's conversion manual.[91] Unlike the manual from thirty years ago that had whittled down the conversion process to an affirmation of Jewish universalism and had pronounced many Jewish rituals to be irrelevant, the new requirements were far more functional and mindful of the sociological basis of Jewishness: they emphasized those things that a non-Jew had to do to be a Jew. The committee insisted, "Proof of the acceptance of our faith lies in the practice thereof. . . . The student is to be trained in home observances, such as candle-lighting, Kiddush, the Seder, and all other forms that honor the Sabbath and holy days."[92]

The new conversion requirements placed a convert's adoption of a new community on a par with his or her initiation into a new belief system. Certainly, the convert was expected to learn the "distinct religious outlook" of Judaism and to understand the core differences between Judaism and his or her old faith (which the rabbis presumed would have been Christianity). Yet rabbis were told to stress, during the three- to six-month instruction period which the committee recommended for a convert, the "community character of Jewish life," so that the "proselyte [will] realize that conversion is a not a private matter."[93]

In the act of emphasizing the sociological dimensions of Jewishness— even if their aim was to show that these elements were as learnable as religious elements—Reform rabbis hastened the decline of the missionary idea. Even supporters were finding themselves unable to stitch together the universalism that mandated a Jewish mission with the particularism encoded in sociological conceptions of Jewishness. Robert Gordis, a Conservative rabbi and supporter of the missionary idea, raised the problem lucidly: "Judaism," he wrote, "is an ethnic faith in which peoplehood is organically bound up with religion."[94] Would a non-Jew ever truly seem like a Jew? *Time* magazine, summarizing Gordis's ideas—in the second column that it published on the Jewish missionary idea in the space of a few years—allowed readers to observe the palpable discomfort Jews felt about opening their door too widely.

In the 1920s, Reform rabbis had been attracted to missionary Judaism precisely because it minimized the specific cultural content of Jewishness in favor of universal claims. They imagined that embracing the universal dimensions of Jewishness was Jews' path to respect and American acceptance. The language of sociology, however, had replaced universalistic claims about Judaism. Still able to equate Jewishness with general—perhaps universal—patterns, sociological language located Jewish survival not in theological precepts but in following the rules that governed and maintained collective life. More than anything else, sociological explanations of Jewishness felt truer than religiously inflected universalistic ones. Universalism had rarely been embodied in Jewish experience, whereas sociology depicted Jewishness as the sum of what Jews did and who they were: where they lived, the jobs they performed, the families they raised, and so on. Some rabbis contended that non-Jews could experience a sociological conversion, and others disputed that there were sociological requirements for Jewishness, but most were content using words like *people* and *community* to describe the boundaries of Jewishness.

Reaching In and Marrying Out

Rabbi Morris Kertzer once recalled that Abraham Joshua Heschel, the eminent rabbi who escaped Nazi Germany and eventually settled in New York City, told him, "I think that the attitude of the Christian community in America has undergone a radical change. Instead of hostility, there is not only respect but an *expectation*—a belief that Jews have a message to convey, insights which others may share. *We mustn't disappoint them*."[95] Kertzer lived his life propelled by that mandate, imagining with every popular article he wrote, every radio address he delivered, and every television appearance he made that non-Jews were hungry for Judaism. Some were, and many were not. Regardless, Jews such as Kertzer and missionary rabbis were themselves hungry to explain and reexplain their Jewishness. In each effort to present Jewishness to the United States lay the opportunity to reformulate who they were and to try anew to ensure Jewish survival. In the words of Rabbi Petuchowski, "As anyone in the educational field knows from his own experience, many a problem that has been unclear to the teacher will be clarified the moment he is charged with presenting it to his students. What the 'mission of Israel' might accomplish for the Jews themselves could be conceived in similar terms."[96] Missionary and outreach efforts, then, were as much about reaching out to non-Jews as they were about reaching into the depths of Jewish self-understanding.

Ironically, just as rabbis, Jewish leaders, and average Jews were becoming increasingly conversant with sociological language to understand Jewishness and its place in the United States, the sociological profile of American Jews was becoming less useful in demarcating the boundaries between Jews and non-Jews. The growth of American suburbs, the expansion and democratization of higher education, and the decline in workplace discrimination all opened channels for greater contact between Jews and non-Jews. It was more and more the case that who or what a Jew was, resembled who or what a non-Jew was.

Nothing highlighted the crumbling of sociological conceptions of Jewishness as forcefully as a wedding between a Jew and a non-Jew, and even more so, the fear that more weddings like it would follow. In the past, intermarriage had most often been an exit strategy. Driven by love or not, Jews who married non-Jews tended to want to leave Jewish life behind. In the era after World War II, intermarriage also became an entrance strategy as more non-Jews than ever before converted to their spouse's faith or agreed to raise their children as Jews. The same problem that had confronted missionary hopefuls erupted in the presence of new marriage patterns: if a non-Jew could marry, create a family with, and even become a Jew, what served to distinguish Jews from non-Jews? The question was a matter of Jewish survival, and it became the ground on which new ideologies of Jewishness emerged. A new vocabulary based on individual choice, or volition, presented a persuasive answer. According to its terms, not the compulsion of law, God, or belief, and not the inevitability of sociological patterns, but the power of individual choice came to define Jewishness. Like any other ideology, however, volitional Jewishness was rife with contradictions and problems, especially when it came to explaining Jewishness to the United States.

CHAPTER 7

A Jewish Marilyn Monroe
and the Civil-Rights-Era Crisis
in Jewish Self-Presentation

Judaizing the American Body

Years after the fact, Norman Mailer wrote that theirs had been a union between the "great American brain" and the "great American body."[1] The brain, Arthur Miller, was Jewish, gawky, and bespectacled. The body, Marilyn Monroe, was beautiful, blonde, and not Jewish. And then in the summer of 1956, moments before her marriage to Miller, she converted. For a time, the American body was Jewish.

For Jews invested in explaining themselves to non-Jews, a Jewish Marilyn Monroe symbolized just how successful—perhaps too successful—their efforts had been. Jewish literary critic Leslie Fiedler, commenting on Miller and Monroe's marriage, said it was as if "the mythical erotic dream girls of us all yearn for Jewish intellectuals and learn to make matzo-balls."[2] When fantasy—beautiful non-Jewish women desiring bookish Jewish men and even cooking Jewish food for them—turned into reality, new fears erupted.

For as long as they had had the resources to do so, Jews had attempted to explain themselves in accessible and appealing ways to non-Jewish Americans. Revelries about ever-increasing permeability between Jews and non-Jews had generally been tempered by reality, which guarded Jewish distinctiveness. Since the 1920s, sociologists had identified social differences—family structure, neighborhood, values, social class, education—as distinguishing Jews from other Americans. Jews did not have to cultivate those social differences; rather, they were simply the sum of what Jews did and how they lived. Unless a person went to great efforts to shed his or her Jewishness, being Jewish was a fact of a Jew's social existence, almost as inevitable and organic as some assumed race to be. It made sense to describe Jewish difference in sociological terms if one imagined that social facts confirmed that Jews were distinct from non-Jews. If, however, social facts—such as where people lived, the values they maintained, and the people they married—indicated very little difference between Jews and non-Jews, then the sociological terms of Jewishness might explain Jewish similarity to other Americans, but they could not safeguard Jewish distinctiveness.

One wishing to witness the bumpy and fractious path away from sociological Jewishness could examine any number of Jewish communal debates about assimilation between the late 1950s and the 1970s. Nothing illustrated the assault on sociological Jewishness more soundly, however, than sociologists' own reports about rising rates of intermarriage and the simultaneous crisis mentality that escalated in the Jewish community. Still, sociological explanations of endogamy, and Jewishness more generally, did not fade easily. Even as research indicated that intermarriage across religious lines was increasing, Jewish communal leaders were reluctant to abandon their allegiance to sociological Jewishness. Many rabbis and Jewish sociologists continued to characterize intermarriage as socially deviant and a threat to American stability, despite the fact that American social structure now provided for greater sociological similarity among religious and ethnic groups. Using sociology less as a tool of description and more as a force of prescription, these rabbis and sociologists advised Americans that the consequences of crossing religious lines in one's most intimate relationships remained dire and could tear apart a marriage, a family, and ultimately, society.

Yet a willed blindness was demanded if one were to continue believing that sociological facts mandated against marriages between Jews and non-Jews. Articles printed in popular magazines and academic journals, and sermons preached from countless pulpits, depicted intermarriage as an emerging norm. Some sources even inflated just how common Jewish intermarriage was in their eagerness to create a sensational story, the kind that would sell magazines, fill pews, and, perhaps, convince people to try to do something to stem the trend. In 1963, reflecting on a series of intermarriage studies performed over the previous few years, a sociologist concluded in the *American Jewish Year Book* that the new data "cast doubt on the doctrine of the persistence of religious endogamy in American life."[3] In the face of Jews' overwhelming support for integration, proscriptions against intermarriage appeared outmoded and even indefensible. As intermarriage and discussions about its implications became more commonplace, rabbis and sociologists had to rethink their descriptions of Jewish difference.

Jewishness, in order to continue serving as an ideology about the relationship between Jews and non-Jews, increasingly had to account for Jews who loved and procreated with non-Jews, non-Jews who loved and procreated with Jews, and non-Jews who became Jews. Some Jewish leaders started to experiment with a new vocabulary of Jewishness that centered on individual choice—what I call volitional Jewishness. Its suppleness was its power; sociological, religious, and biology-based conceptions of Jewishness could fit into a framework of choice, where the individual was free to decide how and when to be Jewish. Its suppleness was also its weakness, making boundaries almost impossible to draw and paying no particular respect to history, tradition, community, or divinity.

This chapter, then, is about the striking success of Jewish efforts to explain themselves to non-Jews, and how that success raised new problems and exacerbated old ones. Marilyn Monroe's short-lived marriage to Arthur Miller issued a public and celebrated challenge to Jewish sociological distinctiveness. If a person who seemed so clearly not Jewish— from her appearance to her family history to her place in American popular culture—could become a Jew, then the sociological assumptions about Jewishness were in jeopardy of unraveling. The Miller-Monroe story is a foray into a larger discussion about the incredible cultural power sociologists and sociological Jewishness had attained by midcentury and, conversely, the shortcomings of sociology. As the spirit of the 1960s swept the United States, Jews found that the ways they had become accustomed to explaining themselves no longer made sense, certainly not in a country where Jews went to school, worked, and lived alongside non-Jews, and where Jews protested segregation and even died for integration. Yet many Jews still maintained faith in Jewish distinctiveness, even if they married a non-Jew, raised a half-Jew, or had once been a Protestant or a Catholic.

The Star, the Playwright, and the Rabbi

The couple stood under the chuppah (a Jewish wedding canopy), she in a simple beige dress and a veil dyed to match, he in a dark suit and thick-framed glasses. Just hours before the wedding, Marilyn Monroe

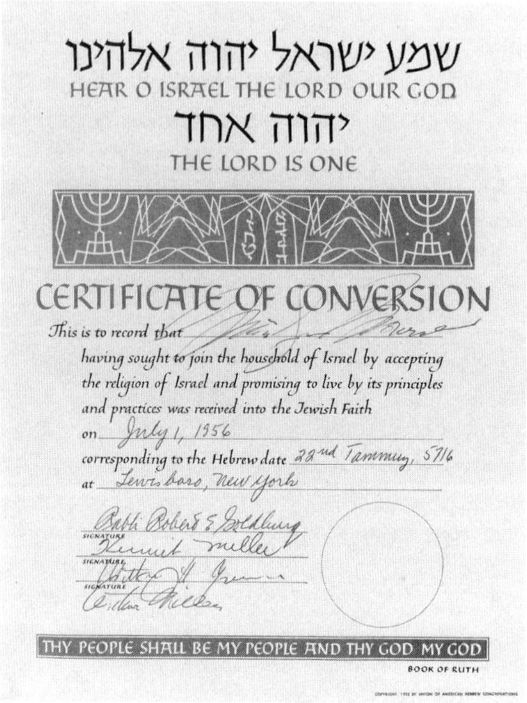

שְׁמַע יִשְׂרָאֵל יְהוָה אֱלֹהֵינוּ
HEAR O ISRAEL THE LORD OUR GOD
יְהוָה אֶחָד
THE LORD IS ONE

CERTIFICATE OF CONVERSION

This is to record that _____

having sought to join the household of Israel by accepting
the religion of Israel and promising to live by its principles
and practices was received into the Jewish Faith

on _July 1, 1956_

corresponding to the Hebrew date _22nd Tammuz, 5716_

at _Lewisboro, New York_

SIGNATURE _Rabbi Robert E. Goldburg_
SIGNATURE _Kermit Miller_
SIGNATURE _Arthur A. Green_
SIGNATURE _Esther Miller_

THY PEOPLE SHALL BE MY PEOPLE AND THY GOD MY GOD
BOOK OF RUTH

FIGURE 10. Marilyn Monroe's conversion certificate.
© Christie's Images, Ltd., 2007.

had signed a certificate of conversion. Decorated with stark modernist line drawings of menorahs and the ten commandments, it attested that Monroe, "having sought to join the household of Israel by accepting the religion of Israel and promising to live by its principles and practices was received into the Jewish Faith on July 1, 1956."[4] Shortly after, according to reports from the star-hungry press, Miller and Monroe "drank wine, exchanged rings, and the bridegroom crushed a goblet in memory of the destruction of Jerusalem by its ancient foes," and they were married as two Jews.[5]

Robert Goldburg, a Reform rabbi at New Haven's Mishkan Israel, sat next to the bride and groom at the small backyard reception in Katonah, New York. In 1970, Rabbi Goldburg tartly told his congregation that no other act—neither his public denunciation of McCarthyism nor his other subversive political activities (which earned him a thick FBI file)—had gained him the recognition that converting Monroe and

FIGURE 11. Marilyn Monroe and Arthur Miller's wedding reception in Katonah, New York, July 1, 1956. Rabbi Robert Goldburg is seated to the left of Monroe. Monroe image by Milton H. Greene © 2008 Joshua Greene, www.archiveimages.com.

officiating at her wedding to Miller had: "Thanks to *Life* magazine and the media around the world, fame or infamy came in this ironic way."[6] Commentators at the time and historians since have not been kind to him. An early biographer of Monroe scripted the scene cynically: "Just prior to the ceremony, Marilyn was closeted with Rabbi Robert Goldburg. . . . He instructed her for two hours . . . in the general theory of Judaism, a humanistic approach. . . . When the indoctrination was over, Marilyn was persuaded that she was finally a Jewess. How profound this feeling was is difficult to know. A sensitive director could convince her that she was also an Archduke's mistress or a cowboy's simple-minded 'angel.'"[7] Morton Miller, Arthur's cousin, characterized Monroe's conversion as "perfunctory."[8] And as recently as 1997, when the encyclopedic *Jewish Women in America* was compiled, its editors made the decision, according to a consistent and well-articulated policy, to omit Monroe.[9]

Goldburg had little patience for Jewish efforts to define who was and was not an insider. In a sermon he delivered in 1958, he chastised Jews for imagining that a clear line divided them from non-Jews and, thus, "forfeit[ing] . . . bright hopes for a better society."[10] A few years later, he complained to his friend, the author Howard Fast, that he was preparing to go to a conference on Jewish assimilation: "With so many more important things to worry about, they brood over this."[11] For Goldburg, the purpose of Judaism—like the purpose of any religion or philosophy—was to improve the world for everyone, a goal that he believed was thwarted by Jews' obsession with distinctiveness and difference. In 1954, he told his congregants that he was "born a Jew by accident," although he assured them that it was a happy accident and one that gave him access to incredible wisdom and ethical teachings.[12]

Still, Goldburg wanted the record to reflect that he took seriously the process of conversion and had not simply been wooed by Monroe's fame or sex appeal. In fact, shortly after Monroe's death in the summer of 1962, Goldburg wrote a lengthy letter to Jacob Rader Marcus, the head of the American Jewish Archives, in which he promised to set out the facts of Monroe's conversion and marriage to Miller. Periodically, over the next two decades, Goldburg sent letters to Marcus, adding details to his recollection and ensuring that history—or at least the archives (he requested the content be "put in a sealed envelope and opened some years later")—would preserve his version of the events.[13]

According to Goldburg, in the late spring of 1956, Miller, whom he considered a friend, told the rabbi that he planned to marry Monroe and that she wished to convert to Judaism. The three arranged a meeting at Monroe's midtown New York City apartment. Goldburg remembered Monroe as sweet and timid. When asked, she explained that she had no religious training, other than "some memories of a Fundamentalist Protestantism which she had long rejected."[14] Monroe did, however, express a powerful attraction to Judaism; the rabbi recalled her saying that she was "impressed with Jewish people she knew, especially Mr. Miller" and was drawn to the "close family" ideal in Judaism.[15] At the end of their first meeting, Goldburg assigned Monroe a list of books to read, including Morris Kertzer's *What Is a Jew?* and Milton Steinberg's *Partisan's Guide to the Jewish Problem.* These were the typical books he assigned to potential converts, and the rabbi remembered discussing them with her at later meetings. While he described Monroe as "not an intellectual person" and possessing only a "limited" attention span, he felt certain that "she understood and accepted the basic principles of Judaism."[16]

Rabbi Goldburg never explained why Monroe's conversion did not occur until moments before the wedding, although he intimated that the time and place of the wedding changed multiple times in order to evade the press.[17] In his estimation, Monroe was sincere in her desire to become Jewish. In a 1986 letter to the archivist, Goldburg emphasized, "No pressure was put on her to convert."[18] Miller, in the few statements he made about the matter, also maintained that Monroe came to the decision on her own, and that he, in fact, saw the whole thing as "rather unnecessary."[19] While Monroe was generally silent about her conversion, she often spoke of her deep affection for Miller's family, which continued even after the marriage ended.[20] A less generous interpretation, offered by one social critic, suggested that Monroe "hankered after intellectual status," something she thought she could attain by marrying Miller and becoming Jewish.[21]

According to Goldburg, Monroe remained connected to Judaism after the wedding; she gave Chanukah presents to Miller's children and attended Passover seders that Goldburg conducted. She never went to synagogue, but Goldburg explained that she avoided most public places for fear of invasive press attention.[22] At certain opportune moments, Monroe was welcomed into the ranks of Jewish life. She and Miller had been invited to appear at a 1957 United Jewish Appeals conference in Miami. According to Goldburg, Monroe agreed to speak briefly about "why she became Jewish and why she believed that Jewish institutions and Israel deserved support." He added parenthetically that he wrote the speech for her.[23] Shortly before the event, Congress's House Un-American Activities Committee indicted Arthur Miller on contempt charges for refusing to name the names of possible members of the Communist Party.[24] The United Jewish Appeals withdrew its invitation to Miller, though its chairman still hoped Monroe would attend. For a brief moment, the red-tinged Jew lost mainstream Jewish acceptance while his formerly non-Jewish wife gained entry. (Monroe declined to make an appearance.)[25] The next year, the couple was once again asked to lend their star power to the organized Jewish community. Miller, following Goldburg's counsel, accepted a speaking engagement at a fundraising dinner for the American Friends of Hebrew University to be held in the fall of 1959. The executive director wanted to make sure that Monroe would accompany her husband, and Goldburg recalled him saying, "Her presence would mean a great fund raising for Hebrew University."[26]

While some Jewish groups may have tried to capitalize on Monroe's Jewishness, the very fact that someone like her could be attracted to Judaism and to a Jewish man vividly challenged the most basic sociological assumptions that rabbis and sociologists had maintained would

FIGURE 12. Arthur Miller, Marilyn Monroe, and Rabbi
Robert Goldburg (from left) attend a fund-raising dinner
for the American Friends of Hebrew University at the
Bellevue Stratford Hotel, in Philadelphia, September 27,
1959. Courtesy of the Jacob Rader Marcus Center of the
American Jewish Archives.

guard Jewish distinctiveness in the United States. Would Goldburg
have performed Miller and Monroe's wedding had Monroe not converted? Most likely, no. The two times he recalled officiating at the marriage between a Jew and a non-Jew were fairly unusual circumstances.[27]
Jewish endogamy was not a practice he could easily eschew, as ingrained
into Jewish tradition as it was. Nonetheless, Goldburg admitted that it
was with a "troubled conscience" that he abided by the Reform movement's long-standing policy of discouraging rabbis from performing
intermarriages.[28] He believed that "the realities of American life" were
more complicated than the dictates of "resolutions which condemn."[29]
Would he have given Monroe a hasty conversion so as to adhere to the

letter, if not the spirit, of Jewish endogamy? He claimed certainly not, but others doubted him and implicitly questioned whether conversion truly solved the problems raised by intermarriage. Regardless of the extent to which Goldburg prepared Monroe for her conversion, he realized that his actions made Jewishness a more complicated matter than some wanted to believe it was.

On January 20, 1961, after a six-month separation, Miller and Monroe divorced.[30] A year and a half later, Monroe was found dead in her Brentwood home. Rabbi Goldburg, away in Europe for a vacation, missed the call from Monroe's former secretary.[31] When he returned, her body had already been laid to rest in a crypt in a Los Angeles cemetery, bereft of the ritual treatment given to the Jewish dead. Neither Miller nor the rabbi who converted her and gave her a Jewish wedding attended the funeral. Instead Joe DiMaggio, an Italian Catholic with an unbeatable hitting streak, played the grieving widower at her funeral, though the two had been divorced since 1955.[32] Years later, in recollecting the end of his marriage to Monroe and her subsequent breakdown, Miller remarked, "How I wished I still had my religion and she hers."[33]

The Prescriptive Power of Sociology

Miller believed that, in trying to become who she was not, Monroe had lost her sense of self. Her conversion to Judaism was only one small piece in her struggle to reinvent herself and in her ultimate alienation from herself. Yet well before the 1950s, sociologists and many rabbis had spoken of religion as a sociological identity, and had explained that changing one's religious identity necessitated a complete, perhaps impossible, self-transformation. Few could articulate what exactly a non-Jew could do to become a full-fledged Jew. In one sense, marrying a Jew may have been the first step; after all, in tying himself or, as was more often the case until the 1970s, herself to a Jewish spouse, a non-Jew could more easily assume the sociological status of being Jewish. Rabbis and many sociologists, however, were reluctant to endorse marriages between Jews and those born as non-Jews, no matter the circumstances. Even if non-Jews showed every sign of pledging their loyalty to the Jewish people (a fact alone about which some rabbis were traditionally skeptical), it was difficult to see how the sociological integrity of Jewishness could survive the entrance of non-Jews into the Jewish fold. Whether Monroe had converted or not, her marriage to Miller symbolized the narrowing of a sociological gap between Jews

and non-Jews, made all the narrower by new educational and professional opportunities for Jews and postwar measures to end structural
Jewish exclusion. Were that sociological gap to close, the apparent differences between Jews and non-Jews threatened to become invisible or
nonexistent.

Changing historical and sociological realities to the contrary, many
Jews were unwilling to abandon their reliance on sociological language
as an assurance of Jewish survival. As an American idiom, it was too
powerful and functional to be surrendered hastily. The putatively unbiased authority of sociology gave rabbis, especially liberal ones, a way of
defending endogamy without appearing to prescribe it. Throughout
the 1950s and 1960s, as data accumulated that punctured old theories
about unchanging religious endogamy, rabbis nonetheless employed
the language of sociological rules to assert endogamy as an ongoing
norm. In the early 1960s, for example, when Rabbi Kertzer sought to
convince his Long Island Reform congregation that intermarriage was
best avoided, he informed them that "deeply ingrained in America is
what sociologists called the 'triple melting pot.'"[34]

Orthodox rabbis, whose congregants were less likely to marry non-
Jews, and who tended to feel more comfortable speaking in the language
of religious decree, also recognized the efficacy of using sociological
vocabulary to mandate endogamy.[35] In 1958, an Orthodox rabbi told a
group of rabbis and Jewish communal workers about the telephone calls
he most dreaded: "A sweet voice [asks]: 'Are you Rabbi Jung? May I have
the pleasure of an interview?' And she comes in, Mary McSomething or
Ruth Williams. She asks, 'Would you be good enough to receive me into
your faith?' And I would say to her, 'What is his name?' That is how the
problem is brought home to me."[36] The rabbi explained that he tried to
convince these women, whom he imagined were motivated solely by
their suitors, that becoming Jewish was not as easy as falling in love or
changing one's last name. The arguments he made were sociological:
these women came from non-Jewish families, and their backgrounds
would make it almost impossible for them to become Jewish women,
wives, and mothers. It was only the extraordinary non-Jew, motivated to
study, follow rituals scrupulously, and abide by Jewish law, who could
become a true Jew and evade sociological realities.

Although early American Reform rabbis would have similarly measured true Jewishness by religious standards (though they focused on
belief and ethics, not ritual observance), by the middle of the twentieth
century Reform and Conservative rabbis spoke almost exclusively in the

language of sociology when it came to defining Jewishness. Sociology carried authority that many rabbis envied. An essential piece of the apparatus of American expert culture, sociology promised to describe social patterns with precision and, thus, instruct Americans in what was normal and what was not. Liberal rabbis knew that most of their congregants did not organize their lives around the categories of Jewish law, and many rabbis questioned the relevance of those categories as well. Anchoring their own prescriptive statements against intermarriage to the empirical vocabulary of sociology gave rabbis the ability to speak with authority about their congregants' intimacies without appearing meddlesome, directive, or even biased. As a language of prescription, nothing was more powerful than a language like sociology, which, ironically, claimed only to describe.

Articles published in the popular press fueled a commonsense suspicion of intermarriage while, simultaneously, indicating that intermarriage was becoming more common and thus more newsworthy. Most reports, like those published in *Woman's Home Companion* and *Good Housekeeping*, warned against intermarriage, describing it as disruptive to social and family harmony. Reporters relied on sociologists and clergy to make the case against intermarriage, generally without noting whether these sources had a personal investment in convincing readers to avoid intermarrying. A 1956 article printed in *Redbook* that promised to offer a "full factual report" on intermarriage asserted, "An interfaith marriage is inevitably subject to more strain and stress than a marriage between persons of the same faith."[37] To substantiate this fact, the reporter quoted Rabbi Maurice Eisendrath, an important leader of the Reform movement, who explained in clearly sociological terms, "A lack of religious unity lowers the chances of marital success."[38] Certainly, the rabbi had a specific investment in dissuading Americans from marrying across faith lines, yet the reporter accepted his dicta as fact, much as the rabbi had accepted sociological models of marital success as fact. In 1960, when Rabbi Levi Olan addressed listeners of a Dallas radio station, he explained that "authorities"—sociologists and other social scientists—had proven that "two young people who come from radically different religious backgrounds are bound to confront . . . differences between themselves which in critical times become dividing factors. . . . The general community is usually unprepared to accept wholly such a mixed religious home and adds to its complexity."[39]

With striking circularity, some sociologists even relied on clergy to validate their conclusions that religious endogamy was the best path for social stability. A *New York Times* article written by a sociologist in 1956 asserted that religious leaders "have long known what recent sociological studies verify": that intermarriages made precarious unions at best.[40] Blurring empirical research with religious doctrine and cultural mores, journalists, rabbis, and sociologists held tight to the norm of religious endogamy, whether motivated by faith-based concerns, fear about the havoc that social mixing could wreak on American and minority life, or as often was the case, both.

Little vivified the sociological case against intermarriage more effectively than studies and, even more so, stories that portrayed children as innocent victims of their parents' selfish and aberrant marital decisions. Playing upon the cold war valorization of religion as essential to America's strength, and the cultural discourse that conceived of children as in constant need of protection, rabbis along with some sociologists constructed an emotionally and politically stirring case for endogamy.[41] Intermarriage, according to one family expert, precipitated a "cold war" at home, as dangerous for children as the international cold war was for humanity.[42] Even if rabbis, sociologists, or social commentators might hesitate to tell adults how to live their lives, children were an entirely different matter; when parents failed to act in the best interest of their offspring, other adults and institutions had a responsibility to step in. "Above all," a rabbi instructed in 1949, "every child is entitled to a religious upbringing—to *one* religious upbringing which will be a source of security and not an occasion of inner conflict."[43]

Admonishments from rabbis, however, could not match the emotional percussiveness of firsthand accounts written by children and their parents. In 1952 and 1953, *Commentary* published two such articles that chronicled the plight of children whose parents had breached sociological categories and left them suspended in the void. The first was written by Eleanor Felder, a guilt-ridden Presbyterian married to a Jewish man and mother of a son. While neither she nor her husband was a religiously minded person, she was certain that "children have a *right* to be exposed to religion."[44] With a sentimentality that did not match her own beliefs, she continued, "The concept of a God who watches over each sparrow may give the child a deep sense of warmth and protection."[45] Even more, she believed, religion gave children a place in the world. Describing her son's religious liminality, she asked pleadingly, "What becomes of children like ours? Where do they end, with what identifying tag?"[46] One reader dismissed Felder's assumption that, in order to "belong," children had to have a religion: "Parents are under no obligation to teach what they know to be false, puerile, and utterly unrealistic."[47] His response found few supporters; most readers echoed Felder's concern with their own stories and solutions. One offered: "The son takes the identity of the father. A young 'Levy' is what the name implies, just as a young 'O'Neill' is what that name implies."[48] Of course, the reader did not mention that mothers often shouldered the responsibility for their children's religious upbringing, even if they did not pass on the family name.

Writing in *Commentary* a few months later, Richard Goldhurst confirmed Felder's fears and testified to the trauma of being raised, as he wrote, "between two worlds." Using a pseudonym, the grown child of a Catholic mother and Jewish father explained that studies of intermarriage authored by "non-participants" could not possibly capture the "feelings and motivations of the individuals involved."[49] What he described was a life of pain, of being caught in the middle between battling parents, and of not knowing where to locate himself. His mother tried to make her boys into good Catholics, taking them to church and making certain they took communion. Yet nothing she did could erase the fact that "society at large understood us best as Jews."[50] He and his brother, however, had no sense of what it meant to be Jewish. Their father had fled tradition when he married their mother, and he seemed as uncomfortable with his Jewishness as he was with his wife's Catholicism. Their Jewish grandfather, far from ushering them into the Jewish world, baited them about "the *shikse*" at every visit. "I was fifteen," Goldhurst tartly recalled, "before I discovered that *shikse* didn't mean 'mother.'"[51] He attributed his "metaphysical skepticism" to his parents' marriage. "Children exposed to warring religious faith," according to Goldhurst's generalization, grew up with no faith at all.[52] Bristling at her son's bitterness and reproach, Goldhurst's mother wrote to the editor, "At least the union produces sons who can write for *Commentary*."[53] Few experts, however, would have seen this as adequate recompense for a lifetime spent without religion and the sense of identity religion ostensibly transmitted.

Marriage experts writing in popular magazines in the 1950s and 1960s also tended to portray children as helpless victims of their parents' brash marital decisions. An article published in *Cosmopolitan* in 1956 warned, "The real trouble in a mixed marriage begins when children arrive."[54] The authors maintained that children deserve a coherent religious background. Without one, "children will grow up in a spiritual and moral vacuum and in the end will probably choose no religion at all."[55] Even if two adults believed their religious differences were inconsequential, the birth of a child would threaten to "set off dormant tensions between husband and wife," according to a *Redbook* reporter, also in 1956.[56] Another article, published in 1963, similarly explained, "Religion causes so much 'trouble' because it is far more deeply grounded in our hearts and our tradition, our hopes and assumptions, than we think."[57] In other words, religion remained an intrinsic part of who a person was and paid no heed to an individual's efforts to circumvent or change it. Furthermore, even if two individuals could ignore their religious differences, any children they produced would suffer from a sense of dislocation: "Where," Felder had asked with self-recrimination, "do our children belong?"[58]

Parents who married across religious lines were accused of valuing their romantic whims over the spiritual and moral well-being of their children. If the doctrines of their own faiths could not convince them to marry within their religions, the consequences for yet-born children would perhaps give them pause. Yet the very fact that a growing number of children had mixed-faith parentage challenged the rhetoric of deviance that had been used to shore up the sociological case against intermarriage. Marshall Sklare, a sociologist employed by the American Jewish Committee who was invested in defending Jewish endogamy, wrote forebodingly in 1964, "It is precisely the 'healthy' modern inter-marriages which raise the most troubling questions of all to the Jewish community."[59] That intermarriages could be healthy, and that their children could be normal, Sklare realized, was a reflection of social changes against which Jews would have to fight if they wanted to maintain their endogamy. Sociology, ever increasingly a tool for measuring higher rates of intermarriage, was losing its power to describe or prescribe Jewish endogamy as a norm.

The Bad Politics of Endogamy

"Only certain types of intermarriages are viewed with concern as social problems," a sociologist had argued in 1958, "namely, those intermarriages which mirror areas of prejudice and threaten vested interests in our society."[60] While sociological wisdom over the preceding three decades had tended to defend certain lines of social division as being essential for individual, family, and social harmony, by the 1960s public and legal battles against segregationist policies were calling such pronouncements into question. In an interview with a *Redbook* reporter in 1963, one sociologist asserted, "I believe that mixed marriages are a good thing, since they break down barriers between people."[61]

Political, demographic, and economic shifts were inexorably eroding the sociological factors that had assured endogamy. In postwar America, opportunities for people to interact and become intimate with others who did not share their religion increased, thanks to the expansion of higher education, legislation barring discrimination in housing and employment practices, mass culture, and suburban growth. Yet closely tied to these structural shifts were ideological ones. The case for inmarriage, refracted through increasingly popular integrationist ideals, seemed bound to flounder. A commitment to integration meant that categorical difference, whether defined by law, sociology, religion, or an individual's attitudes, was an embattled concept. Indeed, many Jews were ardent in their support for mid-twentieth-century liberalism because they saw their own survival as dependent on it, particularly the notion that group difference should be inconsequential to an individual's rights and status.[62] Yet Jewish survival—or the perpetuation of a distinctive Jewish identity—also depended on the existence and assertion of categorical differences between Jews and non-Jews.

With growing self-consciousness, a number of rabbis and sociologists realized their own politics were to blame for turning endogamy into bad politics. As early as 1949, Bernard Bamberger, a Reform rabbi, acknowledged that liberal rabbis like himself were "busily engaged in creating conditions that favor intermarriage." As a result of their fervent fight against segregation and attempts to break down barriers among groups, the rabbi explained, increased social contact between Jews and non-Jews was inescapable and would "sometimes lead to love and marriage."[63] In a 1951 article surveying recent studies of intermarriage, Jewish sociologist Milton Barron, who had written his first book on intermarriage in Derby, Connecticut, similarly observed, "Sending children to public schools and to centers of higher education away from home; the struggle against restrictive covenants, job discrimination, and quota systems; and participation in interfaith activity are but a few practices which lead inevitably to intergroup contacts that sometimes become love and intermarriage."[64] Another Jewish sociologist, writing in the pages of *Commentary* in 1953, exposed the hypocrisy in which he participated: "We have encouraged the cultural and social contacts which lead to intermarriage while condemning intermarriage itself."[65] Still, while many Jews had long felt the chafing between their endogamy and liberalism, it took the civil rights movement to convince them that they were in the throes of a true crisis.

In 1964, the same year Congress passed the Civil Rights Act and the Ku Klux Klan murdered three young men—two Jews and one African American—for registering black voters in Mississippi, *Look* magazine published an article titled "The Vanishing American Jew." A series of bulleted statements, situated directly beneath a photograph of an open Torah scroll, explained just why Jews were vanishing: "New studies reveal loss of Jewish identity, soaring rate of intermarriage."[66] The timing could not have been more provocative. As if it were a zero-sum game, some Jewish voices suggested that Jews could choose either liberalism or survival, not both.

Aware of the weight that their pronouncements about intermarriage carried among rabbis and other clergy, sociologists started to address religious communities more directly than ever before, especially when it came to considering the political ramifications of endogamy. In his 1964 study of assimilation, Milton Gordon urged rabbis, as well as other clergy, to accept that intermarriage was the product of a positive shift in liberal politics. He instructed, "The individual . . . should be allowed to choose freely whether to remain within the boundaries of communality created by his birthright ethnic group, to branch out into multiple interethnic contacts, or even to change his affiliation to that of another ethnic group . . . as a result of religious conversion, intermarriage, or simply private wish."[67] Gordon imagined that, if there were fewer static social boundaries, then less antipathy could be directed toward any particular social group. That same year, another sociologist, equally intent on influencing how clergy thought about intermarriage (he was also a Conservative rabbi himself), argued to the contrary that group differences would always remain in place. And he believed that intermarriage could neither bridge those differences nor function to diminish bigotry; it could only exacerbate social tension. Rabbis, parents, and children were misguided, he wrote, if they believed "human brotherhood" would be achieved through intermarriage.[68] Sociologist Marshall Sklare, writing in *Commentary* in 1964, similarly lambasted Jews for their "complacency" when it came to preventing intermarriage, "a matter more crucial to Jewish survival than any other."[69] Without stating it outright, he pilloried Jewish activism in the civil rights movement and integrationist politics.

Some sociologists, clearly aware of the authority that sociology carried in Jewish communal life, took it as their duty to monitor and even censor their colleagues' work. For example, in 1965 Nathan Hurvitz, a Jewish sociologist, chastised two other sociologists for lacking "an insider's sensitivity to nuances in American Jewish life."[70] The two sociologists, a husband-and-wife team, had written an article suggesting that the vast majority of Jews who intermarried had strong pluralistic values, and thus their intermarriages, far from the cause of cognitive dissonance and psychological turmoil, were simply reflections of their social ideals and liberalism.[71] Hurvitz accused them of coloring their research with their own "negative attitude toward American Jewish life" and implying that only if one were intermarried could he or she be a true supporter of a liberal agenda.[72] In a brief rejoinder, the sociologists acknowledged that research like theirs could tip the precarious balance between integration and endogamy that Jews were trying to achieve. They were certain, however, that old sociological defenses of endogamy—those that equated intermarriage with marital strife, and endogamy with social stability—were a thing of the past, and that it was their professional responsibility to report this shift. Jews who cared about preserving Jewish endogamy, they argued, would have to face new realities and search for more compelling ways to explain the importance of endogamy to themselves, to Americans, and especially to their children, or else it too would become a thing of the past.

The problem, according to Marshall Sklare, who emerged in the 1960s as one of the most vocal sociologists defending Jewish endogamy, was that Jews did not know how to talk about why they should marry other Jews. They had assumed endogamy would simply be a fact of life, and sociologists, along with persistent antisemitism and exclusion from non-Jewish society, had encouraged them in their assumptions. Now as social circumstances changed, and as Jews pledged themselves to the ideals of the civil rights movement, parents lacked the language for persuading their children to marry other Jews. Sklare explained, "The liberalism of the Jewish parent—his commitment to the idea of equality and his belief in the transitory character of the differences which distinguish people from one another—serves to subvert his sense of moral rectitude in opposing intermarriage."[73]

Once again, children rested at the heart of Jewish intermarriage woes. Rabbis and sociologists still worried about the fate of children with intermarried parents (the *Look* article speculated that 70 percent of these children were lost to Judaism). They also started to worry about the fate of children whose parents were both Jewish but who had never heard a compelling argument for endogamy. Leaders of other religious groups shared this anxiety. An article printed in 1963 reported that parents were more likely to teach their children "to be friends with those who are unlike them[,] . . . to practice brotherhood without regard to difference," than to teach them to marry within their own faith.[74] Most people, it seemed, approved of interfaith marriage in the abstract, but according to a survey in the mid-1950s, they "often oppose the idea when their own sons or daughters are involved."[75] It could come as a shock to these children—and certainly would seem to be a sign of their parents' hypocrisy—when they learned that a boyfriend or girlfriend would not be a welcome addition to the family simply on account of his or her religion. Anger would be a likely response, rebellion another.

In a frank assessment, a Conservative rabbi in 1966 explained that many Jewish youth were apt to conclude that their "parents are simply prejudiced against gentiles, using the religious argument to bolster their prejudices."[76] Because Jews tended to support integration—for reasons of self-interest as much as anything else—the problem of Jewish intermarriage became a problem of how to communicate competing ideals to one's children and the larger society, who were as prone to see hypocrisy as they were to appreciate genuine soul-searching.

Here it was, then, the moment when the failure of sociological language, and the irrelevance of religious language in describing Jewishness, created a true crisis, one that struck at the home, had the potential of alienating young Jews, and asked explicit, uncomfortable questions about Jewish prejudices. For many decades already, Jews had sought to explain Jewishness in a way that could prove their Americanness while still preserving their distinctiveness. By the 1960s and 1970s, however, Jews were less self-conscious about asserting their Americanness because most of them simply felt American. More than anything else, their experiences in World War II—as soldiers and as citizens—and their economic and geographic patterns in the postwar years had confirmed their Americanness in their own eyes and in the eyes of other Americans.[77] The declining utility of sociological language to explain Jewishness was itself an indication of how confident Jews had become about their overwhelming similarities to non-Jews. What, then, was the core of Jewish distinctiveness—and what vocabulary, if any, could Jews use to reconcile communal survival, liberal political ideals, and modern assumptions about personhood and individualism?

A Brat-Pack Conversion, Blood, and Volition

The twentieth-century celebrity more well known than Marilyn Monroe for converting to Judaism was Sammy Davis Jr., an African American entertainer. On October 11, 1960, Davis became a Jew, and one month later, in a ceremony held at Temple Hollywood, he wed May Britt, a Swedish-born actress who had also recently converted.[78] In autobiographies and interviews, Davis described his attraction to Judaism as being many years in the making: a chance meeting with the rabbi who served as chaplain in the hospital where Davis recovered from a near-fatal car accident in 1954 had set his journey to Judaism in motion.[79] For her part, Britt pragmatically explained that Judaism "gives us more ties together, something . . . doubly needed in a racially mixed marriage."[80] Yet some Jews were skeptical that Judaism gave these two much of anything in common: not only had neither of them been born Jewish, but one of them was not white and this, it seemed, was more jarring than anything else.

If Rabbi Goldburg thought he received too much of the wrong kind of attention for performing a star-studded marriage, William Mordecai Kramer, the rabbi who officiated at Britt and Davis's wedding, certainly had him beat. Rabbi Kramer, in fact, received so many letters of reprobation that the same archivist to whom Goldburg sent his missives requisitioned the letters "as a record of American sentiment and tolerance in these matters."[81] An angry Jew from Texas, for example, wrote, "Which one of these famed characters is a Jew, the Negro or Mrs. Britt? . . . I have never heard of a rabbi performing a holy Jewish wedding rite for a Negro. . . . It is true no denomation [sic] should be selfish with any religion, however I cannot condone the thought of a Negro marrying a white woman . . . and being married as a Jew."[82] The rabbi also received praise for his actions, but always framed by an acknowledgment of the significant risks he took and the boundaries he had crossed.[83]

That some Jews felt threatened by a black man becoming Jewish and marrying a white woman certainly did not set them apart from other Americans. The Supreme Court, after all, did not declare antimiscegenation legislation—or laws barring mixed race marriages—unconstitutional until 1967, and countless Americans, whether as members of groups or as individuals, systematically discriminated against African Americans.[84] Werner Cahnman, a Jewish sociologist who was interested in both intermarriage and Jewish racial ideologies, tartly described Jews as "thoroughly Americanized, as far as their racial attitudes are concerned."[85] Yet many Jews prided themselves on subscribing to racial liberalism and integrationist politics more completely than other white Americans. Among the ranks of civil-rights workers, Jews were, indeed, overrepresented.[86]

In moments of candor, some rabbis acknowledged that issues of birth and blood—or race—were not irrelevant to Jewish anxiety about intermarriage and conversion. In the 1960s, Solomon Freehof, a past president of the Central Conference of American Rabbis, wrote to one of his colleagues, "Conversion in Judaism means [a] much more intimate, social relationship than conversion in Christianity. Christians may convert a whole continent of Negroes and Chinese and not consider them part of their family, as potential sons-in-law or daughters-in-law. These Negroes and Chinese have been saved from damnation and that is enough. But with us a convert is a 'new-born child.' We are his only relatives now and he may now marry into our families. He is our child, our brother or sister."[87] Rabbi Freehof chose not to illustrate his point by talking about English Protestants or French Catholics. Instead he raised the possibility of nonwhites becoming Jewish. In the rabbi's choice of example, he hoped to highlight the conundrum and perhaps absurdity of visibly non-Jewish people trying to become Jews: even if they accepted the creedal dimensions of Jewishness, their bodies would always betray them as non-Jews. Similarly, in an article about mixed-race Jewish children—that is, products of white Jewish mothers and black non-Jewish fathers—one rabbi argued that these children posed a threat to the terms of Jewish "ethnicity."[88] If Jewish distinctiveness were conceived of as a basic fact of one's birth and background, then people whose bodies seemed clearly to cross the lines between Jewish and not were indeed difficult to assimilate, not to mention a threat to Jewish self-definition.[89]

Yet it was far more often the case that Jews became intimate with and married white Americans, whose bodies less vividly betrayed them as not belonging to the Jewish world. Undoubtedly, people still thought about the bodily significations of Jewishness. Marilyn Monroe's body, which stood as a symbol of midcentury sensuality and desire, likely marked her as non-Jewish, just as Miller's may have marked him as Jewish. Even as many Jews backed away from racial characterizations, the embodied and sociologically complex nature of Jewishness remained central to how Jews thought about themselves and explained themselves to non-Jews.[90]

In the early 1970s, when the Reform movement canvassed expert opinions about intermarriage, one professor suggested that the word *conversion* be replaced by the word *adoption*. He believed the term more accurately reflected the "ethnic familial and communal" dimensions of joining the Jewish faith.[91] Whereas *conversion* connoted an individual's spiritual rebirth, *adoption* implied the invention of biological-like connections to a family, community, or people where none had existed. Unlike purely race-based definitions of Jewishness, it also implied an element of will, not just the happenstance of birth. For an adoption to succeed, both the adopter and the adoptee had to agree to a redefined concept of family, where the kinds of connections usually defined by birth and biology could be approximated by desire and choice. Although the word *adoption* never caught on as a replacement for *conversion*, the spirit behind the semantic suggestion was central to a new vocabulary of Jewishness.

Since the early twentieth century, American sociologists had considered intermarriage a foolproof gauge of assimilation, and arguably for many centuries before that Jews had conflated intermarriage with apostasy: to marry a non-Jew was to abandon being Jewish. Only seismic shifts could account for the observation made by a letter writer to *Commentary* in 1964: "Marrying outside the faith does not necessarily mean a lack of Jewish identification."[92] Similarly, in the late 1970s, Jewish sociologist Herbert Gans illustrated his theory of "symbolic ethnicity" (which had emerged from his earlier work about "symbolic Judaism") in his observation that "by now many Jewish parents realize that intermarriage need not inevitably lead to surrender of Jewish identity."[93]

The causal links between intermarriage and apostasy, and intermarriage and assimilation, were starting to loosen in 1960s America, hastened by a new political order and represented in the shifting vocabulary of Jewishness. Sociological, racial, and religious explanations of Jewishness had become secondary to an overarching discourse of choice. The possibility that Jews could marry non-Jews and still consider themselves Jewish eroded sociological conceptions of Jewishness and stoked the flames of intracommunal strife.[94] Sociological studies, however, remained the weapon of choice. Often armed with their own staffs of sociologists, Jewish organizations bankrolled countless studies and surveys to show the effects of intermarriage on the Jewish people. Whatever their conclusions, whether of crisis or renaissance, the steady stream of studies and efforts to interpret them helped foment a revolution, once again, in how Jews explained themselves—to others and to themselves.

In 1971, a rabbi who admitted to officiating at intermarriages, wrote, "Jews are, generally, frantic about Jewish-Gentile marriage. This reaction is, to my mind, often wildly irrational and destructive. I would hope that we could transcend the 'Jewish-mother' type hysteria, however sophisticated is our modulating."[95] Drawing on unflattering stereotypes of Jews—as tending toward both emotionalism and effeminacy—the rabbi suggested that the shrill cries of crisis were as crippling as the apocryphal Jewish mothers who refused to allow their boys to be real men.[96]

Some sociologists, in their efforts to defuse a rising crisis mentality, suggested that intermarriage could enhance the demographic portrait of American Jews. A team of sociologists who studied intermarriage in Providence, Rhode Island, asserted that, demographically speaking, "the net effects of intermarriage on the overall size of the Jewish population may not be as serious as suggested by several other community studies."[97] In their data, they had found that the youngest generation of Jews, the group whose rate of intermarriage was the highest, also had the highest rate of spousal conversion to Judaism. Furthermore, they argued that the majority of children born to intermarried couples were being raised as Jews. Similarly, in 1972 a rabbi who performed intermarriages reported the results of a survey he had done of all the interfaith couples he had married. His results, he explained, proved that the more welcoming that rabbis were to intermarrying couples, the more likely these couples were to feel committed to Judaism and to raise their children as Jews.[98]

In a world where Jews could choose to marry non-Jews and still feel Jewish, non-Jews could also choose to become Jews, or at least to have Jewish children. In the eyes of some Jewish leaders, far from vanquishing Jewish life, intermarriage could be a great boon to the American Jewish community.[99] Were this to be so, however, Jews would have to embrace a new conception of Jewishness, one that welcomed those who were not born as Jews and that accepted the children of intermarried parents. These new Jews might have backgrounds, family structures, or social patterns different from those who had once defined Jewish life, and they might not be able to trace their ancestry or blood to other Jews. Their Jewishness would instead rest in their desire—or volition—to be seen as Jews.

The most publicized and authoritative voices in Jewish life, nonetheless, tended not to see any silver lining in intermarriage. In the first national Jewish population survey, sponsored by the AJC in 1972, the rising rate of intermarriage—which was, according to the authors, "much higher than in any comparable earlier period"—drew panicked attention.[100] For many commentators, the fact that even Jewish women, who historically had far lower rates of intermarriage than Jewish men, were marrying out confirmed that things truly were amiss.[101] The same team of sociologists who studied intermarriage in Providence discovered that, while one-third of non-Jewish women married to Jewish men converted to Judaism, only one-sixth of non-Jewish men married to Jewish women became Jews. They speculated that Jewish women who intermarried must not have retained a Jewish identity as strong as that of Jewish men, neglecting the gender politics that might have accounted for more women agreeing to convert to their husband's faith than men doing the same for their wives.[102] Considering the sociological data about gender and conversion, one rabbi conjectured, "Daughters who did go so far from their families' standards as to find non-Jewish spouses might have tended to be more negative toward Jewish life than were sons who were freer to roam."[103]

In the name of Jewish unity, Orthodox rabbis issued recriminatory pleas to their Reform and Conservative colleagues to help prevent intermarriage. One reasoned, "If committed Jews of all denominations do not at least agree to hold the line that separates erosion from structure and discontinuity from continuity, the end of American Jewry is already in sight."[104] Whether swayed by Orthodox entreaties or not, Reform rabbis were sobered enough by the new intermarriage statistics to overturn their 1909 resolution. For decades, they had agreed only that rabbis should be "discouraged" from performing intermarriages. Now they emphatically declared "opposition to participation . . . in any ceremony which solemnizes a mixed marriage."[105]

Who Might Be a Jew and Why?

Rabbinic resolutions aside, reports about rising rates of intermarriage stirred new Jewish anxiety and pressed Jewish leaders to rethink how they explained Jewishness in the United States. A full-page advertisement placed in the *New York Times* by the Board of Jewish Education of Greater New York in 1974 was just one sign of the diminishing explanatory power carried by sociological Jewishness. "If You're Jewish, Chances Are Your Grandchildren Won't Be," it warned.[106] The force of the admonishment was in its prediction of the end of sociologically and biologically conferred Jewishness. Implicit in the language of the advertisement was the assumption that in the future a child or grandchild would be able to choose whether or not to be Jewish. Jewishness defined by ancestry and social background had been insulated from individual whim, but choice was predicated on the individual.

Those rabbis and sociologists who perceived a rise in the individual terms of Jewishness imagined that, for Jewish leaders to remain authorities over the terms of Jewishness, they had to learn how to speak a new language to a new audience. Many continued to believe that Jewish leaders had an obligation to popularize Jewishness and make it accessible and appealing. A similar mandate had guided Jews' efforts to present themselves to non-Jews for many decades. By the 1970s, however, Jewish leaders set their sights squarely on Jews. In particular, they turned to young Jews, hoping to influence their future decisions about Jewishness and, most especially, Jewish marriage by addressing them on their own terms, whatever these might be.

One sociologist, who recommended that rabbis and parents emphasize Judaism's positive attitude toward sex, happily quoted a colleague's aphorism: "The motto of some religions is 'Never on Sunday' and the motto of Judaism is 'Twice on Shabbos.'"[107] Writing in 1973, William Abrams, a Conservative rabbi, elaborated: "We must take advantage of the favorable conditions which exist in the society of the seventies for raising a generation of Jews who will be free from the traumas and psychoses which those of us who were raised in a less fortunate generation have had to live with, who will firmly believe that 'Jewish is beautiful.'"[108] Sex, of course, could only help. Young people, he suggested, should be told that Judaism "does not require that human desires . . . be suppressed."[109] Young Jews may have had the power to choose whether to be Jewish, but Jewish leaders, armed with voluminous studies and sociological data, believed they could guide—or even guarantee—the outcome.[110]

When Jews, never more than 4 percent of the American population, married non-Jews, and when non-Jews became Jews, it was more challenging than ever for Jews to explain themselves to the United States and to themselves. But intermarriage, conversion, and the elusiveness of Jewishness were not a shock, even if, taken together, they precipitated a communal identity crisis in late-twentieth-century American Jewish life. A Jewish Marilyn Monroe, a Jewish Sammy Davis Jr., a child with a Jewish father and a non-Jewish mother who felt more Jewish than his friend with two Jewish parents, a rabbi who would wed a Jew and a non-Jew if they promised to raise a Jewish family, a sociologist who by studying intermarriage led the Jewish community to new places: these individuals all could find themselves in Jewishness. Yet the fact that they all believed Jewishness was capacious enough to accommodate them was itself a measure of the new strain placed on Jewishness. These varieties of Jewishness made it difficult to know a Jew from a non-Jew and to explain what it meant to be Jewish. Some saw in the challenge portents of an ominous future, while others glimpsed the inner workings of a system that could remain relevant in all times and places—the markings, perhaps, of something eternal.

Conclusion

Speaking of Jews

Arthur Miller stood in the front of the cavernous sanctuary in the spring of 1994. His old friend Robert Goldburg had invited the playwright to give a sermon for Shabbat HaGadol—the "Great Sabbath" that occurs on the Saturday before the start of Passover. Mishkan Israel, once located in a red brick building trimmed with terra-cotta in downtown New Haven, Connecticut, now sprawled long and low on a ridge in suburban Hamden.[1] In his talk that day, Miller spoke about the tenacity of the group's hold on the individual, even in a modern liberal state like America. "We used to think," he mused, "we were past all that."[2] With the rise of individual rights and the challenges to traditional sources of authority, Miller had believed, even hoped, that group loyalties and the battles that came along with them would become distant memories. In his own life, he had strayed far from his Jewish identity— as he put it, he had "wandered a long way from Bob Goldburg"—yet there was always something that called him back. People, he realized, needed ways to understand "who is me and who is not me."[3] Groups help individuals locate themselves, and they embody and create human distinctions. While some groups define themselves through race or God, Miller explained on that Saturday, group identity may also "be based on poetry, on one's ability and willingness to repeat certain words in unison."[4]

Is language constitutive of identity? Am I what I say I am—or, to put the weight of the collective on the question, are we what we say we are? Jews living in the United States in the twentieth century answered the question with a resounding yes. Believing that they could speak their existence into reality, they toiled to create explanations of themselves. They imagined they had an audience of non-Jews who would listen to their explanations, even as they spent far more time talking to themselves than to non-Jews. What Miller called poetry, and what I have called simply the language of Jewishness, emerged through the encounters—real or not—Jews had with non-Jews and through the ways those interactions pushed Jews to reencounter themselves. It was indispensable to Jewish attempts to create a place for Jews in the United States. While the specific terms of Jewishness changed over time, the purpose remained constant: to create a language of survival and to use language for survival.

The luxury of using words to guard survival was uniquely American in a century when most Jews were denied the opportunity to speak for themselves. Certainly, many non-Jews in the United States did not listen to how Jews explained their Jewishness: some did not care, others were already set in their views about Jews, and still others felt too much disdain for Jews to listen to them. Nonetheless, from the World War I era through the time of the civil rights movement, Americans grew more willing to listen to what Jews had to say about themselves. Already in the interwar years, politicians started to suggest that the United States would resist totalitarianism by adhering to democratic ideals that tolerated both group difference and individualism. By World War II, many American leaders were arguing that the war effort against Nazism depended on the maintenance of these ideals. To insure American stability and unity, diversity could not be ignored; however, leaders attempted to circumscribe and regulate the forms it took according to a particular understanding of which types of difference were nonthreatening. With the cold war came a simultaneous expansion of toleration and narrowing of what activities and ideas were deemed tolerable. Those who came of age during the postwar years witnessed the fundamental hypocrisy of a society that defined itself by democratic ideals—and against, of course, communist ones—without fully extending those ideals to all of its citizens. The civil rights movement emerged as a response, offering Jews, like other white Americans, a chance to redefine democracy, yet also questioning the terms on which they had achieved comfort in postwar America.

By the late 1960s, more non-Jews than in earlier decades would have been willing to listen to Jews explain themselves, and at the same time, Jews did not need to explain themselves nearly as fervently. Their decades-long efforts to present themselves to the United States had succeeded by most material measures. Jews were accepted as part of American society, their contributions were generally recognized, and their differences were very rarely perceived as reason to exclude them from mainstream channels of power or sociability. These material signs of American Jewish success cannot be minimized, especially in an era when one-third of world Jewry was annihilated.

Still, this account of Jews' efforts to explain themselves to non-Jews from World War I through the civil rights era should not be understood simply as a success story. Rather it chronicles just how difficult it was to find a descriptive, meaningful, and efficacious vocabulary of Jewishness. The social-scientific turn and the rise of sociological Jewishness emerged from a new Jewish consciousness about American politics and culture. Early-twentieth-century rabbis, who had so grandly hoped that Judaism would cast its ethical light across the American continent, were replaced by Jewish leaders and intellectuals who spoke the language of group identity and who argued that group life was an essential component of American life. Their faith in sociological Jewishness rested on the assumption that Jewish patterns and behaviors would always, in some measure, be distinguishable from non-Jewish ones. Eventually, however, sociological Jewishness ran into the problem of history: things change. Neither Jews nor the United States stood still. The belief that Jewishness was a sociological inevitability could not survive long without, at the least, begging questions about whether Jews wanted to be different and what their difference meant.

While one problem with sociological Jewishness was circumstantial—Jews by the late 1960s and 1970s, contrary to what some sociologists had predicted, were quite similar to non-Jews—the other was substantive. For all its benefits, the sociological vocabulary never revealed the source and ultimate meaning of Jewish distinctiveness. Functional explanations tend to be silent about origin and fate, choosing instead to describe how things appear—or function—in the present. As I have argued, sociological descriptions of Jewishness contained their own prescriptive force, defining norms and exerting pressure on Jews to conform to them. But the sociological vocabulary occluded Jewish agency and presented Jewishness as a present-tense condition, neither a choice nor a God-ordained necessity. For some Jews, this was a problem of the deepest magnitude.

A man whose life had been shaped by his narrow escape from Nazism, and who became the most public face of Judaism by the 1960s, Rabbi Abraham Joshua Heschel believed that Jewishness was more than a condition described by things like neighborhood, class, and family background. It also contained within it, as he wrote in 1955, "an answer to man's ultimate questions."⁵ But first Jews had to decide to ask these questions and place themselves into a relationship with something beyond themselves and the society in which they lived. Echoing Protestant neoorthodoxy much as Milton Steinberg had, Heschel believed that religion was irreducible: it, in fact, existed whether or not human beings were there to tend to it.⁶ For him, therefore, a sociological conception of Jewishness, functional and driven by collective human-made patterns, was deeply flawed. Yet far from excusing human beings from participating in their ultimate fate, Heschel explained, God searched for human response and partnership.⁷ Drawing on Hasidic ideas and parting company with Christian neoorthodoxy, he argued that human actions in this world mattered. Individuals could make themselves visible to God and enter into a relationship with God through what they chose to do, such as by protesting racism or marching for peace, both things that Heschel did.

Volitional Jewishness, as it emerged in the last three decades of the twentieth century, protested the disembodied character of sociological Jewishness. In his conviction that the ultimate meaning of Jewishness lay in the ineffable moments when man searched for God and God searched for man, Heschel conceived of choice—or volition—as being cosmically larger than an individual pursuit. Yet whether or not God was the source and ultimate meaning in a volitional framework of Jewishness, the individual was the observable actor, deciding when and how to enact his or her Jewishness.⁸ As a vocabulary that empowered the individual—not disembodied social factors—with defining Jewishness, a volitional conception of Jewishness raised new ethical and moral problems for the individual.⁹ Whereas social facts once could be held responsible for determining the boundaries of Jewishness, now individuals were the agents of those decisions—determining who could join a synagogue, qualify for an all-expense paid trip to Israel, or become a Jew. Perhaps individuals were not truly responsible for creating those boundaries. Community, blood, God, economics, or politics may have remained the true operatives. Nonetheless, the individual was increasingly named as the source. Confirming this, a 2000 study found that American Jews believed in a "sovereign self" that acted ultimately on its own authority.¹⁰

Yet was the testimony given by American Jews about their autonomy to be taken at face value?¹¹ Below the surface of the discourse of volition—a language that corresponded to the material conditions of Jewish life in the late twentieth and early twenty-first centuries—were other conceptions of Jewishness lurking?

If one looked hard enough, one could see the sociological model of Jewishness still pulsating in the public ways Jews explained themselves, the behaviors in which they engaged, and the perceptions that non-Jews had about Jewishness. The advent of JDate, an online dating service for Jews, was only one of the most recent confirmations that many Jews believed they would have more in common with a person born and raised as a Jew than with someone who was not, regardless of other volition-based qualities. Of course, one had to choose to post a profile on JDate, and according to a number of reports, a rising number of non-Jews trolled the Web site and even created their own profiles.[12] Yet Jews and some non-Jews subscribed to the Web dating service because they harbored assumptions about generic Jewish traits: their intelligence, the closeness of their families, and their avoidance of certain violent and addictive behaviors. These characteristics were not ascribed to individual choices that a Jew may or may not make. Rather people tended to assume that they marked an entire group, determined by forces beyond any one individual's control.

Similarly, the early-twenty-first-century ascendance of Birthright Israel travel programs evidenced the enduring power of sociological Jewishness. A major philanthropic endeavor to provide every young Jewish person with the chance to visit Israel, Birthright designated Jewishness as a condition, not a choice. Any person with one Jewish parent (whether mother or father) was eligible to participate in a Birthright trip, an indication that the very meaning of being born a Jew was as mutable as it was powerful. Wealthy Jews donated millions of dollars to the program, guided by the belief that even Jews who felt little connection to their Jewishness could be made to feel their true "birthright" if enticed by a free trip. By many measures, the program was successful, especially among Jews who described themselves as being on the margins of Jewish institutional life.[13] Perhaps for these Jews, who had not chosen to mark their Jewishness in normative terms, birth and sociology were all the more important. Clearly, although Jews increasingly described their Jewishness as a sum of choices they made about how to live their lives, traces and sometimes deep imprints of other vocabularies remained.

I have argued that the public language Jews used to explain themselves to non-Jews made a difference in the United States. While my focus has been on the shifting ways that Jewish leaders attempted to explain Jewishness to non-Jews, the theme of self-reflection and self-invention runs steadily throughout each chapter. Certainly, non-Jews learned about Jewishness from listening to Jewish Chautauqua Society rabbis give lectures, from reading books and studies about Jewish life, from watching television programs and tuning into radio shows about Jews, and from many of the other efforts I have described. Yet in deciding how to narrate themselves to others, Jewish leaders often remade and encountered themselves anew. Anthropologists call this reflexivity: the process of coming to a greater comprehension of one's self by way of the Other.[14] For American Jews who formulated new vocabularies of Jewishness in the twentieth century, reflexivity was unavoidable. The terms they used to talk about Jewishness generated new ways for Jews to understand themselves and their relationship to the non-Jewish world. These terms also gave Jews a sense of power in shaping their future and the United States.

The act of presenting Jewishness to the United States—of crafting a message for the new nation Jews hoped to make home—was an act of Jewish survival. Jews invented and appropriated language to instruct Americans on how to accept them, and used it as well to figure out how to accept themselves. Never created in a vacuum, language responds to the forces of history, politics, and culture. Which is not to say, however, that it cannot be generative. A faith in the generative qualities of words and language drove American Jews to explain themselves many times over to America, and it inspires all of us who hope against the odds that a word, a sentence, or a paragraph might make a difference.

Notes

Abbreviations

AJA	American Jewish Archives, Hebrew Union College, Cincinnati, OH
AJC	American Jewish Committee Information Center and Digital Archives, New York
AJHS	American Jewish Historical Society, New York
CCA	Connecticut College Archives, New London
CCARY	*Central Conference of American Rabbis Yearbook*
JCS-NY	Jewish Chautauqua Society Archives, Union of American Hebrew Congregations, New York
MI	Mishkan Israel, Hamden, CT
NHCHS	New Haven Colony Historical Society, New Haven, CT
RA	Ratner Archives, Jewish Theological Seminary, New York
Stanford	Stanford University Libraries Special Collections

Introduction

1. Although to the best of my knowledge the phrase *social-scientific turn* is my own, other scholars have explored the twentieth-century investment that Jews had in the social sciences. See Susan Glenn, "The Vogue of Jewish Self-Hatred in Post–World War II America," *Jewish Social Studies* 12, no. 3 (Spring–Summer 2006): 95–136; Mitchell Hart, *Social Science and the Politics of Modern Jewish Identity* (Stanford, CA: Stanford University Press, 2000); and Andrew Heinze, *Jews and the American Soul: Human Nature in the Twentieth Century* (Princeton, NJ: Princeton University Press, 2004). For a study of how

social-scientific scholarship was linked to Jewish educational campaigns, see Stuart Svonkin, *Jews against Prejudice: American Jews and the Fight for Civil Liberties* (New York: Columbia University Press, 1997). Finally, Arnold Eisen's work on the practice-oriented nature of modern Judaism has influenced my thinking about the turn toward social-scientific explanations of Jewishness in the twentieth century. See Arnold M. Eisen, *Rethinking Modern Judaism: Ritual, Commandment, Community* (Chicago: University of Chicago Press, 1998).

2. All of the social sciences—anthropology, psychology, sociology, economics, and political science—received federal funding and became tied to national interests during and after World War II. See Terrence Ball, "The Politics of Social Science in Postwar America," in *Recasting America: Culture and Politics in the Age of Cold War,* ed. Lary May (Chicago: University of Chicago Press, 1989); and Ellen Herman, *The Romance of American Psychology: Political Culture in the Age of Experts* (Berkeley: University of California Press, 1995).

3. On the sway of social-scientific experts and surveys, see Sarah Igo, *The Averaged American: Surveys, Citizens, and the Making of a Mass Public* (Cambridge, MA: Harvard University Press, 2007).

4. See Hart, *Social Science.*

5. In the United States, African Americans, like Jews, were attracted to sociology as a political strategy for improving the lot of minorities. See Jonathan Holloway, *Confronting the Veil: Abram Harris Jr., E. Franklin Frazier, and Ralph Bunche, 1919–1941* (Chapel Hill: University of North Carolina Press, 2002); and James Blackwell and Morris Janowitz, eds., *Black Sociologists: Historical and Contemporary Perspectives* (Chicago: University of Chicago Press, 1974).

6. Mordecai Kaplan, *Judaism as a Civilization: Toward a Reconstruction of American-Jewish Life* (Philadelphia: Jewish Publication Society, 1994 [1934]), 177. My understanding of Kaplan's sociological basis has been influenced most by Eisen, *Rethinking Modern Judaism;* Noam Pianko, "Diaspora Jewish Nationalism and Jewish Identity in America, 1914–1967" (PhD diss., Yale University, 2004); and Mel Scult, *Judaism Faces the Twentieth Century: A Biography of Mordecai M. Kaplan* (Detroit: Wayne State University Press, 1993). See also *Jewish Social Studies* 12, no. 2 (Winter 2006), the entire issue of which is devoted to Kaplan and his legacy.

7. For the genesis of this idea, see Émile Durkheim, *The Elementary Forms of Religious Life,* trans. K. Fields (New York: Free Press, 1995 [1912]).

8. I am indebted to the work of a number of historians whom I cite throughout this book for their explorations of popular culture in American Jewish life. For a useful reference work on the subject, see Paul Buhle, ed., *Jews and American Popular Culture* (Westport, CT: Praeger, 2006).

9. Two recent studies of European Jewish life provocatively argue that the new conditions of modernity, enlightenment, and emancipation compelled Jews to reformulate both what it meant to be Jewish and what it meant to be modern. See Jonathan Hess, *Germans, Jews, and the Claims of Modernity* (New Haven, CT: Yale University Press, 2002); and Ronald Schechter, *Obstinate*

Hebrews: Representations of Jews in France, 1715–1815 (Berkeley: University of California Press, 2003). Yuri Slezkine makes a somewhat similar, though far wider-reaching point in his recent study of the twentieth century: *The Jewish Century* (Princeton, NJ: Princeton University Press, 2004). For a recent and useful history of the Jewish Enlightenment, see Shmuel Feiner, *The Jewish Enlightenment*, trans. Chaya Naor (Philadelphia: University of Pennsylvania Press, 2004). Also see Pierre Birnbaum and Ira Katznelson, eds., *Paths of Emancipation: Jews, States, and Citizenship* (Princeton, NJ: Princeton University Press, 1995).

10. See Jon Butler, *Becoming America: The Revolution before 1776* (Cambridge, MA: Harvard University Press, 2000).

11. A number of historians discuss the persistent tension in American life between social diversity and national unity. See Gary Gerstle, *American Crucible: Race and Nation in the Twentieth Century* (Princeton, NJ: Princeton University Press, 2001); David Hollinger, "How Wide the Circle of the 'We'? American Intellectuals and the Problem of the Ethnos since World War II," *American Historical Review* 98, no. 2 (April 1993): 317–337; William Hutchison, *Religious Pluralism in America: The Contentious History of a Founding Ideal* (New Haven, CT: Yale University Press, 2003); and Matthew Frye Jacobson, *Whiteness of a Different Color: European Immigrants and the Alchemy of Race* (Cambridge, MA: Harvard University Press, 1998).

12. For a study on American liberalism generally, see Alan Brinkley, *Liberalism and Its Discontents* (Cambridge, MA: Harvard University Press, 1998). For some of the most interesting attempts to explain Jewish liberalism and Jews' turn away from liberalism, see Michael Alexander, *Jazz Age Jews* (Princeton, NJ: Princeton University Press, 2001); Murray Friedman, *The Neoconservative Revolution: Jewish Intellectuals and the Shaping of a Public Policy* (New York: Cambridge University Press, 2005); Daniel Greene, "The Crisis of Jewish Freedom: The Menorah Association and American Pluralism, 1906–1934" (PhD diss., University of Chicago, 2004); Marc Dollinger, *Quest for Inclusion: Jews and Liberalism in Modern America* (Princeton, NJ: Princeton University Press, 2000); Michael Staub, *Torn at the Roots: The Crisis of Jewish Liberalism in Postwar America* (New York: Columbia University Press, 2002); and Joshua Zeitz, *White Ethnic New York: Jews, Catholics, and the Shaping of Postwar Politics* (Chapel Hill: University of North Carolina Press, 2007).

13. Since Moses Rischin's 1962 examination of Jews in New York City, historians of American Jews have been centrally interested in the question of Jewish accommodation to American patterns, debating whether assimilation, acculturation, or resistance was the most common strategy Jews employed in their encounter with America. In the 1970s, Arthur Goren's esteemed study of early-twentieth-century Jewish leaders' efforts to organize a centralized authority structure (a kehillah) in New York City was guided by a similar interest in understanding how Jews accommodated themselves to the American landscape. A decade later, Deborah Dash Moore, one of the most eminent

American Jewish historians, studied second-generation American Jews and the ways in which they created their own patterns within existing American institutions and frameworks. A five-volume series published by Johns Hopkins University Press in 1992 chronicling Jewish life from 1654 through the present also focused on the tensions of Jewish accommodation in America. Most recently, Hasia Diner and Jonathan Sarna have both examined the tension between American and Jewish norms as a framework for understanding the sweep of American Jewish history, although Diner also highlights the importance of ethnic choices in her narrative. Finally, Eli Lederhendler, a scholar who clearly wishes to revise what he believes are standard narratives of American Jewish history, is still invested in the tensions of Jewish accommodation in America, though his conclusions about how these tensions were resolved tend to be less sanguine than other historians' assessments. See Hasia Diner, *The Jews of the United States, 1654–2000* (Berkeley: University of California Press, 2004); Arthur A. Goren, *New York Jews and the Quest for Community: The Kehillah Experiment, 1908–1922* (New York: Columbia University Press, 1970); Eli Lederhendler, *New York Jews and the Decline of Urban Ethnicity, 1950–1970* (Syracuse, NY: Syracuse University Press, 2001); Deborah Dash Moore, *At Home in America: Second Generation New York Jews* (New York: Columbia University Press, 1981); Moses Rischin, *The Promised City: New York's Jews, 1870–1914* (Cambridge, MA: Harvard University Press, 1962); and Jonathan Sarna, *American Judaism: A History* (New Haven, CT: Yale University Press, 2004). The titles in the Hopkins series, all published in 1992 in Baltimore by Johns Hopkins University Press, are: Hasia Diner, *A Time for Gathering: The Second Migration, 1820–1880;* Eli Faber, *A Time for Planting: The First Migration, 1654–1820;* Henry Feingold, *A Time for Searching: Entering the Mainstream, 1920–1945;* Edward Shapiro, *A Time for Healing: American Jewry since World War II;* and Gerald Sorin, *A Time for Building: The Third Migration, 1880–1920.*

14. In my mind, some of the key texts in this discussion include Kwame Anthony Appiah, *Cosmopolitanism: Ethics in a World of Strangers* (New York: Norton, 2006); Hollinger, "How Wide the Circle of the 'We'? American Intellectuals and the Problem of the Ethnos since World War II"; and Michael Walzer, *On Toleration* (New Haven, CT: Yale University Press, 1997).

15. Joseph Zeitlin concluded that Reform rabbis, though they may not have had as much sway over the centers of Jewish population, had more contact with non-Jews and were pressed more often than other rabbis to teach non-Jews about Judaism and Jewishness. See *Disciples of the Wise: The Religious and Social Opinions of American Rabbis* (New York: Bureau of Publications Teachers College–Columbia University, 1945), 56.

16. For a thorough history of Reform Judaism, in both its European and American contexts, see Michael A. Meyer, *Response to Modernity: A History of the Reform Movement in Judaism* (New York: Oxford University Press, 1988).

17. See Leonard Dinnerstein, *Antisemitism in America* (New York: Oxford University Press, 1994).

Chapter 1. Spiritual Missions after the Great War

1. Kaufmann Kohler, "The Mission of Israel and Its Application to Modern Times," *CCAR* 29 (1919): 265–288.

2. Ibid., 288.

3. Ibid., 280.

4. "Jewish Chautauqua Society and Summer Schools," *Jewish Exponent* 69, no. 21 (August 22, 1919): 2.

5. Historians note that the early church was threatened by Jewish success at gaining converts, and through ecclesiastical edicts and, often, coercion directed against converts and Jews, church fathers attempted to prevent any conversions to Judaism, or so-called Judaizing. Also, a number of policies were enacted to limit the contact that Jews could have with Christians. By the end of the medieval period—particularly in the wake of the Spanish Inquisition and other efforts to expel Jews—few Jews were involved in proselytizing efforts. Even in places like England, where, as historian Todd Endelman explains, Jews gained considerable rights between the late eighteenth and early nineteenth centuries, Jews still recoiled from converting Christians who wanted to join Judaism, because they worried about the reactions from the dominant Christian world. See Mark Cohen, *Under Crescent and Cross: The Jews in the Middle Ages* (Princeton, NJ: Princeton University Press, 1994); Todd Endelman, *The Jews of Georgian England, 1714–1830: Tradition and Change in Liberal Society* (Philadelphia: Jewish Publication Society of America, 1979), chapter 9; and Leonard Glick, *Abraham's Heirs: Jews and Christians in Medieval Europe* (Syracuse, NY: Syracuse University Press, 1999).

In general, Orthodox and most Conservative rabbis opposed any Jewish attempts to proselytize non-Jews. Melach Schachter, for example, an Orthodox rabbi and professor at Yeshiva University, wrote in 1965, "Unlike other religions, Judaism shuns missionary activity." See Schachter, "The Problem of Conversion Today," *New York: Union of Orthodox Jewish Congregations of America* (May–June 1965): 14. Found in Max Routtenberg Papers, Box 2, Folder 9, RA. Also see David Ellenson, "The Development of Orthodox Attitudes to Conversion in the Modern Period," *Conservative Judaism* 36, no. 4 (Summer 1983): 57–73.

6. See Perry Miller, *Errand into the Wilderness* (Cambridge, MA: Harvard University Press, Belknap Press, 1956).

7. For biographical information about Kohler and a commentary on his theology, see Lee Levinger, "The Theology of Kaufmann Kohler," *CCAR Journal*, no. 24 (January 1959): 10–11. Also see Michael A. Meyer, *Response to Modernity: A History of the Reform Movement in Judaism* (New York: Oxford University Press, 1988), 264–295; and Karla Goldman, *Beyond the Synagogue Gallery: Finding a Place for Women in American Judaism* (Cambridge, MA: Harvard University Press, 2000), 151–171.

8. Kaufmann Kohler, *Jewish Theology* (New York: Ktav Publishing House, 1968 [1918]), 8.

9. Ibid., 327. Dana Evan Kaplan argues that many turn-of-the-century Reform rabbis, despite their allegiance to universalism, were cool to the idea of extending Judaism beyond the Jewish people. See "W. E. Todd's Attempt to Convert to Judaism and Study for the Reform Rabbinate in 1896," *American Jewish History* 83, no. 4 (December 1995): 429–444.

10. *CCARY* 29 (1919): 278.

11. For a general history of the German Reform movement, see Meyer, *Response to Modernity,* chapters 1–5.

12. Arnold Eisen's study on chosenness offers valuable insight about the disjuncture between the chosen-people idea and post-Enlightenment values. See Arnold Eisen, *The Chosen People in America: A Study in Jewish Religious Ideology* (Bloomington: Indiana University Press, 1983). See also Shmuel Feiner, *The Jewish Enlightenment,* trans. Chaya Naor (Philadelphia: University of Pennsylvania Press, 2004); Jacob Katz, *Out of the Ghetto: The Social Background of Jewish Emancipation, 1770–1870* (Cambridge, MA: Harvard University Press, 1973); and David Sorkin, *The Transformation of German Jewry, 1780–1840* (Detroit: Wayne State University Press, 1999), for insightful histories about Jewish involvement in and reaction to the Enlightenment and emancipation efforts.

13. *CCARY* 29 (1919): 269. Also see Isaiah 42:6–7, and 49:6.

14. *Second Biennial Report of the Jewish Publication Society,* 28, quoted in Jonathan Sarna, *JPS: The Americanization of Jewish Culture, 1888–1988* (Philadelphia: Jewish Publication Society, 1989), 97.

15. Max Wiener, a critic of the Reform mission theology, wrote that Reformers tied their vision of Judaism to ideals they manufactured—like universalism—and not the lives they led. See Max Wiener, "The Conception of Mission in Traditional and Modern Judaism," *YIVO Annual of Jewish Social Science* 2–3 (1947–1948): 9–24.

16. On the Jewish attraction to race-based definitions of identity, see John Efron, *Defenders of the Race: Jewish Doctors and Race Science in Fin-de-Siècle Europe* (New Haven, CT: Yale University Press, 1994); Susan Glenn, "In the Blood? Consent, Descent, and the Ironies of Jewish Identity," *Jewish Social Studies* 8, no. 2–3 (Winter–Spring 2002); Eric Goldstein, *The Price of Whiteness: Jews, Race, and American Identity* (Princeton, NJ: Princeton University Press, 2006); and Michael Marrus, *The Politics of Assimilation: A Study of the French Jewish Community at the Time of the Dreyfus Affair* (Oxford: Clarendon Press, 1971), chapter 1.

17. See Elazar Barkan, *The Retreat of Scientific Racism: Changing Concepts in Britain and the United States between the World Wars* (New York: Cambridge University Press, 1992); Matthew Frye Jacobson, *Whiteness of a Different Color: European Immigrants and the Alchemy of Race* (Cambridge, MA: Harvard University Press, 1998); Alexandra Minna Stern, *Eugenic Nation: Faults and Frontiers of Better Breeding in Modern America* (Berkeley: University of California Press, 2005); and George W. Stocking, *Race, Culture, and Evolution: Essays in the History of Anthropology* (Chicago: University of Chicago Press, 1982).

18. *CCAR* 29 (1919): 280.

19. See Gary Gerstle, *American Crucible: Race and Nation in the Twentieth Century* (Princeton, NJ: Princeton University Press, 2001); and Matthew Frye Jacobson, *Barbarian Virtues: The United States Encounters Foreign Peoples at Home and Abroad, 1876–1917* (New York: Hill and Wang, 2000). Both Jacobson and Gerstle explain that faith in assimilation was based on a belief that newcomers had to be properly regimented and controlled. The large regulatory state, a legacy of progressivism, manifested the belief that America's greatness needed to be managed and guarded.

20. The same pattern of a rhetorical commitment to the universal appeal of democracy, paired with a fear of immigrants, can be observed with regard to earlier immigration restriction acts, particularly those that restricted Chinese and Japanese immigrants in the late nineteenth and early twentieth centuries. See Charles J. McClain, *In Search of Equality: The Chinese Struggle against Discrimination in Nineteenth-Century America* (Berkeley: University of California Press, 1994); George Anthony Peffer, *If They Don't Bring Their Women Here: Chinese Female Immigration before Exclusion* (Urbana: University of Illinois Press, 1999); Lucy E. Salyer, *Laws Harsh as Tigers: Chinese Immigrants and the Shaping of Modern Immigration Law* (Chapel Hill: University of North Carolina Press, 1995); and Ronald T. Takaki, *Strangers from a Different Shore: A History of Asian Americans* (New York: Penguin Books, 1990). On the 1924 immigration restriction act and the category of illegal immigrant that emerged from it, see Mae Ngai, *Impossible Subjects: Illegal Aliens and the Making of Modern America* (Princeton, NJ: Princeton University Press, 2004).

21. *CCAR* 29 (1919): 286.

22. Ibid.

23. Ibid., 288.

24. Ibid., 287–288.

25. Ibid., 303.

26. Ibid., 302.

27. John Higham coined and defined the term *Tribal Twenties*. See John Higham, *Strangers in the Land: Patterns of American Nativism, 1860–1925* (New York: Atheneum, 1963).

28. For more on American nativism and antisemitism, see Leonard Dinnerstein, *Antisemitism in America* (New York: Oxford University Press, 1994).

29. "Why the Jews Are Not Missionaries," *Literary Digest* 62, no. 36 (August 30, 1919): 36.

30. For an excellent examination of the goodwill movement and so-called ecumenicism, see Benny Kraut, "A Wary Collaboration: Jews, Catholics, and the Protestant Goodwill Movement," in *Between the Times: The Travail of the Protestant Establishment in America, 1900–1960*, ed. William Hutchison (New York: Cambridge University Press, 1989): 203–204. William Hutchison argued that the 1920s were generally a vibrant period for American missionary thought

and activity, but also noted that an underlying critique of missionary behavior was gaining strength. See *Errand to the World: American Protestant Thought and Foreign Missions* (Chicago: University of Chicago Press, 1987), especially chapter 6.

31. Kraut, "A Wary Collaboration," 207. For information on Christian missions to Jews, also see Yaakov Ariel, *Evangelizing the Chosen People: Missions to the Jews in America, 1880–2000* (Chapel Hill: University of North Carolina Press, 2000); and Jonathan Sarna, "The American Jewish Response to Nineteenth-Century Christian Missions," *Journal of American Jewish History* 68, no. 1 (1981): 35–51. For a European counterpart, Elisheva Carlebach provides an excellent account of both forced and voluntary Jewish conversions to Christianity in Germany between 1500 and 1750. See *Divided Souls: Converts from Judaism in Germany, 1500–1750* (New Haven, CT: Yale University Press, 2001). Also see Todd Endelman, *Radical Assimilation in English Jewish History, 1656–1945* (Bloomington: Indiana University Press, 1990). Endelman is also working on a new transnational study of radical Jewish assimilation, in which he considers the force of Christian missionary activity and state assimilationist policies.

32. S. Fyne, "The New Year—the Index of the Jew's Mission," *Jewish Exponent* 76, no. 26 (September 18, 1925): 12.

33. Samuel Goldenson, "What We Jews a Mission? *[sic]*" (sermon) November 18, 1923, Samuel Goldenson Papers, Box 1, Folder 3, MS 81, AJA, 3–4.

34. Ibid., 14.

35. Samuel Schulman, "The 'Jewish Mission': Two Views," *Menorah Journal* 10, no. 4 (August–September 1924): 318.

36. Ibid., 319.

37. Johan Smertenko, "The 'Jewish Mission': Two Views," *Menorah Journal* 10, no. 4 (August–September 1924): 324. On Smertenko, see "Johan J. Smertenko, 86, Dies; Author and Activist for Israel," *New York Times,* May 5, 1983.

38. "Preliminary Report: Committee for the Preparation of a Manual for the Instruction of Proselytes," *CCARY* 35 (1925): 109. This committee had existed in a slightly different form prior to 1924, as the Committee on the Preparation of a Manual for Conversion. See *CCARY* 34 (1924): 49.

39. "Preliminary Report: Committee for the Preparation of a Manual for the Instruction of Proselytes," 110.

40. Letter from Samuel Schulman to Joseph Rauch, June 13, 1927, Samuel Schulman Papers, Box 7, Folder 7, MS 90, AJA.

41. "Preliminary Report: Committee for the Preparation of a Manual for the Instruction of Proselytes," 111. In his letter to Rabbi Rauch, Schulman also indicated that he believed the manual should be free of apologetic statements. See Letter from Schulman to Rauch, June 13, 1927, AJA.

42. "Preliminary Report: Committee for the Preparation of a Manual for the Instruction of Proselytes," 111.

43. Ibid.

44. Ibid., 110.

45. *CCARY* 37 (1927): 194.

46. Letter from Schulman to Joseph Rauch, June 13, 1927, AJA.

47. *CCARY* 37 (1927): 195.

48. In the late nineteenth and early twentieth centuries, religious leaders, like other American leaders, worried about the feminization of American culture and religion. See Gail Bederman, *Manliness and Civilization: A Cultural History of Gender and Race in the United States, 1880–1917* (Chicago: University of Chicago Press, 1995); Ann Braude, "Women's History *Is* American Religious History," in *Retelling U.S. Religious History,* ed. Thomas Tweed (Berkeley: University of California Press, 1997); Ann Douglas, *The Feminization of American Culture* (New York: Avon Books, 1978); and Clifford Putney, *Muscular Christianity: Manhood and Sports in Protestant America, 1880–1920* (Cambridge, MA: Harvard University Press, 2003).

49. A body of literature on early religion and ritual studies has influenced my view that religious practice often functions to separate believer from nonbeliever or member from nonmember. See, for example, Shaye Cohen, *The Beginnings of Jewishness: Boundaries, Varieties, Uncertainties* (Berkeley: University of California Press, 1999); Mary Douglas, *Purity and Danger* (New York: Praeger, 1966); and Eviatar Zerubavel, *The Fine Line: Making Distinctions in Everyday Life* (Chicago: University of Chicago Press, 1991).

50. *CCARY* 35 (1925): 110.

51. Ibid., 111.

52. Mordecai Kaplan, *Judaism as a Civilization: Toward a Reconstruction of American-Jewish Life* (Philadelphia: Jewish Publication Society, 1994 [1934]), 91–92.

53. Henry Pereira Mendes, "Orthodox Judaism: Part III—the Future," *Jewish Forum* 3, no. 4 (April 1920): 227–234. For information about Rabbi Mendes, see *The Universal Jewish Encyclopedia,* vol. 7.

54. A number of sources have contributed to my understanding of late-nineteenth- and twentieth-century Christian liberalism and modernism. Most important, see William Hutchison, *The Modernist Impulse in American Protestantism* (Cambridge, MA: Harvard University Press, 1976). On the social gospel, see Charles Hopkins, *The Rise of the Social Gospel in American Protestantism, 1865–1915* (New Haven, CT: Yale University Press, 1940); and Henry Farnham May, *Protestant Churches and Industrial America* (New York: Harper, 1949). Both of these books focus particularly on the development of Protestant liberalism. For sources on Catholic liberalism, see Aaron Ignatius Abell, *American Catholicism and Social Action: A Search for Social Justice, 1865–1950* (Garden City, NY: Hanover House, 1960); and Robert D. Cross, *The Emergence of Liberal Catholicism in America* (Cambridge, MA: Harvard University Press, 1958). Although his book focuses on the development of Christian fundamentalism, George M. Marsden also provides useful information on the rise of Christian liberalism. See *Fundamentalism and American Culture: The Shaping of Twentieth-Century Evangelicalism, 1870–1925* (New York: Oxford University Press, 1980). For a recent and important study that considers the rise

of liberalism and pacifism among Christian leaders from World War I through the early civil rights era, see Joseph Kosek, "Spectacles of Conscience: Christian Nonviolence and the Transformation of American Democracy, 1914–1956 (PhD diss., Yale University, 2004). Lastly, in his comprehensive history of American religion, Sydney Ahlstrom dwells fruitfully on the characteristics of theological liberalism. See *A Religious History of the American People* (New Haven, CT: Yale University Press, 1972), chapters 46 and 47.

55. Kaplan, *Judaism as a Civilization,* 92, 99.

56. This is, of course, a play on Ahad Ha'am's famous statement: "More than Israel has kept the Sabbath, the Sabbath has kept Israel." He initially wrote this statement in an essay "Shabbat v'tzionut" ("Sabbath and Zionism") published in *Hashiloah,* a Zionist journal, in 1898. A reprint of the essay can be found in *Kol kitvei ahad ha'am* (Jerusalem: Hozaah Ivrit, 1956).

57. For information about the Chautauqua Society, see Joseph Gould, *The Chautauqua Movement: An Episode in the Continuing American Revolution* (New York: State University of New York, 1961); Andrew Rieser, *The Chautauqua Moment: Protestants, Progressives, and the Culture of Modern Liberalism* (New York: Columbia University Press, 2003); and Jeffrey Simpson, *Chautauqua: An American Utopia* (New York: Harry N. Abrams, 1999). For an informative, though hagiographic, account of Berkowitz's life written by his son, see Max Berkowitz, *The Beloved Rabbi: An Account of the Life and Works of Henry Berkowitz* (New York: Macmillan, 1932).

58. Berkowitz, "A Jewish Summer Assembly," *JCS Summer Assemblies* (August 15, 1894): 3, JCS-NY. Berkowitz details the process of becoming part of the Chautauqua Literary and Scientific Circle, and thus being given permission to use the Chautauqua name in, "The Jewish Chautauqua Society," *Chautauquan* 39, no. 5 (July 1904): 447–448. On the middle-class roots of the Chautauqua (not Jewish) Society, see Rieser, *The Chautauqua Moment.* For two studies about turn-of-the-century leisure culture, see Kathy Lee Peiss, *Cheap Amusements: Working Women and Leisure in Turn-of-the-Century New York* (Philadelphia: Temple University Press, 1986); and Roy Rosenzweig, *Eight Hours for What We Will: Workers and Leisure in an Industrial City, 1870–1920* (New York: Cambridge University Press, 1983). For a longitudinal institutional history of the JCS, see Peggy Kronsberg Pearlstein, "Understanding through Education: One Hundred Years of the Jewish Chautauqua Society, 1893–1993" (PhD diss., George Washington University, Washington, DC, 1993).

59. Others have explained that Roosevelt believed American unity was best achieved by delineating a clear line between those fit for inclusion and those who were not—most notably African Americans. Americanism, in his mind, was about taming excessively feminized civilization and increasing American pluralism around a distinctly racialized model of citizenship. See Gerstle, *American Crucible,* especially chapters 1 and 2. For an excellent study that provides the context for Roosevelt's warrior mentality, see T. J. Jackson Lears, *No Place of Grace: Antimodernism and the Transformation of American Culture: 1880–1920* (New York: Pantheon Books, 1981).

60. "Roosevelt Speaks," *Jewish Chautauqua Assembly Record* 4, no. 5 (July 27, 1900): 4, JCS-NY.

61. See Naomi Wiener Cohen, *Encounter with Emancipation: The German Jews in the United States, 1830–1914* (Philadelphia: Jewish Publication Society, 1984); and Hasia R. Diner, *A Time for Gathering: The Second Migration, 1820–1880* (Baltimore: Johns Hopkins University Press, 1992). On Jewish efforts to attain middle-class respectability in the United States, see Goldman, *Beyond the Synagogue Gallery.*

62. On American progressivism and efforts to uplift immigrants to middle-class standards, see Bederman, *Manliness and Civilization;* Jacobson, *Barbarian Virtues;* and Daniel Rodgers, *Atlantic Crossings: Social Politics in a Progressive Age* (Cambridge, MA: Harvard University Press, Belknap Press, 1998).

63. For a comprehensive history of the National Council of Jewish Women, see Faith Rogow, *Gone to Another Meeting: The National Council of Jewish Women, 1893–1993* (Tuscaloosa: University of Alabama Press, 1993).

64. *Proceedings of the Thirteenth Annual Summer Assembly of the Jewish Chautauqua Society* (Philadelphia: Jewish Chautauqua Society, 1909): 31, JCS-NY.

65. The American Jewish Committee was founded in 1906 and the Anti-Defamation League, under the auspices of B'nai Brith, in 1913. See Naomi Wiener Cohen, *Not Free to Desist: The American Jewish Committee, 1906–1966* (Philadelphia: Jewish Publication Society of America, 1972); and Deborah Dash Moore, *B'nai B'rith and the Challenge of Ethnic Leadership* (Albany: State University of New York Press, 1981). The Centralverein (founded the same year as the JCS) was a German precedent to Jewish-American defense organizations. See Ismar Schorsch, *Jewish Reactions to German Anti-Semitism, 1870–1914* (New York: Columbia University Press, 1972).

66. Historian David Biale has pointed out that, over the span of history, Jews have drawn on the political strategy of de-emphasizing their power in order to, in fact, maintain some semblance of it. See *Power and Powerlessness in Jewish History* (New York: Schocken Books, 1986).

67. Berkowitz, *The Beloved Rabbi,* 185–186. On the Jewish Publication Society, see Jonathan Sarna, *JPS: The Americanization of Jewish Culture, 1888–1988.* In the United States, philosemitism had a long tradition, wrapped up with messianic claims. Claxton's philosemitism, however, may have been part of a broader postbellum trend in the South, in which politicians and preachers often drew parallels between the vanquished South and the Israelites of the Hebrew Bible. This aspect of "Lost Cause" religion is chronicled in Charles Reagan Wilson, *Baptized in Blood: The Religion of the Lost Cause, 1865–1920* (Athens: University of Georgia Press, 1980). I thank Anne Rose for pointing out this possible connection.

68. *Proceedings of the Thirteenth Annual Summer Assembly of the Jewish Chautauqua Society* (Philadelphia: Jewish Chautauqua Society, 1909): 141, JCS-NY.

69. "Profiles: Dr. Philander P. Claxton," *American Judaism* 6, no. 3 (January 1957): 23.

70. Although the South had been a relatively hospitable place for Jews to live, the level of antisemitism there increased, as it did throughout the United States, with the influx of eastern European Jewish immigrants. See Clive Webb, *Fight against Fear: Southern Jews and Black Civil Rights* (Athens: University of Georgia Press, 2001).

71. In 1929, Salo Baron was appointed by Columbia as the first chair in Jewish history at an American university. Throughout the following decades, a few American universities offered Jewish history courses, but until the 1960s the majority did not. It was not until 1969 that the Association for Jewish Studies was founded as a professional organization for scholars in the new field of Jewish studies. For an excellent and comprehensive history of Jewish studies in the United States, see Paul Ritterband and Harold S. Wechsler, *Jewish Learning in American Universities: The First Century* (Bloomington: Indiana University Press, 1994). Also see Susanne Klingenstein, *Jews in the American Academy, 1900–1940: The Dynamics of Intellectual Assimilation* (Syracuse, NY: Syracuse University Press, 1998).

72. "Jewish Chautauqua Society and Summer Schools," *Jewish Exponent* 69, no. 21 (August 22, 1919): 2.

73. Ibid.

74. "Angles of Jewish Influence in America," in *Aspects of Jewish Power in the United States: Volume IV of the International Jew, the World's Foremost Problem* (Dearborn, MI: Dearborn Publishing, 1922): 50. This reference is drawn from Pearlstein, "Understanding through Education," 310. For a study of Henry Ford's relationship to the Jews in America, see Neil Baldwin, *Henry Ford and the Jews: The Mass Production of Hate* (New York: Public Affairs, 2001).

75. "Jewish Chautauqua Assembly in Cleveland," *Jewish Exponent* 27, no. 14 (December 31, 1920): 2.

76. The Conservative and Orthodox movements developed institutional bases by the 1920s, and an experiment to unify New York City's Jews failed in the same decade. See Arthur A. Goren, *New York Jews and the Quest for Community: The Kehillah Experiment, 1908–1922* (New York: Columbia University Press, 1970); Jeffrey S. Gurock, *The Men and Women of Yeshiva: Higher Education, Orthodoxy, and American Judaism* (New York: Columbia University Press, 1988); and Jack Wertheimer, "The Conservative Synagogue," in *The American Synagogue*, ed. Jack Wertheimer (Hanover, NH: Brandeis University Press, 1987).

77. Max Berkowitz, "The Jewish Chautauqua Society," *Jewish Layman* 17, no. 7 (April 1943): 7. Also, I am grateful to Hollace Weiner for unearthing many heretofore forgotten records about Goldberg's life and accomplishments. See Hollace Ava Weiner, "The Jewish Junior League: The Rise and Demise of the Fort Worth National Council of Jewish Women, 1901–2002" (master's thesis, University of Texas, Arlington, 2005).

78. Letter from Jeanette Miriam Goldberg to Abraham Feldman, October 23, 1923, Abraham Feldman Papers, Box 18, Folder 9, MS 38, AJA.

79. Letter from Jeanette Miriam Goldberg to Abraham Feldman, January 14, 1924, Abraham Feldman Papers, Box 18, Folder 9, MS 38, AJA.

80. Ibid. This was clearly typical behavior on Goldberg's part. For a similar example of her hands-on approach, see her correspondence with Rabbi Hyman Enelow throughout 1926, Hymen Enelow Papers, Box 7, Folder 12, MS 11, AJA.

81. Letter from Abraham Feldman to Jeanette Miriam Goldberg, January 18, 1924, Abraham Feldman Papers, Box 18, Folder 9, MS 38, AJA.

82. Letter from Abraham Feldman to Jeanette Miriam Goldberg, July 11, 1924, Abraham Feldman Papers, Box 18, Folder 9, MS 38, AJA.

83. "Chautauqua Society Building Good Will," *Los Angeles Jewish Community Press,* June 26, 1936, from "Clippings Book," JCS-NY.

84. "'Defend Free Speech,' Says Rabbi Fink," *Jewish Transcript,* June 28, 1935, from "Clippings Book," JCS-NY.

85. "Rabbi Lewis Lectures on Jewish Law," *Daily Iowan,* June 25, 1935, from "Clippings Book," JCS-NY.

86. *Atlanta Southern Israelite,* January 17, 1936; and "Rabbi Bazell Jewish Chaut Speaker at Lexington on June 22," *Louisville Kentucky Jewish Chronicle,* June 11, 1937. Both are from "Clippings Book," JCS-NY.

87. Jerome Sinsheimer, "Ways and Means for Jewish Chautauqua Society Support," *Proceedings of the Ninth Biennial Convention of the NFTB* (1941): 10, JCS-NY.

Chapter 2. *The Ghetto* and Beyond

1. Thomas Haskell has argued that social scientists were guided by a belief in the interconnectedness of the whole society and its small constituent parts. See *The Emergence of Professional Social Science: The American Social Science Association and the Nineteenth-Century Crisis of Authority* (Urbana: University of Illinois Press, 1977). Also see Dorothy Ross, *The Origins of American Social Science* (New York: Cambridge University Press, 1991).

2. Andrew Heinze's thorough study of Jewish involvement in American psychology offers a nuanced interpretation of the relationship between Jewish experience and psychological theories. See *Jews and the American Soul: Human Nature in the Twentieth Century* (Princeton, NJ: Princeton University Press, 2004).

3. Robert Salerno, *Louis Wirth: A Bio-Bibliography* (New York: Greenwood Press, 1987), 6, 20. Fred Matthews explains that Park encouraged his students to choose a research subject to which they had personal connections. Fred Matthews, "Louis Wirth and American Ethnic Studies: The Worldview of Enlightened Assimilationism, 1925–1950," in *The Jews of North America,* ed. Moses Rischin (Detroit: Wayne State University Press, 1987), 125.

4. See Elizabeth Wirth Marvick, "Biographical Memorandum on Louis Wirth," in *Louis Wirth on Cities and Social Life,* ed. Albert J. Reiss (Chicago: University of Chicago Press, 1964), 335. For more biographical information on Wirth, see also Hasia Diner, "Introduction to the Transaction Edition," in *The Ghetto,* by Louis Wirth (New Brunswick, NJ: Transaction Publishers, 1998).

5. The most important book about the social gospel movement in the United States remains Henry Farnham May, *Protestant Churches and Industrial America* (New York: Harper, 1949). Scholars have specifically argued that Christian reform movements sculpted early sociology in the United States. See Cecil Greek, *The Religious Roots of American Sociology* (New York: Garland Publishing, 1992); R. Laurence Moore, "Secularization: Religion and the Social Sciences," in *Between the Times: The Travail of the Protestant Establishment in America, 1900–1960,* ed. William Hutchinson (Cambridge: Cambridge University Press, 1989); and Anne Rose, "'Race' Speech—'Culture' Speech— 'Soul' Speech: The Brief Career of Social-Science Language in American Religion during the Fascist Era," *Religion and American Culture* 14, no. 1 (Winter 2004): 83–108.

6. The Chicago school of sociology is described in a number of sources. For focused studies, see Andrew Abbott, *Department and Discipline: Chicago Sociology at One Hundred* (Chicago: University of Chicago Press, 1999); Fred Matthews, *Quest for an American Sociology: Robert E. Park and the Chicago School* (Montreal: McGill-Queen's University Press, 1977); Stow Persons, *Ethnic Studies at Chicago, 1905–1945* (Chicago: University of Illinois Press, 1987); and Luigi Tomasi, ed., *The Tradition of the Chicago School of Sociology* (Brookfield, VT: Ashgate, 1998). I have also drawn on Morris Janowitz's introduction to the third edition of Park and Burgess's important textbook on sociology. See Ernest Burgess and Robert Park, *Introduction to the Science of Sociology* (Chicago: University of Chicago Press, 1969 [1921]). A number of review articles about American immigration history also examine the Chicago school, since, in many ways, immigration history started with the sociological studies emerging from the University of Chicago. See, for example, Gary Gerstle, "Liberty, Coercion, and the Making of Americans," *Journal of American History* 84, no. 2 (September 1997): 524–558; Jon Gjerde, "New Growth on Old Vines—the State of the Field: The Social History of Immigration to and Ethnicity in the United States," *Journal of American Ethnic History* 18, no. 4 (Summer 1999): 40–66; and Russell Kazal, "Revisiting Assimilation: The Rise, Fall, and Reappraisal of a Concept in American Ethnic History," *American Historical Review* 100, no. 2 (April 1995): 437–471.

7. Between 1895 and 1946, twenty-two African Americans earned doctorates in the social sciences. (If one includes history as a social science, the number jumps to seventy-seven.) See Harry Greene, *Holders of Doctorates among American Negroes* (Boston: Meador Publishing Company, 1946), cited in Jonathan Holloway, *Confronting the Veil: Abram Harris Jr., E. Franklin Frazier, and Ralph Bunche, 1919–1941* (Chapel Hill: University of North Carolina Press, 2002), 222n43. In this same book, Holloway argues that social science was an important grounding for many shifts in black intellectual life. On African American social scientists, also see James Blackwell and Morris Janowitz, eds., *Black Sociologists: Historical and Contemporary Perspectives* (Chicago: University of Chicago Press, 1974).

8. Quoted in Matthews, *Quest for an American Sociology,* 83.

9. On the black migration to Chicago, see James Grossman, *Land of Hope: Chicago, Black Southerners, and the Great Migration* (Chicago: University of Chicago Press, 1989).

10. Robert Park, "Human Migration and the Marginal Man," *American Journal of Sociology* 33, no. 6 (May 1928): 888.

11. For Simmel's essay on the stranger, see Kurt Wolff, ed., *The Sociology of Georg Simmel* (Glencoe, IL: Free Press, 1950), 402–408. On Simmel, see Lewis Coser, *Masters of Sociological Thought: Ideas in Historical and Social Context* (New York: Harcourt Brace Jovanovich, 1977).

12. Robert Park, *Race and Culture* (Glencoe, IL: Free Press, 1950), 376. Also see Persons, *Ethnic Studies at Chicago, 1905–1945*, chapter 6.

13. Park, "Human Migration and the Marginal Man," 892.

14. Hortense Powdermaker, *Stranger and Friend: The Way of an Anthropologist* (New York: Norton, 1966), 15. For an analysis of Powdermaker's Jewish identity, see Nancy Scheper-Hughes, "Hortense Powdermaker, the Berkeley Years (1967–1970): A Personal Reflection," *Journal of Anthropological Research* 47, no. 4 (Winter 1991): 457–471. See also Hortense Powdermaker, *After Freedom: A Cultural Study of the Deep South* (New York: Russell and Russell, 1968 [1939]).

15. On European-Jewish sociologists, see Mitchell Hart, *Social Science and the Politics of Modern Jewish Identity* (Stanford: Stanford University Press, 2000). The assumption that sociology was Jewish in nature, it seemed, was related to the belief that both Jews and sociologists aimed to undermine established social structures. For information about the 1930s survey in America, see Joseph Zeitlin, *Disciples of the Wise: The Religious and Social Opinions of American Rabbis* (New York: Bureau of Publications Teachers College–Columbia University, 1945), 46. Werner Cahnman calculated the proportion of Jews to non-Jews in the American Sociological Association. He also found that Jews occupied about one-quarter of the editorial and top positions for the *American Sociological Review* and *American Journal of Sociology*. See "Sociology," *Encyclopaedia Judaica* 15 (1971): 62–69. Jews also constituted a significant presence in the social sciences more broadly. See Heinze, *Jews and the American Soul;* David A. Hollinger, *Science, Jews, and Secular Culture: Studies in Mid-Twentieth-Century American Intellectual History* (Princeton, NJ: Princeton University Press, 1996); Jack Porter, *The Jew as Outsider: Historical and Contemporary Perspectives, Collected Essays, 1974–1980* (Washington, DC: University Press of America, 1981), chapter 4; and Stephen Steinberg, *The Academic Melting Pot: Catholics and Jews in American Higher Education* (New York: McGraw-Hill, 1974). Steinberg presents data from the 1969 Carnegie Commission Survey on Faculty and Student Opinion, and illustrates that Jews were disproportionately more involved in the social sciences compared to Catholics and Protestants (120).

16. Quoted in Howard Odum, *American Sociology: The Story of Sociology in the United States through 1950* (New York: Longmans, Green, and Co., 1951), 230.

17. Quoted in Salerno, *Louis Wirth*, 9.

18. Louis Wirth, *The Ghetto* (Chicago: University of Chicago Press, 1928), 10.

19. Ibid., 285.

20. Ibid., vii.

21. Wirth drew considerably on the work done by earlier Jewish historians, most notably Israel Cohen, Joseph Jacobs, David Philipson, and Arthur Ruppin, to describe the historical development of the ghetto.

22. On race science, see Elazar Barkan, *The Retreat of Scientific Racism: Changing Concepts in Britain and the United States between the World Wars* (New York: Cambridge University Press, 1992); Matthew Frye Jacobson, *Whiteness of a Different Color: European Immigrants and the Alchemy of Race* (Cambridge, MA: Harvard University Press, 1998); Alexandra Stern, *Eugenic Nation: Faults and Frontiers of Better Breeding in Modern America* (Berkeley: University of California Press, 2005); and George W. Stocking, *Race, Culture, and Evolution: Essays in the History of Anthropology* (Chicago: University of Chicago Press, 1982). For a more specific study of Jewish involvement in social science through race science, see Todd Endelman, "Anglo-Jewish Scientists and the Science of Race," *Jewish Social Studies* 11, no. 1 (Fall 2004): 52–92; and John M. Efron, *Defenders of the Race: Jewish Doctors and Race Science in Fin-de-Siècle Europe* (New Haven, CT: Yale University Press, 1994). For a provocative study of the relationship between Boas's Jewishness and his anthropological work, see Geyla Frank, "Jews, Multiculturalism, and Boasian Anthropology," *American Anthropologist* 99, no. 4 (1997): 731–735.

23. Wirth, *The Ghetto*, 261.

24. Ibid., 130.

25. See Marvick, "Biographical Memorandum on Louis Wirth," 333–340. Marshall Sklare, who earned his master's degree in sociology from University of Chicago in the 1940s and later became an important Jewish sociologist of American Jews, recalled hearing that Wirth "was proud of the fact he had married a Gentile woman" (7). It should be mentioned that Sklare himself disapproved of Wirth's assimilationism and noted that he never felt comfortable discussing Jewish issues with him. See Marshall Sklare, *Observing America's Jews* (Hanover, NH: Brandeis University Press, 1993).

26. Many immigrants were, in fact, never naturalized. See Zane Miller, "Pluralism, Chicago Style: Louis Wirth, the Ghetto, the City, and 'Integration,'" *Journal of Urban History* 18, no. 3 (May 1992): 254.

27. Marvick, "Biographical Memorandum on Louis Wirth," 337.

28. In a new edition of *The Ghetto*, Hasia Diner persuasively suggests that Wirth's Jewishness was not inconsequential to his initial rejection from Chicago's department. Although she admits that there is little conclusive evidence on this point, she believes that, while Park admired his student, he also shared antisemitic stereotypes prevalent in American universities. Wirth's daughter, however, traces his early career moves without mentioning his initial rejection from Chicago's department. Diner also interprets Wirth's decision to steer clear of Jewish topics after he wrote his dissertation as, in part, a reflection

of his realization that the academic world of sociology was loath to accept a study of Jews as true scholarship. See Diner, "Introduction to the Transaction Edition"; and Marvick, "Biographical Memorandum on Louis Wirth."

29. Robert Bannister, "Principle, Politics, Profession: American Sociologists and Fascism, 1930–1950," in *Sociology Responds to Fascism,* ed. Stephen Turner and Dirk Käsler (New York: Routledge, 1992), 196. W. F. Ogburn wrote this remark to a friend at Smith in 1930.

30. Quoted in Odum, *American Sociology,* 228. While criticizing the abstruse nature of some social science and also pleading for more government funding, Wirth reiterated his belief that the modern world could not come to grips with the seismic changes in its midst without the aid of social science. See Louis Wirth, "Responsibility of Social Science," *Annals of the American Academy of Political and Social Science* 249 (January 1947): 143–151.

31. On the rise of antisemitism in the interwar era, see Leonard Dinnerstein, *Antisemitism in America* (New York: Oxford University Press, 1994).

32. Morris Raphael Cohen, *A Dreamer's Journey: The Autobiography of Morris Raphael Cohen* (Boston: Beacon Press, 1949), 241.

33. Cohen most clearly attests to his faith in reason and science in his book *Reason and Nature: An Essay on the Meaning of Scientific Method* (Glencoe, IL: Free Press, 1953 [1931]). In his biography of Cohen, David Hollinger offers an excellent analysis of Cohen's philosophical view on scientific inquiry. Cohen believed science was the best possible way to avoid parochialism and to organize society; thus he believed that pure scientific inquiry would never undermine truth and morality. See David Hollinger, *Morris R. Cohen and the Scientific Ideal* (Cambridge, MA: MIT Press, 1975). On positivism in the social sciences, see Ross, *The Origins of American Social Science,* chapter 10. For a specific study on the rise of objectivism in American sociology, see Robert Bannister, *Sociology and Scientism* (Chapel Hill: University of North Carolina Press, 1987). Bannister argues that, starting in the 1920s and peaking during the interwar period, objectivism or scientism rose in the American social sciences because people were looking for some standard according to which to comprehend an increasingly fragmented and diverse world. R. Laurence Moore makes a similar point about the attempt to see social science as neutral and value-free in the interwar era. See Moore, "Secularization."

34. Although the influence of the actual institutions that grew out of *Wissenschaft des Judentums* may have been small, the general movement toward the scientific study of Judaism and Jewishness was a significant force in Jewish Enlightenment and emancipation. See Jacob Katz, *Out of the Ghetto: The Social Background of Jewish Emancipation, 1770–1870* (Cambridge, MA: Harvard University Press, 1973); David Myers, *Re-inventing the Jewish Past: European Intellectuals and the Zionist Return to History* (New York: Oxford University Press, 1995); Ismar Schorsch, *From Text to Context: The Turn to History in Modern Judaism* (Hanover, NH: Brandeis University Press, 1994); and David Sorkin, *The Transformation of German Jewry, 1780–1840* (New York: Oxford University Press, 1987).

35. Leopold Zunz, *Zur Geschichte und Literatur* (Berlin: Veit und Comp, 1845). Cited in Schorsch, *From Text to Context*, 152.

36. Derek Penslar, Mitchell Hart, and John Efron have fruitfully studied the ideological dimensions of European Jewish social science. Penslar even argues that the agencies that collected statistics about Jewish social life were themselves engaged in the process of "consciousness raising" (218). See Efron, *Defenders of the Race;* Hart, *Social Science and the Politics of Modern Jewish Identity;* and Derek Penslar, *Shylock's Children: Economics and Jewish Identity in Modern Europe* (Berkeley: University of California Press, 2001).

37. For example, YIVO and the German Centralverein were both defense organizations established by the early twentieth century that depended on scientific research to make their case against antisemitism. See Cecile Kuznitz, "The Origins of Yiddish Scholarship and the YIVO Institute for Jewish Research" (PhD diss., Stanford University, 2000); and Ismar Schorsch, *Jewish Reactions to German Anti-Semitism, 1870–1914* (New York: Columbia University Press, 1972). In the United States, the American Jewish Committee stood at the helm of Jewish defense activities. See Naomi Wiener Cohen, *Not Free to Desist: The American Jewish Committee, 1906–1966* (Philadelphia: Jewish Publication Society, 1972).

38. He recounts his turn away from religion in Cohen, *A Dreamer's Journey*, 69.

39. For biographical information on Cohen, see Hollinger, *Morris R. Cohen and the Scientific Ideal;* and Milton Konvitz, *Nine American Jewish Thinkers* (New Brunswick: Transaction Publishers, 2000). On Cohen's teaching method, see Leonara Cohen Rosenfield, "Morris R. Cohen, the Teacher," *Journal of the History of Ideas* 18, no. 4 (October 1957): 552–571.

40. See Hollinger, *Science, Jews, and Secular Culture*, 17–18, 48–49.

41. Morris Raphael Cohen, *Reflections of a Wondering Jew* (Glencoe, IL: Free Press, 1950), 17. Cohen's daughter has argued that there was a "Judaic" basis for his thought and philosophy. See Leonora Cohen Rosenfeld, "The Judaic Values of a Philosopher: Morris Raphael Cohen, 1880–1947," *Jewish Social Studies* 42, no. 3–4 (Summer–Fall 1980): 189–202.

42. See Cohen's letter to Robert Goldman, December 18, 1936, *Jewish Social Studies* Papers, Box 11, Folder "CJR 1938," MS 0670, Stanford. Cohen describes this meeting in some detail in his autobiography. See Cohen, *A Dreamer's Journey*, chapter 27.

43. Hollinger, *Morris R. Cohen and the Scientific Ideal*, 59.

44. Robison published some of her work in *Jewish Social Studies,* and she also edited and compiled much of the data for a volume of population studies that the conference sponsored.

45. On Baron, see Robert Liberles, *Salo Wittmayer Baron: Architect of Jewish History* (New York: New York University Press, 1995); and Paul Ritterband and Harold S. Wechsler, *Jewish Learning in American Universities: The First Century* (Bloomington: Indiana University Press, 1994), chapter 7.

46. A copy of Einstein's letter, sent on March 12, 1936, is in Box 13, Folder "1940–42, re Prof Cohen," MS 0670, Stanford. In 1953, Einstein wrote another

letter in support of the financially struggling organization at the behest of a board member, although he did not host another dinner party. See letter from Einstein to David Rosenstein, November 29, 1953, Box 3, Folder "Copies of Correspondence with Einstein," MS 0670, Stanford.

47. Transcript of February 7, 1937, Conference on Jewish Relations Dinner Address, Box 12, Folder unmarked, MS 0670, Stanford, 9. Cohen expressed this sentiment in a number of places. See Cohen, *A Dreamer's Journey*, 241–257; and Cohen, *Reflections of a Wondering Jew*, 3.

48. Transcript of February 7, 1937, Conference on Jewish Relations Dinner Address, Box 12, Folder unmarked, MS 0670, Stanford, 9. In the 1940s, the conference published some of its research in a volume edited by Sophia Robison. See *Jewish Population Studies* (New York: Conference on Jewish Relations, 1943). This and other projects are mentioned in a memo, "Projects of the Conference on Jewish Relations," n.d. [1943?], Box 13, Folder "1943," MS 0670, Stanford. The data compiled by the conference quickly drew interest from Jewish organizations. Cohen mentions a number of organizations—including the AJC, B'nai Brith, the Jewish Welfare Board, the National Council of Jewish Women, and the Union of American Hebrew Congregations—that all relied on the data gathered by the Conference on Jewish Relations. See Cohen, *A Dreamer's Journey*, 249.

49. On the importance of *maskilim* journals, see Shmuel Feiner, *The Jewish Enlightenment*, trans. Chaya Naor (Philadelphia: University of Pennsylvania Press, 2004). On the *Menorah Journal*, see Daniel Greene, "The Crisis of Jewish Freedom: The Menorah Association and American Pluralism, 1906–1934" (PhD diss., University of Chicago, 2004); and Lauren Strauss, "Staying Afloat in the Melting Pot: Constructing an American Jewish Identity in the *Menorah Journal* of the 1920s," *American Jewish History* 84, no. 4 (December 1996): 315–331.

50. See, for example, Letter from Koppel Pinson (first editor of *Jewish Social Studies*) to George Boas, Oct 8, 1937, Box 12, Folder "K. Pinson, 1937–39," MS 0670, Stanford.

51. See Milton Konvitz, "The Life and Mind of Morris R. Cohen," in *Freedom and Reason: Studies in Philosophy and Jewish Culture*, ed. Salo Baron, Ernest Nagel, and Koppel Pinson (Glencoe, IL: Free Press, 1951), 14. Some of the history of the establishment of *Jewish Social Studies* is also recounted in Liberles, *Salo Wittmayer Baron*.

52. Morris Cohen, "Publisher's Foreword," *Jewish Social Studies* 1, no. 1 (January 1939): 3.

53. Ibid., 3–4.

54. Franz Boas, "Heredity and Environment," *Jewish Social Studies* 1, no. 1 (January 1939): 14.

55. See Alan Steinweis, *Studying the Jew: Scholarly Antisemitism in Nazi Germany* (Cambridge, MA: Harvard University Press, 2006), 8. Also, Hart provides a brief discussion about the various invidious uses to which social research performed by Jews about Jews was put. See Hart, *Social Science and the Politics of Modern Jewish Identity*, 219–220.

56. Recounted in Harry Lurie and Max Weinreich, eds., *Jewish Social Research in America: Status and Prospects,* vol. 4, *YIVO Annual of Jewish Social Science* (New York: Yiddish Scientific Institute—YIVO, 1949): 161.

57. Recounted in Hollinger, *Morris R. Cohen and the Scientific Ideal,* 209.

58. Letter from Morris Cohen to Louis Caplan, December 21, 1936, Box 11, Folder "CJR 1938," MS 0670, Stanford.

59. This address was republished in a posthumous collection of Cohen's essays. See Cohen, *Reflections of a Wondering Jew,* 7.

60. I have chosen to define a "substantive" article about Jewish topics as one that contains the word *Jews, Jewish,* or *antisemitism* in its title or abstract and that appears to deal with Jewish matters in a more than cursory way. Given these criteria, a JSTOR search of the *American Journal of Sociology* and the *American Sociological Review* arrived at twenty-five articles between 1939 and 1959. This search was done on July 9, 2004. In a survey about Jewish social research, *Jewish Social Studies* was recognized as the chief channel through which significant studies were disseminated. See Howard Odum, "Toward the Dynamic Study of Jewish Culture," *Social Forces* 29, no. 4 (May 1951): 250.

61. A useful index of articles published from 1939 to 1953 can be found in *Jewish Social Studies* 15 (1953): 2-8.

62. See *Jewish Social Studies* 8, no. 1 (January 1946). Baron first served as the chair for the Commission on Jewish Cultural Reconstruction, but eventually the commission became independent from the conference. Stanford houses material about the commission, Boxes 16 and 17, MS 0670.

63. YIVO, the Yiddish Scientific Institute, was founded in Vilna in 1925 to document the history and language of Jewish life. It relocated to New York City in 1940. See Kuznitz, "The Origins of Yiddish Scholarship."

64. See Conference on Jewish Relations Annual Report of the President [Cohen], June 10, 1940, Box 3, Folder "William Gresser," MS 0670, Stanford, 2.

65. See Steinweis, *Studying the Jew.*

66. Conference on Jewish Adjustment in America, December 26-27, 1945, Domestic Affairs Division-2: 73-74, AJC.

67. In one article, Wirth had indicated some doubts about the value of Jewish assimilation, but his public statements continued to rail against those Jews who worked to preserve Jewish distinctiveness. See Louis Wirth, "Education for Survival: The Jews," *American Journal of Sociology* 48, no. 6 (May 1943): 682-691.

68. See Herbert Blumer, "In Memoriam: Louis Wirth, 1897-1952," *American Journal of Sociology* 58, no. 1 (July 1952): 69; Ernest Burgess, "Louis Wirth, 1897-1952," *American Sociological Review* 17, no. 4 (August 1952): 499; E. Franklin Frazier, "Louis Wirth: An Appreciation," *Phylon* 13, no. 1 (1952): 167; and Rupert Vance, "Louis Wirth, 1897-1952," *Social Forces* 31, no. 1 (October 1952): 96.

69. Rabbi Jacob Weinstein, "Eulogy to Louis Wirth" (May 6, 1952), delivered at Mendel Hall, University of Chicago, from Louis Wirth's Biographical File, University of Chicago Archives, Regenstein Library.

70. *The Ghetto* was reprinted in 1956 by University of Chicago and then again in 1998, with a foreword by Hasia Diner, by Transaction Publishers (New Brunswick, NJ). For just a smattering of sources that heavily rely on his book (more often for specific details about Jewish life than for its actual argument), see Nathan Glazer, *American Judaism* (Chicago: University of Chicago Press, 1957); Oscar Handlin, *Adventure in Freedom: Three Hundred Years of Jewish Life in America* (New York: McGraw-Hill, 1954); C. Bezalel Sherman, *The Jew within American Society: A Study in Ethnic Individuality* (Detroit: Wayne State University Press, 1965 [1960]); and Marshall Sklare, *Conservative Judaism: An American Religious Movement* (Glencoe, IL: Free Press, 1955).

71. Odum, *American Sociology,* 232.

Chapter 3. The Sacred and Sociological Dilemma of Jewish Intermarriage

1. Felix Mendelsohn, "Intermarriage: A Sociological Problem" (sermon), December 29, 1939, Temple Israel, Chicago, Intermarriage Nearprint File, AJA: 1.

2. Ibid.

3. For two studies that discuss the development of Jewish endogamy, see Shaye Cohen, *The Beginnings of Jewishness: Boundaries, Varieties, Uncertainties* (Berkeley: University of California Press, 1999), prologue and chapter 8; and Christine Hayes, *Gentile Impurities and Jewish Identities: Intermarriage and Conversion from the Bible to the Talmud* (New York: Oxford University Press, 2002). Also see Michael Satlow, *Jewish Marriage in Antiquity* (Princeton, NJ: Princeton University Press, 2001).

4. Napoleonic France offers the best illustration of this. See Paula Hyman, *The Jews of Modern France* (Berkeley: University of California Press, 1998).

5. On the ways in which American identity has been forged through inter-marriage, see David Hollinger, "Amalgamation and Hypodescent: The Question of Ethnoracial Mixture in the History of the United States," *American Historical Review* 108, no. 5 (December 2003): 1363–1390; and Hollinger, "How Wide the Circle of the 'We'? American Intellectuals and the Problem of the Ethnos since World War II," *American Historical Review* 98, no. 2 (April 1993): 317–337. On *The Melting Pot,* see Neil Larry Shumsky, "Zangwill's *The Melting Pot:* Ethnic Tensions on Stage," *American Quarterly* 27, no. 1 (March 1975): 29–41. On *Abie's Irish Rose,* see Ted Merwin, "The Performance of Jewish Ethnicity in Anne Nichols' *Abie's Irish Rose,*" *Journal of American Ethnic History* 20, no. 2 (Winter 2001): 3–37. For a study of literary portrayals of intermarriage in the early twentieth century, see Adam Sol, "Longings and Renunciations: Attitudes toward Intermarriage in Early Twentieth Century Jewish American Novels," *American Jewish History* 89, no. 2 (June 2001): 215–230.

6. For a general historical and sociological overview of intermarriage (not just Jewish) in America, see Paul Spickard, *Mixed Blood: Intermarriage and*

Ethnic Identity in Twentieth-Century America (Madison: University of Wisconsin Press, 1990).

7. An excerpt from Hitler's September 15, 1935, speech and the specific text of the law prohibiting Jews from marrying Aryans can be found in Paul Mendes-Flohr and Jehuda Reinharz, eds., *The Jew in the Modern World* (New York: Oxford University Press, 1980), 491–492. Although specific statistics vary, it is clear that rates of intermarriage were unusually high in pre-Nazi Weimar Germany. In 1947, Uriah Engelman compiled statistics that showed a steady increase in intermarriage between 1901 and 1929. At points, for every hundred Jewish-Jewish marriages, there were fifty intermarriages. Marion Kaplan has computed statistics for those same years and found that, between 1914 and 1918, 29.86 percent of Jewish men and 21 percent of Jewish women intermarried. Nathan Stoltzfus, relying upon German primary and secondary sources, believes that by 1933, 44 percent of German Jews who married chose to marry non-Jews. See Uriah Zevi Engelman, "Intermarriage among Jews in Germany, U.S.S.R., and Switzerland," *Jewish Social Studies* 2, no. 1 (January 1940): 157–178; Marion Kaplan, *The Making of the Jewish Middle Class: Women, Family, and Identity in Imperial Germany* (New York: Oxford University Press, 1991); and Nathan Stoltzfus, *Resistance of the Heart: Intermarriage and the Rosenstrasse Protest in Nazi Germany* (New York: Norton, 1996). For another commentary on high intermarriage rates in pre-Nazi Germany, see Shulamit Volkov, "German Jews between Fulfillment and Disillusion," in *In Search of Jewish Community: Jewish Identities in Germany and Austria, 1918–1933,* ed. Michael Brenner and Derek Penslar (Bloomington: Indiana University Press, 1998). On antimiscegenation law, see Peggy Pascoe, "Miscegenation Law, Court Cases, and Ideologies of 'Race' in Twentieth-Century America," *Journal of American History* 83, no. 1 (June 1996): 44–69; and Peter Wallenstein, *Tell the Court I Love My Wife: Race, Marriage, and Law—an American History* (New York: Palgrave Macmillan, 2002). In total, forty-one colonies and states had antimiscegenation laws. When antimiscegenation laws were ruled unconstitutional in 1967, sixteen states still had them on the books. See Martha Hodes, *White Women, Black Men: Illicit Sex in the Nineteenth Century South* (New Haven, CT: Yale University Press, 1993), 1, 213n1.

8. See Joseph Jacobs, *Studies in Jewish Statistics, Social, Vital, and Anthropometric* (London: D. Nutt, 1891), v–vi.

9. Arthur Ruppin is an example of a Jewish social scientist who embedded his racial interpretation of Jewish endogamy in his Zionist commitments. See Arthur Ruppin, *The Jews of To-Day* (New York: Henry Holt and Co., 1913). On the multiple—and often contradictory—ways that Jews deployed their racial views for ideological purposes, see Mitchell Hart, *Social Science and the Politics of Modern Jewish Identity* (Stanford: Stanford University Press, 2000); John M. Efron, *Defenders of the Race: Jewish Doctors and Race Science in Fin-de-Siècle Europe* (New Haven, CT: Yale University Press, 1994); and Eric Goldstein, *The Price of Whiteness: Jews, Race, and American Identity* (Princeton, NJ: Princeton University Press, 2006).

10. On the ways that sexual boundaries and racial boundaries correlated in political, legal, and cultural realms, see Hodes, *White Women, Black Men;* Matthew Frye Jacobson, *Whiteness of a Different Color: European Immigrants and the Alchemy of Race* (Cambridge, MA: Harvard University Press, 1998); Elise Lemire, *"Miscegenation": Making Race in America* (Philadelphia: University of Pennsylvania Press, 2002); Pascoe, "Miscegenation Law"; and Wallenstein, *Tell the Court I Love My Wife.*

11. Maurice Fishberg, *The Jews: A Study of Race and Environment* (New York: Walter Scott Publishing, 1911), 205. Also see Maurice Fishberg, "Intermarriage between Jews and Christians," *Eugenics in Race and State* (Baltimore: Williams and Wilkins Company, 1923), volume 2.

12. For a discussion of the larger contours of this shift, see Elazar Barkan, *The Retreat of Scientific Racism: Changing Concepts in Britain and the United States between the World Wars* (New York: Cambridge University Press, 1992).

13. For biographical information about Drachsler, see "Julius Drachsler, Sociologist, Dead," *New York Times,* July 23, 1927, 13; entry in *Who Was Who in America,* vol. 1 (1897–1942); and personnel files from Smith College Archives and City College of the City University of New York Division of Archives and Special Collections. See Paul Mendes-Flohr and Jehuda Reinharz, eds., *The Jew in the Modern World* (New York: Oxford University Press, 1995), 706, for comparative immigration statistics.

14. On Jewish immigrants and the public school experience, see Stephan Brumberg, *Going to America, Going to School: The Jewish Immigrant Public School Encounter in Turn-of-the-Century New York City* (New York: Praeger, 1986).

15. Julius Drachsler, *Intermarriage in New York City: A Statistical Study of the Amalgamation of European People* (New York: Columbia University Press, 1921), 17–18.

16. Marriage licenses recorded only the nationality of people who were not born in the United States, so in all other cases he had to infer nationality from surnames and clergy titles. Ibid., 23.

17. Specifically, these percentages were determined by calculating the number of marriages that involved at least one Jew or one "colored" person and then determining how many of those were intermarriages. See ibid., 49–50.

18. Drachsler, *Democracy and Assimilation: The Blending of Immigrant Heritages in America* (New York: Macmillan, 1920), 93.

19. Ibid.

20. Ibid., 91.

21. Ibid., 163.

22. Ibid., 157.

23. See John Higham, *Strangers in the Land: Patterns of American Nativism, 1860–1925* (New York: Atheneum, 1963), chapter 9.

24. Kallen delineated his theory of cultural pluralism in a two-part article printed on February 18 and 25, 1915, in the *Nation.* Reprinted in Horace Kallen, *Culture and Democracy in the United States* (New York: Arno Press, 1970). On

Kallen, see Daniel Greene, "A Chosen People in a Pluralist Nation: Horace Kallen and the Jewish-American Experience," *Religion and American Culture* 16, no. 2 (June 2006): 161–193; Milton Konvitz, "Horace M. Kallen," in *The "Other" New York Jewish Intellectuals,* ed. Carole Kessner (New York: New York University Press, 1994); and William Toll, "Ethnicity and Freedom in the Philosophy of Horace M. Kallen," in *The Jews of North America,* ed. Moses Rischin (Detroit: Wayne State University Press, 1987). I am drawing on a critique of Kallen's theory offered by Philip Gleason. See Gleason, "American Identity and Americanization," in *Harvard Encyclopedia of American Ethnic Groups,* ed. Stephan Thernstrom (Cambridge, MA: Harvard University Press, 1980).

25. See Rebecca Davis, "'Not Marriage at All, but Simple Harlotry': The Companionate Marriage Controversy," *Journal of American History* 94, no. 4 (March 2008): 1137–1163; John D'Emilio and Estelle Freedman, *Intimate Matters: A History of Sexuality in America* (Chicago: University of Chicago Press, 1997); Peter Laipson, "'Kiss without Shame, for She Desires It': Sexual Foreplay in American Marital Advice Literature, 1900–1925," *Journal of Social History* 29, no. 3 (Spring 1996): 507–525; Jessamyn Neuhaus, "The Importance of Being Orgasmic: Sexuality, Gender, and Marital Sex Manuals in the United States, 1920–1963," *Journal of the History of Sexuality* 9, no. 4 (October 2000): 447–473; and Christina Simmons, "Companionate Marriage and the Lesbian Threat," *Frontiers* 4, no. 3 (Fall 1979): 54. On the increase in the divorce rate in the United States, see Elaine Tyler May, *Great Expectations: Marriage and Divorce in Post-Victorian America* (Chicago: University of Chicago Press, 1980). According to May, between the end of the Civil War and 1929, the divorce rate in America increased by 2,000 percent (p. 1). Also see Jenna Weissman Joselit, *The Wonders of America: Reinventing Jewish Culture, 1880–1950* (New York: Hill and Wang, 1994), chapter 1, for an analysis of the substantial anxiety that Jews in this era felt about marriage and intermarriage.

26. Although parts of his theory were published earlier, for the fullest expression of it see Ernest Burgess and Leonard Cottrell, *Predicting Success or Failure in Marriage* (New York: Prentice-Hall, 1939), chapter 6.

27. Reuben Resnik, "Some Sociological Aspects of Intermarriage of Jew and Non-Jew," *Social Forces* 12, no. 1 (October 1933): 94–102.

28. For an early theorist of social interactionism, and an important early twentieth-century school of thought in sociology, see Charles Cooley, *Human Nature and the Social Order* (New York: Schocken, 1964 [1902]).

29. In the post-World-War-II era, social-scientific studies of interracial marriage tended to focus on the psychological deficiencies of those people who married across the color line. See Renee Romano, *Race Mixing: Black-White Marriage in Postwar America* (Cambridge, MA: Harvard University Press, 2003), 53–58.

30. Resnik, "Some Sociological Aspects of Intermarriage of Jew and Non-Jew," 96.

31. Ray Baber, "A Study of 325 Mixed Marriages," *American Sociological Review* 2, no. 5 (October 1937): 709 (italics in original).

32. At the time, in continental Europe (with the exception of France) there were no legal means to contract a marriage between a Jew and a non-Jew without the conversion of one of the partners to the other's faith, and no states in Germany allowed for the children of a mixed union to be raised as Jews. See Alan Levenson, "Reform Attitudes, in the Past, toward Intermarriage," *Judaism* 38, 3 (Summer 1989): 320–332; and Michael A. Meyer, *Response to Modernity: A History of the Reform Movement in Judaism* (New York: Oxford University Press, 1988), 134–135.

33. Mendel Silber, *CCARY* 18 (1908): 267.

34. *CCARY* 19 (1909): 179.

35. Ibid., 175.

36. Ibid., 115.

37. Louis Mann, "Intermarriage as a Practical Problem in the Ministry," *CCARY* 47 (1937): 310.

38. Ibid., 317 (emphasis in original).

39. Ibid., 316.

40. Ibid., 319.

41. On the development of marriage counseling, see Beth Bailey, "Scientific Truth . . . and Love: The Marriage Education Movement in the United States," *Journal of Social History* 20 (Summer 1987): 711–732; Rebecca Davis, "'The Wife Your Husband Needs': Marriage Counseling, Religion, and Sexual Politics in the United States, 1930–1980" (PhD diss., Yale University, 2006); and Eva Moskowitz, *In Therapy We Trust: America's Obsession with Self-Fulfillment* (Baltimore: Johns Hopkins University Press, 2001), chapter 3.

42. George Sokolsky, "My Mixed Marriage," *Atlantic Monthly* 152, no. 2 (August 1933): 139.

43. Ibid., 138.

44. "I Married a Jew," *Atlantic Monthly* 163, no. 1 (January 1939): 38–46; and "I Married a Gentile," *Atlantic Monthly* 163, no. 3 (March 1939): 321–326.

45. "The Shadow of Anti-Semitism," *American Magazine* 128, no. 5 (November 1939): 29. My own judgment is that this article is much more likely a sincere expression of one man's situation than the two published in the *Atlantic Monthly*.

46. Jacob J. Weinstein, "The Jew and Mixed Marriage," *Reconstructionist* 7, no. 10 (June 17, 1941): 6.

47. Ibid., 7.

48. Ibid., 8.

49. Ibid., 7.

50. Ibid., 9.

51. Paula Hyman explains that middle-class women were often simultaneously saddled with the duty of socializing their children to modern norms and guarding tradition. See *Gender and Assimilation in Modern Jewish History: The Roles and Representation of Women* (Seattle: University of Washington Press, 1995), particularly chapter 5. In modern Jewish history, the only serious exception to the pattern of disproportionately high male exogamy occurred

in late-eighteenth-century Berlin and is wonderfully documented in Deborah Hertz, *Jewish High Society in Old Regime Berlin* (New Haven, CT: Yale University Press, 1988). Many scholars have noted the gender imbalance in intermarriage and conversion to Christianity. See, for example, Todd Endelman's introduction to *Jewish Apostasy in the Modern World*, ed. Todd Endelman (New York: Holmes and Meier, 1987). In the United States, until well into the 1970s, sociologists reported that Jewish men married out much more often than women, but by the 1980s the numbers had evened out. See Susan Weidman Schneider, *Intermarriage: The Challenge of Living with Difference between Christians and Jews* (New York: Free Press, 1989), 6.

52. Milton Barron, "The Incidence of Jewish Intermarriage in Europe and America," *American Sociological Review* 11, no. 1 (February 1946): 8.

53. Ellen Rothman contextualizes this sexual double standard as a central component of post-Civil-War courtship practices. See *Hands and Hearts: A History of Courtship in America* (New York: Basic Books, 1984), part 3. Also see Nancy F. Cott, *Public Vows: A History of Marriage and the Nation* (Cambridge, MA: Harvard University Press, 2000).

54. On the Judeo-Christian idea, see Mark Silk, *Spiritual Politics: Religion and America since World War II* (New York: Simon and Schuster, 1988).

55. For a broader study of pluralism and religion, see William Hutchison, *Religious Pluralism in America: The Contentious History of a Founding Ideal* (New Haven, CT: Yale University Press, 2003). Gary Gerstle offers an incisive analysis of how race, specifically African American identity, was excluded from an otherwise broadening sphere of American belonging in the World War II era. See *American Crucible: Race and Nation in the Twentieth Century* (Princeton, NJ: Princeton University Press, 2001), chapter 5.

56. Ruby Jo Reeves Kennedy, "Single or Triple Melting Pot? Intermarriage Trends in New Haven, 1870–1940," *American Journal of Sociology* 49, no. 4 (January 1944): 331–339. For biographical information on Kennedy, see *Who Was Who in America* 5 (1973): 391; and *New London Day*, April 7, 1945, copy in Ruby Jo Reeves Kennedy File, Box 8, Folder 1, CCA. On wartime religious designations, see Deborah Dash Moore, "Jewish GIs and the Creation of the Judeo-Christian Tradition," *Religion and American Culture* 8, no. 1 (Winter 1998): 31–53.

57. For criticism of Kennedy's work, see Paul Besanceney, *Interfaith Marriages: Who and Why* (New Haven, CT: College and University Press, 1970), 66; and John L. Thomas, "The Factor of Religion in the Selection of Marriage Mates," *American Sociological Review* 16, no. 4 (August 1951).

58. Milton Barron, *People Who Intermarry: Intermarriage in a New England Industrial Community* (Syracuse, NY: Syracuse University Press, 1946), xii. For other sociological studies influenced by Kennedy's model, see Loren Chancellor and Thomas Monahan, "Religious Preferences and Interreligious Mixtures in Marriages and Divorces in Iowa," *American Journal of Sociology* 61, no. 3 (1955): 233–239; Will Herberg, *Protestant-Catholic-Jew: An Essay in American Religious Sociology* (Chicago: University of Chicago Press, 1983 [1955]); and August

Hollingshead, "Cultural Factors in the Selection of Marriage Mates," *American Sociological Review* 15, no. 5 (October 1950): 619–627.

59. Ruby Jo Reeves Kennedy, "Single or Triple Melting Pot? Intermarriage in New Haven, 1870–1950," *American Journal of Sociology* 58, no. 1 (July 1952): 57.

60. Kennedy, "Single or Triple Melting Pot? Intermarriage Trends in New Haven, 1870–1940," 334.

61. Ibid., 331.

62. Address delivered by President Charles Shain at Kennedy Memorial Service, January 8, 1970, Ruby Jo Reeves Kennedy File, Box 8, Folder 1, CCA. Kennedy was one of the few women in a male-dominated profession, but as yet I do not have any concrete evidence that speaks to the role of her gender in her work.

63. Her paper was published as "What Has Social Science to Say about Intermarriage?" in *Conference on Intermarriage and Jewish Life,* ed. Werner Cahnman (New York: Herzl Press and Jewish Reconstructionist Press, 1963).

64. Newspaper clippings documenting synagogue appearances in New Haven, Connecticut (November 1964), and Manchester, Connecticut (April 1966), can be found in the Ruby Jo Reeves Kennedy File, Box 8, Folder 1, CCA.

65. For a discussion of Groves, see Judson Landis and Mary Landis, *Building a Successful Marriage* (New York: Prentice-Hall, 1948), 12; and Moskowitz, *In Therapy We Trust,* 82–87.

66. Ernest R. Groves, "The Problem of Mixed Marriage," *Ladies' Home Journal* 58, no. 16 (June 1941): 92.

67. Ibid.

68. See Carl Bacal, "The Risks You Take in Intermarriage," *Good Housekeeping* 149 (July 1959): 62–63, 97–98, 100; James Bossard, "Eight Reasons Why Marriages Go Wrong," *New York Times,* June 25, 1956, 21; Eugene Fleming and George Walsh, "Mixed Marriage," *Cosmopolitan* 141, no. 5 (November 1956): 72–73; Murray Leiffer, "Mixed Marriages and Church Loyalties," *Christian Century* 66, no. 3 (January 19, 1949): 78–80; Murray Leiffer, "Mixed Marriages and the Children," *Christian Century* 66, no. 4 (January 26, 1949): 106–108; Norman Lobsenz, "How Successful Are Interfaith Marriages?" *Redbook* 107 (October 1956): 36–39, 94–96; Morton Sontheimer, "Would You Approve Your Child's Marrying a Protestant? A Catholic? A Jew?" *Woman's Home Companion* 80 (March 1953): 30–31, 100; and "Interfaith Marriages," *Time* 53, no. 5 (January 31, 1949): 63.

69. The three most important studies that correlated interfaith marriage with increased divorce rates were Howard Bell, *Youth Tell Their Story* (Washington, DC: American Council on Education, 1938); Judson Landis, "Marriages of Mixed and Non-Mixed Religious Faith," *American Sociological Review* 14, no. 3 (June 1949): 401–407; and H. Ashley Weeks, "Differential Divorce Rates by Occupations," *Social Forces* 21, no. 3 (March 1943): 334–337.

70. See Elaine Tyler May, *Homeward Bound: American Families in the Cold War Era* (New York: Basic Books, 1988); and Riv-Ellen Prell, *Fighting to Become Americans: Jews, Gender, and the Anxiety of Assimilation* (Boston: Beacon Press,

1999). On the cultural power of women's magazines, see Moskowitz, *In Therapy We Trust,* 162–163; and Joanne Meyerowitz, "Beyond the Feminist Mystique: A Reassessment of Postwar Mass Culture, 1946–1958," *Journal of American History* 79, no. 4 (March 1993): 1455–1482.

71. See, for example, Albert I. Gordon, "Intermarriage: A Personal View," *Jewish Spectator* 29, no. 9 (November 1964): 8–13; and Joseph Rosenbloom, "Is Intermarriage Inevitable?" *National Jewish Monthly* 72–73 (April 1959): 17, 50–52.

72. *CCARY* 57 (1947): 178.

73. On Jewish chaplains, see Philip Bernstein, *Rabbis at War: The CANRA Story* (Waltham, MA: American Jewish Historical Society, 1971); and Deborah Dash Moore, *GI Jews: How World War II Changed a Generation* (Cambridge, MA: Harvard University Press, 2004).

74. See W. Gunther Plaut, *Unfinished Business* (Toronto: Lester and Orpen Dennys, 1981), for Rabbi Plaut's autobiography. Plaut was quite prolific. For an example of his work on Reform Judaism, see W. Gunther Plaut, *The Rise of Reform Judaism,* 2 vols. (New York: World Union for Progressive Judaism, 1963–65).

75. *CCARY* 57 (1947): 180.

76. Ibid., 174, 182.

77. Ibid., 179.

78. Ibid. Morgenstern made a similar comment in a letter to a layperson in Florida who wanted to know if it was acceptable for intermarriages to be performed in Reform temples. See letter from Morgenstern to C. J. Heinberg, January 28, 1947, Julian Morgenstern Papers, Box 5, Folder 9, MS 30, AJA.

79. *CCARY* 57 (1947): 180.

80. Ibid.

81. Ibid., 181.

82. Ibid.

83. Mordecai Kaplan, *Judaism as a Civilization: Toward a Reconstruction of American-Jewish Life* (Philadelphia: Jewish Publication Society, 1994 [1934]), 50.

84. See Endelman, *Jewish Apostasy in the Modern World,* for a number of essays that show the connection between intermarriage and conversion to Christianity. For two other studies that remark on this connection, see Hyman, *Gender and Assimilation in Modern Jewish History;* and Hertz, *Jewish High Society in Old Regime Berlin.* On an individual level, intermarriage did not always represent the repudiation of Jewishness, but often it did, and almost always it was perceived as such, until the 1970s, when it became much more common. For an argument about the ways that some early-twentieth-century Jewish women may have retained their Jewishness while intermarrying, see Keren McGinity, "Still Jewish: A History of Women and Intermarriage in America" (PhD diss., Brown University, 2005). Also, on some of the creative family arrangements that emerged out of intermarriage (not just Jewish), see Anne C. Rose, *Beloved Strangers: Interfaith Families in Nineteenth-Century America* (Cambridge, MA: Harvard University Press, 2001).

Chapter 4. Serving the Public Good and Serving God in 1940s America

1. "A Tribute from the Highest Authority in the Land," *Jewish Layman* 17, no. 7 (April 1943): 16–17.

2. In 1945, the JCS sent rabbis to thirty-one African American schools. See Executive Secretary's Report, November 1, 1945, in *Minutes Executive Board, National Board of Temple Brotherhoods and Jewish Chautauqua Society, 1944–1946:* 3, JCS-NY.

3. See Abraham Shusterman, "Chautauqua Addresses the Negro," *Jewish Layman* 17, no. 1 (October 1942): 9–10. The article did not explicitly say which colleges Rabbi Shusterman visited; however, according to the minutes of the JCS, rabbis visited North Carolina College for Negroes in Durham and Shaw University and Saint Augustine's College in Raleigh that fall. See National Federation of Temple Brotherhoods and JCS Minutes, March 15, 1943, appendix designated "Universities Served by the Jewish Chautauqua Society," JCS-NY.

4. On the history of the Conservative movement in the United States, see Moshe Davis, *The Emergence of Conservative Judaism* (Philadelphia: Jewish Publication Society, 1963); Daniel Judah Elazar and Rela Mintz Geffen, *The Conservative Movement in Judaism: Dilemmas and Opportunities* (Albany: State University of New York Press, 2000); Neil Gillman, *Conservative Judaism: The New Century* (West Orange, NJ: Behrman House, 1993); and Jack Wertheimer, "The Conservative Synagogue," in *The American Synagogue,* ed. Jack Wertheimer (Hanover, NH: Brandeis University Press, 1987). The classic work on American suburbanization is Kenneth T. Jackson, *Crabgrass Frontier: The Suburbanization of the United States* (New York: Oxford University Press, 1985), though in the past decade the literature has become significantly vaster. In 1994, the *American Quarterly* published a symposium about suburban history (see vol. 46, no. 1 [March 1994]), a useful place to start in order to think about scholarship on the suburb. Also, the *Journal of Urban History* devoted an issue in 2001 to assessing the state of suburban scholarship (see vol. 27, no. 3 [March 2001]).

5. See especially Gary Gerstle, *American Crucible: Race and Nation in the Twentieth Century* (Princeton, NJ: Princeton University Press, 2001), chapter 5.

6. Mark Silk, "Notes on the Judeo-Christian Tradition in America," *American Quarterly* 36, no. 1 (Spring 1984): 67.

7. "A Trumpet for All Israel," *Time* 58, no. 16 (October 15, 1951): 54.

8. Albert Gordon, "The Rabbi," delivered at the Conference on the Role of Judaism in the Modern World, April 19, 1942, Chicago, Record Group 41, p. 18, RA. For a biographical note, see Albert Gordon, *Jews in Suburbia* (Boston: Beacon Press, 1959).

9. Herman Hailperin, "The Seminary as Interpreter of Judaism to the World," delivered at the Conference on the Role of Judaism in the Modern World, April 19, 1942, Chicago, Record Group 41, p. 83, RA (emphasis in original).

10. See Jenna Weissman Joselit, "By Design: Building the Campus of the Jewish Theological Seminary," in *Tradition Renewed: A History of the Jewish*

Theological Seminary, ed. J. Wertheimer (New York: Jewish Theological Seminary of America, 1997).

11. Simon Greenberg, "The Seminary: A Link between the Past and Future," delivered at the Conference on the Role of Judaism in the Modern World, April 19, 1942, Chicago, Record Group 41, 168–169, RA.

12. Quoted in Michael Greenbaum, *Louis Finkelstein and the Conservative Movement: Conflict and Growth* (Binghamton, NY: Global Publications, 2001), 49.

13. On the genesis of Conservative Judaism, see Ismar Schorsch, *From Text to Context: The Turn to History in Modern Judaism* (Hanover, NH: Brandeis University Press, 1994), chapter 13.

14. "'Justice, Justice Shalt Thou Pursue . . .' Resolutions on Social Action adopted by the constituent bodies of the Conservative Movement in Judaism," n.d., Papers of Rabbi Ben Zion Bokser, Box 22, Folder "Joint Commission on Social Action," 69, RA.

15. Mordecai Kaplan, *Judaism as a Civilization: Toward a Reconstruction of American-Jewish Life* (Philadelphia: Jewish Publication Society, 1994 [1934]), chapter 14. More generally on Kaplan's philosophy, see Arnold M. Eisen, *Rethinking Modern Judaism: Ritual, Commandment, Community* (Chicago: University of Chicago Press, 1998). On Kaplan's relationship to the Conservative movement, see Mel Scult, *Judaism Faces the Twentieth Century: A Biography of Mordecai M. Kaplan* (Detroit: Wayne State University Press, 1993), 229–232.

16. Marshall Sklare, *Conservative Judaism: An American Religious Movement* (Glencoe, IL: Free Press, 1955).

17. My interpretation of Finkelstein's goals is based closely on Michael Greenbaum and Fred Beuttler's analyses of him. See Fred Beuttler, "Organizing an American Conscience: The Conference on Science, Philosophy, and Religion, 1940–1968" (PhD diss., University of Chicago, 1995); Fred Beuttler, "For the World at Large: Intergroup Activities at the Jewish Theological Seminary," in *Tradition Renewed: A History of the Jewish Theological Seminary,* ed. Jack Weirtheimer (New York: Jewish Theological Seminary of America, 1997); and Greenbaum, *Louis Finkelstein and the Conservative Movement.*

18. Jessica Feingold, "Up from Isolation—Intergroup Activities at the Seminary," *Judaism* 27, no. 3 (Summer 1978), 291.

19. Quoted in Greenbaum, *Louis Finkelstein and the Conservative Movement,* 64.

20. "Fifty-Five Years of Service," *New York Times,* December 1, 1942.

21. For the classic article on American civil religion, see Robert Bellah, "Civil Religion in America," *Daedalus* 96 (Winter 1967): 1–21.

22. Ira Eisenstein, "The New Diaspora in American Democracy," *Proceedings of the Rabbinical Assembly of America* 13 (1949): 260–261.

23. Ibid., 290.

24. "Justice, Justice Shalt Thou Pursue . . . ," 80. See also Alan Heil, *Voice of America: A History* (New York: Columbia University Press, 2003).

25. Conservative rabbis were clearly aware of the dangers of supporting public expressions of religion, evidenced, for example, by their disavowal of religion in public schools. See "Justice, Justice Shalt Thou Pursue . . . ," 40, 55, 58–59. Also see Jonathan Sarna, "Church-State Dilemmas of American Jews," in *Jews and the American Public Square: Debating Religion and Republic,* ed. Alan Mittleman, Jonathan D. Sarna, and Robert Licht (New York: Rowman and Littlefield, 2002).

26. Louis Finkelstein, Robert McIver, and Lyman Bryson, eds., *Approaches to National Unity: Fifth Symposium of the Conference on Science, Philosophy, and Religion in Their Relation to the Democratic Way of Life* (New York: Harper and Brothers, 1945), x.

27. One estimate put the total number of participants in all of the conferences, institutes, and workshops at seventy-five thousand. See Feingold, "Up from Isolation—Intergroup Activities at the Seminary," 289.

28. See Exodus 27:20.

29. Louis Finkelstein, foreword to *The Eternal Light,* by Morton Wishengrad (New York: Crown, 1947).

30. Quoted in Greenbaum, *Louis Finkelstein and the Conservative Movement,* 74.

31. See Joon-Mann Kang, "Franklin D. Roosevelt and James L. Fly: The Politics of Broadcast Regulation, 1941–1944," *Journal of American Culture* 10, no. 2 (Summer 1987): 23.

32. Jeffrey Shandler and Elihu Katz, "Broadcasting American Judaism: The Radio and Television Department of the Jewish Theological Seminary," in *Tradition Renewed: A History of the Jewish Theological Seminary,* ed. Jack Wertheimer (New York: Jewish Theological Seminary of America, 1997), 369–371. Also see Barbara Savage, *Broadcasting Freedom: Radio, War, and the Politics of Race* (Chapel Hill: University of North Carolina Press, 1999).

33. Shandler and Katz, "Broadcasting American Judaism," 372–373.

34. All these quotes are taken from a digest of readers' letters culled by the Jewish Theological Seminary's Communications Department. See "Eternal Light Listener Comments," Record Group 11C-26–40, RA.

35. For scripts to some of the earliest episodes, see Wishengrad, *The Eternal Light.* For summaries and discussions of other episodes, see Marjorie Wyler, "*The Eternal Light:* Judaism on the Airwaves," *Conservative Judaism* 39, no. 2 (Winter 1986–87): 18–22.

36. Wishengrad, *The Eternal Light,* 157.

37. Ibid., 159.

38. For discussions of this particular episode, see Shandler and Katz, "Broadcasting American Judaism," 367; and Wyler, "*The Eternal Light.*"

39. Leonard Levin, "The Legacy of Milton Steinberg," *Conservative Judaism* 32, no. 4 (Summer 1979): 84.

40. Letter from Milton Steinberg to Solomon Goldman, February 1, 1945, Solomon Goldman Papers, Box 16, Folder 14, MS 203, AJA.

41. Samuel Goldman, opening remarks for evening session, Conference on the Role of Judaism in the Modern World, April 19, 1942, Chicago, Record

Group 41, RA. For another criticism of Finkelstein's work, see the discussion that follows Ira Eisenstein, "The New Diaspora in American Democracy," *Proceedings of the Rabbinical Assembly of America* 13 (1949): 286.

42. Milton Steinberg, "What's Wrong with Conservative Judaism?" n.d. [1940s], Milton Steinberg Collection, P-369, Box 12, Folder 2, AJHS. Also see Milton Steinberg "Crisis in Conservative Judaism," n.d. [1940s], Milton Steinberg Collection, P-369, Box 12, Folder 2, AJHS.

43. For a thorough biography of Steinberg, see Simon Noveck, *Milton Steinberg: Portrait of a Rabbi* (New York: Ktav Publishing House, 1978). Steinberg's son has also written a fascinating analysis of Steinberg's intellectual biography. See Jonathan Steinberg, "Milton Steinberg, American Rabbi— Thoughts on His Centenary," *Jewish Quarterly Review* 95, no. 3 (Summer 2005): 579–600.

44. See Sherry Gorelick, *City College and the Jewish Poor: Education in New York, 1880–1924* (New Brunswick, NJ: Rutgers University Press, 1981).

45. Charles Shulman, "A Memoir on Milton Steinberg," sermon given at Riverdale Temple, New York, n.d. [1963], Charles Shulman Papers, Box 9, Folder 1, MS 124, AJA.

46. Kaplan was known especially for teaching homiletics. See Scult, *Judaism Faces the Twentieth Century.*

47. In a letter to Kaplan in 1945, Steinberg wrote that he was in Kaplan's "debt for an entire system of thought." See Letter from Milton Steinberg to Mordecai Kaplan, May 21, 1945, Milton Steinberg Collection, P-369, Box 5, Folder 6, AJHS.

48. Mordecai Kaplan, "Milton Steinberg's Contribution to Reconstructionism," *Reconstructionist* 16, no. 9–16 (May 1950), 9.

49. Milton Steinberg, *A Partisan Guide to the Jewish Problem* (New York: Bobbs-Merrill, 1945), 140.

50. For an epistolary record of their courtship, see Milton Steinberg Collection, P-369, Boxes 1–3, AJHS. Also see the semifictionalized account that Edith wrote about her marriage: Milton Steinberg Collection, P-369, Box 5, Folder 9, AJHS. Finally, see Noveck, *Milton Steinberg,* 50.

51. Milton Steinberg, *The Making of the Modern Jew* (New York: Bobbs-Merrill, 1933), 24.

52. Steinberg, *A Partisan Guide to the Jewish Problem,* 182.

53. Steinberg, *The Making of the Modern Jew,* 291–292.

54. Milton Steinberg, "To Be or Not to Be a Jew," *Common Ground* (Spring 1941), reprinted by Jewish Reconstructionist Foundation, Reconstructionist Pamphlet, no. 3, copy in Milton Steinberg Collection, P-369, Box 11, Folder 3, AJHS, 14.

55. Ibid., 12.

56. Ibid., 11.

57. Ibid., 13–14.

58. Noveck, *Milton Steinberg.*

59. Milton Steinberg, *Basic Judaism* (New York: Harcourt, Brace, and World, 1947), vii.

60. Quoted in Noveck, *Milton Steinberg*, 206. Within its first month, the book sold five thousand copies, and before the end of the year it had gone into a third reprint. See Noveck, *Milton Steinberg*, 211.

61. Steinberg, *Basic Judaism*, viii.

62. Letter from Milton Steinberg to Jay Goldin, February 7, 1947, Milton Steinberg Collection, P-369, Box 5, Folder 5, AJHS.

63. Ibid.

64. "A Jew on Judaism," *Newsweek*, no. 11 (September 15, 1947): 74.

65. For a useful overview of the history of the *Reconstructionist*, see Richard Hirsch, "American Jewish Life since 1935: A Reconstructionist Retrospective," *Reconstructionist* 70, no. 1 (Fall 2005): 5–14.

66. Milton Steinberg, "The Common Sense of Religious Faith," published in three installments in the *Reconstructionist* 13, no. 1–3 (February 21, March 7, and March 21, 1947), reprinted in Milton Steinberg, *Anatomy of Faith* (New York: Harcourt, Brace, and Company, 1960), 108.

67. Steinberg delivered this remark during a four-part lecture series he delivered in January 1950. See "New Currents in Religious Thought," in Milton Steinberg, *Anatomy of Faith* (New York: Harcourt, Brace, and Company, 1960), 248–249.

68. Irving Kristol, "How Basic Is 'Basic Judaism'?" *Commentary* 5, no. 1 (January 1948), 28.

69. On Niebuhr, see Richard Fox, *Reinhold Niebuhr: A Biography* (New York: Pantheon Books, 1985).

70. Will Herberg, "The Religious Thinking of Milton Steinberg," *Commentary* 12, no. 5 (November 1951), 499.

71. Ibid., 500.

Chapter 5. Constructing an Ethnic America

1. For an excellent analysis of the tercentennial, see Arthur A. Goren, *The Politics and Public Culture of American Jews* (Bloomington: Indiana University Press, 1999), chapter 9.

2. "Papers and Proceedings of the Tercentenary Conference on American Jewish Sociology," *Jewish Social Studies* 17, no. 3 (July 1955): 7.

3. Ibid.

4. Ibid., 8.

5. Werner Cahnman [executive secretary of the Conference on Jewish Relations], "Tercentenary Conference on American Jewish Sociology," Box 1, Folders "Sociology Conference: Biographical Notes, Summaries of Papers, Actual Papers," and "Program and Planning: 1954 American Sociology Conference," MS 0670, Stanford.

6. "Papers and Proceedings of the Tercentenary Conference on American Jewish Sociology," 115.

7. In the minutes from their meetings, the conference committee noted that they planned to ask Handlin to present a paper. See Committee on Tercentenary

Conference on American Jewish Sociology Minutes, January 19, 1954, Box 1, Folder "Sociology Conference 1954," MS 0670, Stanford. For a list of invitees to the conference lunch, see List of Invitees, Box 1, Folder "Sociology Conference: Lists—Names of People Sent Invitations," MS 0670, Stanford.

8. Glazer was a student during some of the war; he did not graduate from college until January 1944. See Nathan Glazer, "From Socialism to Sociology," in *Authors of Their Own Lives: Intellectual Autobiographies by Twenty American Sociologists,* ed. Bennett Berger (Berkeley: University of California Press, 1990), 197; and interview with Nathan Glazer, December 9, 2004, 6 (cited hereafter as Glazer transcript). I do not know specifically how Handlin avoided serving in the war. By the war years, he had received his doctorate and was teaching full-time at Harvard.

9. For a genealogy of the words *ethnic* and *ethnicity,* see Werner Sollors, *Beyond Ethnicity: Consent and Descent in American Culture* (New York: Oxford University Press, 1986), chapter 1.

10. On the power of social science to sculpt norms and project a unified, even if imagined, American community, see Sarah Igo, *The Averaged American: Surveys, Citizens, and the Making of a Mass Public* (Cambridge, MA: Harvard University Press, 2007); and Ellen Herman, *The Romance of American Psychology: Political Culture in the Age of Experts* (Berkeley: University of California Press, 1995).

11. On the funding of the social sciences, see Terrence Ball, "The Politics of Social Science in Postwar America," in *Recasting America: Culture and Politics in the Age of Cold War,* ed. Lary May (Chicago: University of Chicago Press, 1989).

12. See Daniel Horowitz, *Vance Packard and American Social Criticism* (Chapel Hill: University of North Carolina Press, 1995).

13. For a history of the American Jewish Committee, see Naomi Wiener Cohen, *Not Free to Desist: The American Jewish Committee, 1906–1966* (Philadelphia: Jewish Publication Society, 1972).

14. Martin Jay, *The Dialectical Imagination: A History of the Frankfurt School and the Institute of Social Research, 1923–1950* (Boston: Little, Brown and Company, 1973). For information on the founding of the AJC department, see Conference Proceedings, May 20–21, 1944, Box "Scientific Research Department, General Subject Files, 1945–48, Administrative Files, 1945–50, and Poll Files, 1945–48," Folder "Report of Social Scientists Research in Field of Anti-Semitism (1944)," Records of the AJC Scientific Research Division, DIS (Discontinued AJC Divisions and Departments) 12–18, AJC, 1.

15. "Progress Report of the Scientific Department," June 22, 1945, Box "Scientific Research Department, General Subject Files, 1945–48, Administrative Files, 1945–50, and Poll Files, 1945–48," Folder "Scientific Research Department, Monthly Reports, 1949–1950," Records of the AJC Scientific Research Division, DIS (Discontinued AJC Divisions and Departments) 12–18, AJC.

16. Conference on Jewish Adjustment in America, December 26–27, 1945, Domestic Affairs Division-2: 235–236, AJC.

17. See Gunnar Myrdal, *An American Dilemma: The Negro Problem and Modern Democracy* (New York: Harper and Row, 1962 [1944]). For background information and a critical assessment of the study, see Walter Jackson, *Gunnar Myrdal and America's Conscience: Social Engineering and Racial Liberalism, 1938–1987* (Chapel Hill: University of North Carolina Press, 1990); and Stephen Steinberg, *Turning Back: The Retreat from Racial Justice in American Thought and Policy* (Boston: Beacon Press, 1995). The *New York Times* paid a great deal of attention to Myrdal's book. See, for example, Frances Gaither, "Democracy—the Negro's Hope," review of *An American Dilemma*, by Gunnar Myrdal, *New York Times Book Review*, April 12, 1944, 7.

18. Conference on Jewish Adjustment in America, 235–236.

19. Ibid., 247.

20. Isacque Graeber and Steuart Henderson Britt, ed., *Jews in a Gentile World: The Problem of Anti-Semitism* (New York: Macmillan, 1942).

21. See, for example, AJC discussions about whether educational materials ever reached true antisemites, and whether these materials were capable of overturning prejudice. "A Study Proposal: Gentleman's Agreement and Crossfire," Box "Scientific Research Department, General Subject Files, 1945–48, Administrative Files, 1945–50, and Poll Files, 1945–48," Folder "Scientific Research Department," Records of the AJC Scientific Research Division, DIS (Discontinued AJC Divisions and Departments) 12–18, AJC, 1.

22. On the Studies in Prejudice series, see Stuart Svonkin, *Jews against Prejudice: American Jews and the Fight for Civil Liberties* (New York: Columbia University Press, 1997), 32–40. For a perceptive analysis of some of the theories, especially that of Jewish self-hatred, developed in various AJC studies, see Susan Glenn, "The Vogue of Jewish Self-Hatred in Post–World War II America," *Jewish Social Studies* 12, no. 3 (Spring–Summer 2006): 95–136. Stephen Steinberg has argued that post-World-War-II social science defined racism as a belief of the individual, not an aspect of the structure of society as a whole, and therefore was unable to predict the civil rights crisis of the 1960s. See Steinberg, *Turning Back*.

23. Glazer transcript, 5. Glazer's sense of their ongoing commitment to finding Marxist solutions to social problems, as well as their anxiety about being "found out" by the AJC, is confirmed in Martin Jay's account of the Frankfurt school's relationship to the AJC. See Jay, *The Dialectical Imagination*, chapter 7.

24. Elliot Cohen, "An Act of Affirmation: Editorial Statement," *Commentary* 1, no. 1 (November 1945): 1. On the early years of *Commentary*, see Nathan Abrams, "'America Is Home': *Commentary* Magazine and the Refocusing of the Community of Memory, 1945–1960," in *Commentary in American Life*, ed. Murray Friedman (Philadelphia: Temple University Press, 2005); Neil Jumonville, *Critical Crossings: The New York Intellectuals in Postwar America* (Berkeley: University of California Press, 1991), 63–65; and Steven Zipperstein, "*Commentary* and American Jewish Culture in the 1940s and 1950s," *Jewish Social Studies* 3, no. 2 (Winter 1997): 18–28.

25. Cohen, "An Act of Affirmation," 2.

26. See Barbara Miller Solomon, "A Portrait of Oscar Handlin," in *Uprooted Americans: Essays to Honor Oscar Handlin,* ed. Richard L. Bushman, Neil Harris, David Rothman, Barbara Miller Solomon, Stephan Thernstrom (Boston: Little, Brown and Company, 1979), 4; and Bruce Stave, *The Making of Urban History: Historiography through Oral History* (Beverly Hills: Sage Publications, 1977), 146.

27. Handlin first recounted this story in "History: A Discipline in Crisis?" *American Scholar* 40 (Summer 1971); republished in Oscar Handlin, *Truth in History* (Cambridge, MA: Harvard University Press, 1979), quote taken from p. 3.

28. Handlin, *Truth in History,* 3.

29. Interview with Oscar Handlin, December 10, 2002, 4 (cited hereafter as Handlin transcript).

30. See Seymour Martin Lipset and David Riesman, *Education and Politics at Harvard* (New York: McGraw-Hill, 1975); Stephen Steinberg, *The Ethnic Myth: Race, Ethnicity, and Class in America* (New York: Atheneum, 1981), 238–249; and Marcia Graham Synnott, *The Half-Opened Door: Discrimination and Admissions at Harvard, Yale, and Princeton, 1900–1970* (Westport, CT: Greenwood Press, 1979).

31. According to Peter Novick, Arthur Schlesinger wrote this letter. See Peter Novick, *That Noble Dream: The "Objectivity Question" and the American Historical Profession* (New York: Cambridge University Press, 1988), 172–173.

32. Handlin transcript, 9. David Brody, a Jewish man who studied under Handlin both as an undergraduate and as a graduate student from 1948 through 1958, told me that, although everyone at Harvard knew Handlin was Jewish, Handlin made an effort to separate the scholarship he did on Jewish topics from his scholarship at Harvard. Brody believes that Handlin was able to identify himself and his success almost fully with Harvard, an experience that Brody, also a Jew, did not share. Phone interview with David Brody, March 3, 2004.

33. Portions of this chapter rest on evidence from oral histories I conducted with Oscar Handlin and Nathan Glazer in December 2002. There is a rich theoretical literature about the process of conducting oral histories and doing ethnographic research. My own identity as, at the time, a youngish female graduate student certainly affected the responses I was able to elicit from both men. The placement of one's own self in ethnography, often termed reflexivity, is discussed in Barbara Babcock, "Reflexivity: Definitions and Discriminations," *Semiotica* 30 (1980): 1–14; Lynn Davidman, *Tradition in a Rootless World* (Berkeley: University of California Press, 1991); and Elaine Lawless, *Holy Women, Wholly Women: Sharing Ministries of Wholeness through Life Stories and Reciprocal Ethnography* (Philadelphia: University of Pennsylvania Press, 1993). Manuals about conducting oral histories and recording life stories also offer excellent advice on how to structure an interview and how to elicit the deepest and richest responses. See, for example, Elliot Mishler, "The Analysis of Interview-Narratives," in *Narrative Psychology: The Storied Nature of Human Conduct,* ed. Theodore Sarbin (New York: Praeger, 1986). See also Lewis P. Hinchman and Sandra K. Hinchman, eds., *Memory, Identity, Community: The*

Idea of Narrative in the Human Sciences (Albany: State University of New York Press, 1997). I also consulted a body of literature written by historians grappling with ways to use oral histories as historical sources. The *Journal of American History* had an informative symposium on oral history. See *Journal of American History* 86, no. 2 (September 1999): 698–733. See also Barbara Allen, "Story in Oral History: Clues to Historical Consciousness," *Journal of American History* 79, no. 2 (September 1992): 606–611; and Alistair Thomson, "Fifty Years On: An International Perspective on Oral History," *Journal of American History* 85, no. 2 (September 1998): 581–595. The journal *Oral History Review,* published since 1973, is also a valuable resource. Finally, on the way that our memories of the past are inflected through our present, see Edward Casey, *Remembering: A Phenomenological Study* (Bloomington: Indiana University Press, 1987); and Daniel Schachter, *The Seven Sins of Memory: How the Mind Forgets and Remembers* (Boston: Houghton Mifflin, 2001).

34. Technically speaking, this is not absolutely true. Before being offered a position at Harvard, Handlin taught for a year (1938–39) at his alma mater, Brooklyn College. See Solomon, "A Portrait of Oscar Handlin," 6.

35. Handlin transcript, 3. For a brief account of his family, see also Solomon, "A Portrait of Oscar Handlin," and Stave, *The Making of Urban History,* 145–156.

36. Handlin transcript, 2–3. Handlin recounts a similar story in the second edition of *The Uprooted*. See Oscar Handlin, *The Uprooted: The Epic Story of the Great Migrations That Made the American People* (Boston: Little, Brown and Company, 1973 [1951]), 301.

37. Arthur Schlesinger, *In Retrospect: The History of a Historian* (New York: Harcourt, Brace, and World, 1963), 6.

38. Handlin transcript, 7. David Brody, in fact wrote a paper about Jews for a seminar that Handlin offered in social history in 1953. In 1955, Brody published the essay in the *Publications of the American Jewish Historical Society* and received a five-hundred-dollar prize from the American Jewish Historical Society. See David Brody, "American Jewry, the Refugees, and Immigration Restriction (1932–1942)," *Publications of the American Jewish Historical Society* 44, no. 1–4 (September 1954–June 1955): 219–248; and "Historical News and Comments: Report of the Fifty-Third Annual Meeting," *Publications of the American Jewish Historical Society* 44, no. 1–4 (September 1954–June 1955): 240. Phone interview with Brody, March 3, 2004.

39. Milton Gordon, *Assimilation in American Life: The Role of Race, Religion, and National Origins* (New York: Oxford University Press, 1964), 224.

40. Christopher Lasch, *The New Radicalism in America, 1889–1963* (New York: W. W. Norton and Company, 1965), ix.

41. For an excellent analysis of the turn away from a belief in intellectual objectivity, see Novick, *That Noble Dream.*

42. This theory has been noted elsewhere. See, for example, Jumonville, *Critical Crossings;* and Jack Porter, *The Jew as Outsider: Historical and Contemporary Perspectives, Collected Essays, 1974–1980* (Washington, DC: University Press of America, 1981).

43. Glazer's biography has been recounted a number of places. See Joseph Dorman's documentary *Arguing the World*, and its companion book *Arguing the World: The New York Intellectuals in Their Own Words* (New York: Free Press, 2000). Also see Jumonville, *Critical Crossings;* and Leonard Dinnerstein and Gene Koppel, *Nathan Glazer: A Different Kind of Liberal* (Tucson: University of Arizona, 1973). For Glazer's account of his father's socialism, see Dorman, *Arguing the World,* 30–31, 36. According to Alexander Bloom, Thomas received nine hundred thousand votes in 1932, even though only seventeen thousand Americans were members of the Socialist Party. See *Prodigal Sons: The New York Intellectuals and Their World* (New York: Oxford University Press, 1986), 43. Glazer's father's decision to vote socialist was part of a broader trend of Jewish support for socialist candidates in New York City in the 1920s and 1930s. However, as Deborah Dash Moore argues, during those same years more and more Jews were won over by the ideals of the Democratic Party. See *At Home in America: Second Generation New York Jews* (New York: Columbia University Press, 1981), chapter 8.

44. Glazer, "From Socialism to Sociology," 191–192.

45. Glazer transcript, 6. According to Glazer, Avukah was a leftist group that believed in a binational Palestine. Avukah was founded in 1925 in Washington, DC. Among its early activities were a summer school program and the publication of *Brandeis Avukah Annual* (1932). In 1934, the newsletter *Avukah Bulletin* was started, replaced in 1938 by *Avukah Student Action*. For a descriptive entry about Avukah, see *The Universal Jewish Encyclopedia* (New York: Universal Jewish Encyclopedia, 1939), 1: 649–650.

46. Glazer, "From Socialism to Sociology," 195.

47. On the New York intellectuals, see Terry Cooney, *The Rise of New York Intellectuals: Partisan Review and Its Circle* (Madison: University of Wisconsin Press, 1986); Alan Wald, *The New York Intellectuals: The Rise and Decline of the Anti-Stalinist Left from the 1930s to the 1980s* (Chapel Hill: University of North Carolina Press, 1987); and Hugh Wilford, *The New York Intellectuals: From Vanguard to Institution* (New York: Manchester University Press, 1995).

48. See Jumonville, *Critical Crossings,* 197; and Glazer, "From Socialism to Sociology," 196.

49. Both Gary Gerstle and Lizabeth Cohen argue that working-class unionism and, at times, socialism created common cause among workers across ethnic lines, but only in limited instances. See Lizabeth Cohen, *Making a New Deal: Industrial Workers in Chicago, 1919–1939* (New York: Cambridge University Press, 1990); and Gary Gerstle, *Working-Class Americanism: The Politics of Labor in a Textile City, 1914–1960* (New York: Cambridge University Press, 1989). On Jewish socialism, see Tony Michels, *A Fire in Their Hearts: Yiddish Socialists in New York* (Cambridge, MA: Harvard University Press, 2005).

50. Jumonville sets Glazer's abandonment of socialism as part of a broader trend common to other New York Jewish intellectuals. See Jumonville, *Critical Crossings,* chapter 2.

51. Stephen Steinberg believes that the state's involvement and investment in social-scientific research accounts for the failure of the social sciences to take a critical view of postwar America. See Steinberg, *Turning Back*. Also see David Hollinger, *Science, Jews, and Secular Culture: Studies in Mid-Twentieth-Century American Intellectual History* (Princeton, NJ: Princeton University Press, 1996).

52. According to historians, the reasons for the failure of socialism are many and vague, but most explanations at least mention the conflict between pro-Stalinist and anti-Stalinist socialists, America's victory in the war, and the apparent success of New Deal reform and social welfare. See John Laslett and Seymour Martin Lipset, eds., *Failure of a Dream? Essays on the History of American Socialism* (New York: Anchor Press/Doubleday, 1974). See as well Alan Brinkley, *The End of Reform: New Deal Liberalism in Recession and War* (New York: Knopf, 1995); Melvyn Dubofsky, *The State and Labor in Modern America* (Chapel Hill: University of North Carolina Press, 1994); Steve Fraser and Gary Gerstle, eds., *The Rise and Fall of the New Deal Order, 1930–1980* (Princeton, NJ: Princeton University Press, 1989); and George Lipsitz, *A Rainbow at Midnight: Labor and Culture in the 1940s* (Urbana: University of Illinois Press, 1994).

53. Glazer, "From Socialism to Sociology," 200.

54. Ibid., 209. Glazer recounted this same transition from socialism to sociology when I met with him. See Glazer transcript, 10.

55. Glazer, "From Socialism to Sociology," 203.

56. Glazer transcript, 5, 13.

57. Nathan Glazer, "Personal Reflections on the Early Period" (delivered at the "*Commentary*, the American Jewish Community and American Culture" conference sponsored by the American Jewish Committee and the Feinstein Center of Temple University, New York City, March 10, 2003). His remarks have been published, in slightly altered form, in Nathan Glazer, "*Commentary*: The Early Years," in *Commentary in American Life*, ed. Murray Friedman (Philadelphia: Temple University Press, 2005).

58. Milton Steinberg, "*Commentary* Magazine—Benefit or Detriment to American Judaism?" sermon given at Park Avenue Synagogue, November 18, 1949, Milton Steinberg Collection, P-369, Box 11, Folder 6, AJHS, 2. Historian Steven Zipperstein has also described *Commentary* as often flouting normative Jewish ideas. See "*Commentary* and American Jewish Culture in the 1940s and 1950s," *Jewish Social Studies* 3, no. 2 (Winter 1997): 18–28.

59. Steinberg, "*Commentary* Magazine," 2.

60. Glazer transcript, 7.

61. Nathan Glazer, "The Study of Man," *Commentary* 1, no. 1 (November 1945): 84.

62. Ibid.

63. I discuss the Chicago school in chapter 2. See, as well, Morris Janowitz's introduction to the third edition of Ernest Burgess and Robert Park, *Introduction to the Science of Sociology* (Chicago: University of Chicago Press,

1969 [1921]); and Fred Matthews, *Quest for an American Sociology: Robert E. Park and the Chicago School* (Montreal: McGill-Queen's University Press, 1977).

64. Irving Howe, *Selected Writings, 1950–1990* (New York: Harcourt Brace Jovanovich, 1990), 264. Interestingly, neither Glazer nor Handlin changed· his last name, although Howe did. For biographical information about Howe, see Gerald Sorin, *Irving Howe: A Life of Passionate Dissent* (New York: New York University Press, 2002).

65. For many years, historians have contended that until the 1960s American Jews did not confront the atrocities of World War II. Some historians, especially Hasia Diner and Kirsten Fermaglich, contest this claim to show a much earlier and more immediate set of Jewish reactions to the war. See Hasia Diner, "Before 'The Holocaust' American Jews Confront Catastrophe, 1945–1962" (David W. Belin Lecture in American Jewish Affairs, University of Michigan, March 17, 2004); Hasia Diner, *The Jews of the United States, 1654–2000* (Berkeley: University of California Press, 2004), 261–265; and Kirsten Fermaglich, *American Dreams and Nazi Nightmares: Early Holocaust Consciousness and Liberal America, 1957–1965* (Waltham, MA: Brandeis University Press, 2006).

66. Nathan Glazer, "America's Ethnic Pattern: 'Melting Pot' or 'Nation of Nations'?" *Commentary* 15, no. 4 (April 1953): 408. Here he was invoking the Law of the Third Generation, as first proposed by Marcus Hansen. See Marcus Hansen, *The Problem of the Third Generation Immigrant* (Rock Island, IL: Augustana Historical Society, 1938). See Matthew Frye Jacobson's discussion of the creation of an American founding myth that situated Ellis Island, not Plymouth Rock, as the birthplace of the nation, a trend in which Handlin and Glazer clearly participated. Matthew Frye Jacobson, *Roots Too: White Ethnic Revival in Post–Civil Rights America* (Cambridge, MA: Harvard University Press, 2006).

67. Oscar Handlin, "America Recognizes Diverse Loyalties," *Commentary* 9, no. 3 (March 1950): 220–226.

68. In her book about race during the cold war, Mary L. Dudziak similarly argues that the United States attempted to prove the worth of its democratic system by showing its tolerance of difference, although this policy clearly had limited effectiveness in the case of African Americans. *Cold War Civil Rights: Race and the Image of American Democracy* (Princeton, NJ: Princeton University Press, 2000).

69. Harry Lurie and Max Weinreich, eds., "Jewish Social Research in America: Status and Prospects," *YIVO Annual of Jewish Social Science* 4 (1949): 220.

70. Handlin, *The Uprooted*, 3.

71. Ibid., 273. Also see Reed Ueda, "Immigration and the Moral Criticism of American History: The Vision of Oscar Handlin," *Canadian Review of American Studies* 21, no. 2 (Fall 1990): 183–201.

72. "Mary Handlin, Historian, Dies; Co-Author of Books on America," *New York Times,* May 25, 1976.

73. Phone interview with Brody, March 3, 2004. Brody also mentioned that Mary was a constant presence in Handlin's office and would shoo students out

when she thought they had taken enough of the professor's time. When I interviewed Handlin, his current wife, Lillian Handlin, was in the office when I arrived; she left for our interview, but she returned about an hour later and rather clearly, though quite politely, indicated that my time was up.

74. For her coauthored books, see *Commonwealth: A Study of the Role of Government in American Economy* (New York: New York University Press, 1947); *The Dimensions of Liberty* (Cambridge, MA: Harvard University Press, Belknap Press, 1961); *Facing Life: Youth and the Family in American History* (Boston: Little, Brown and Company, 1971); and *The Wealth of the American People: A History of American Affluence* (New York: McGraw-Hill, 1975). Shulamit Reinharz observes that many professors' wives similarly aided their husbands but received only infrequent recognition. See Reinharz's entry for "Sociology," in *Jewish Women in America*, ed. Paula Hyman and Deborah Dash Moore (New York: Routledge, 1997), 1273–1278.

75. Historians of gender and social science note that social science itself emerged as a male field, in contradistinction to social work, a field that was often seen as feminine. After World War II, when the federal government invested heavily in the social sciences, men dominated the field and created a social-scientific agenda that tended to prioritize male experience as the key for understanding society. See Barbara Laslett, "Gender in/and Social Science History," *Social Science History* 16, no. 2 (Summer 1992): 177–195; and Helene Silverberg, "Introduction: Toward a Gendered Social Science History," in *Gender and American Social Science: The Formative Years*, ed. Helene Silverberg (Princeton, NJ: Princeton University Press, 1998).

76. Oscar and Mary Handlin, *Danger in Discord: Origins of Anti-Semitism in the United States* (New York: Anti-Defamation League of B'nai Brith, 1948), 7.

77. Ibid., 8.

78. In a footnote, Glazer wrote, "The term 'ethnic group' refers to an element in a population that feels itself, to some extent, part of a single nationality, nation, people or race." *American Judaism* (Chicago: University of Chicago Press, 1957), 4. Handlin simply used the word *ethnic* (such as in "ethnic attachment") without an explicit definition.

79. Oscar Handlin, *Adventure in Freedom: Three Hundred Years of Jewish Life in America* (New York: McGraw-Hill, 1954), viii–ix.

80. Handlin transcript, 4.

81. In an article, Handlin briefly mentioned that he begrudged the tercentenary organizers for rejecting his proposal to create a full documentary history of Jewish American life. See Oscar Handlin, "A Twenty Year Retrospect of American Jewish Historiography," *American Jewish Historical Quarterly* 65, no. 4 (June 1976): 296–297.

82. See Nathan Glazer, "Social Characteristics of American Jews, 1654–1954," *American Jewish Year Book* 56 (1955).

83. Glazer transcript, 12.

84. Glazer, *American Judaism*, viii.

85. Many historians have noted that religion gained a new place of prominence during the 1950s. See James Hudnut-Beumler, *Looking for God in the Suburbs: The Religion of the American Dream and Its Critics, 1945–1965* (New Brunswick, NJ: Rutgers University Press, 1944); William O'Neill, *American High: The Years of Confidence, 1945–1960* (New York: Free Press, 1986); and Stephen Whitfield, *The Culture of the Cold War* (Baltimore: Johns Hopkins University Press, 1991).

86. Will Herberg, *Protestant-Catholic-Jew: An Essay in American Religious Sociology* (Chicago: University of Chicago Press, 1983 [1955]). On Herberg, see Harry Ausmus, *Will Herberg: From Right to Right* (Chapel Hill: University of North Carolina Press, 1987).

87. Glazer, *American Judaism,* 130.

88. Handlin, *Adventure in Freedom,* 250.

89. Ibid, 260.

90. C. Bezalel Sherman, "Misadventure in History," *Congress Weekly* 21, no. 33 (December 6, 1954): 7. I am grateful to Deborah Dash Moore for bringing this review to my attention. Handlin's book generally received mixed reviews. Most reviewers accepted his historical material, but those who took issue with the book (mainly Jewish reviewers) questioned the value of its speculations on the present and future of American Jews. Most of the negative reviewers believed, like Sherman, that Handlin had neglected the importance of Jewish distinctiveness and had tried to sweep tensions and conflicts between Jewishness and Americanness under the carpet. See Ludwig Lewisohn, "Two Histories," *Saturday Review* (September 18, 1954): 20–21; Albert Mordell, "Book Reviews: *Adventure in Freedom,*" *Publication of the American Jewish Historical Society* 44 (1954–55): 120–123; and Ellis Rivkin, "Review of *Adventure in Freedom,*" *American Jewish Archives* 9, no. 1 (April 1957): 48–53.

91. Handlin transcript, 12. Handlin often maintained that Jewish issues simply manifested more general trends and patterns. For example, Handlin spoke out against creating a unified and authoritative body to represent American Jews. See Oscar Handlin, "Freedom or Authority in Group Life?" *Commentary* 14, no. 6 (December 1952): 547–554.

92. Arthur Cohen, "Revival in Judaism, Too," *Christian Century* 74, no. 42 (October 16, 1957): 1232.

93. Glazer, *American Judaism,* 122.

94. Handlin transcript, 8.

95. Ibid., 9.

96. Ibid., 8.

97. Ibid., 11–12.

98. Ibid.

99. Ibid.

100. Oscar Handlin, *The Uprooted,* 322.

101. Ibid.

102. Glazer, *American Judaism,* 149.

103. Nathan Glazer and Daniel P. Moynihan, *Beyond the Melting Pot: The Negroes, Puerto Ricans, Jews, Italians, and Irish of New York City* (Cambridge, MA: MIT Press, 1963), 17.

104. Ibid, 20.

105. For autobiographical information, see Herbert Gans, *Making Sense of America: Sociological Analyses and Essays* (New York: Rowman and Littlefield, 1999), appendix A, "An Autobiographical Account." I also gathered more information about Gans's life from a personal conversation with him on April 21, 2004, at Columbia University.

106. Herbert Gans, "American Jewry: Present and Future," *Commentary* 21, no. 5 (May 1956): 427.

107. Handlin first made this statement in a forum published by the *National Jewish Monthly*. See Oscar Handlin, "The Goals of Survival: What Will U.S. Jewry Be Like in 2000? . . . Two Views," *National Jewish Monthly* (May 1957): 5, 32–33. Shortly after its publication, the *New York Times* summarized the article. See "Big Changes Seen for Jews in U.S.," *New York Times*, May 13, 1957, 11. The museum analogy was a popular one. A year before Handlin made this statement, Gans observed in *Commentary* that second-generation Jews tended to objectify their religion into "museum pieces and collector's items" (428). Gans, however, believed that even these fairly anesthetized objects of Jewish culture could still express meaning for Jews. See Gans, "American Jewry: Present and Future."

108. Glazer, *American Judaism*, 142.

109. Ibid., 141.

110. C. Bezalel Sherman, *The Jew within American Society: A Study in Ethnic Individuality* (Detroit: Wayne State University Press, 1965 [1960]). He had written earlier versions of this book in Yiddish (1948) and Hebrew (1954). For biographical information about Sherman, see his obituary: "Charles Sherman, Sociologist, Active in Jewish Affairs, Dies," *New York Times*, January 3, 1971, 69.

111. John Appel, "Book Review of *The Jew within American Society*," *Jewish Social Studies* 29, no. 4 (October 1967): 245–246.

112. See Nathan Glazer, *Ethnic Dilemmas* (Cambridge, MA: Harvard University Press, 1983); and Nathan Glazer, "Individualism and Equality in the United States," in *On the Making of Americans: Essays in Honor of David Riesman*, ed. Nathan Glazer, Herbert Gans, Joseph Gusfield, and Christopher Jencks (Philadelphia: University of Pennsylvania Press, 1979). Handlin made his attitudes toward affirmative action and identity politics less public. He clearly disagreed with affirmative action policies, however. See Oscar Handlin, "A Discipline in Crisis," in *Truth in History*, 6. Daryl Michael Scott specifically designates Glazer and Handlin as the leaders of a 1960s neoconservative movement that blamed blacks and other racial minorities for their inability to attain the same achievements as white Americans and refused to see any larger social forces at work. I think he oversimplifies Handlin's attitude, especially given his 1959 study on blacks and Puerto Ricans, but he is right to see the two as sharing a disdain for systemic—as opposed to individualized—explanations of

group difference. See Daryl Michael Scott, *Contempt and Pity: Social Policy and the Image of the Damaged Black Psyche, 1880–1996* (Chapel Hill: University of North Carolina Press, 1997).

113. Nathan Glazer, "New York's Puerto Ricans," *Commentary* 26, no. 6 (December 1958): 469–478. In many ways, these same attitudes informed Glazer's coauthored study of ethnicity in New York. See Glazer and Moynihan, *Beyond the Melting Pot.*

114. See Oscar Handlin, *The Newcomers: Negroes and Puerto Ricans in a Changing Metropolis* (Cambridge, MA: Harvard University Press, 1967 [1959]), 87.

115. Ibid, 119.

116. For perspectives on the way that the civil rights movement pushed many social scientists to revise their models of ethnic success and become involved in social protest, see Charles Smith and Lewis Killian, "Black Sociologists and Social Protest," in *Black Sociologists: Historical and Contemporary Perspectives,* ed. James Blackwell and Morris Janowitz (Chicago: University of Chicago Press, 1974); and Steinberg, *Turning Back.*

117. Handlin originally wrote these words in 1970, in a book coauthored with his wife, Mary Flug Handlin. Reprinted as "Ethnicity and the New History" in Handlin, *Truth in History,* 383–402. He railed against "new historians," those historians writing after the civil rights movement who focused on the "victimization" of groups, and described them as producing "familiar endless, pointless, vacuous soap-operas, useless as history, as formula for action, or as a source of faith" (402). His polemic is full of contradictions, including his refutation of present-concerned history; he himself often claimed that history was a guide for the present.

118. I should note that, in the 1990s, Glazer appeared to have softened his animus against affirmative action and thus rethink the way social, economic, and political forces might operate quite differently depending on one's group identity. See James Traub, "Nathan Glazer Changes His Mind, Again," *New York Times,* June 28, 1998, sec. 6, p. 23.

119. Oscar Handlin, "Living in a Valley," *American Scholar* 46 (Summer 1977): 301.

120. Glazer transcript, 14.

Chapter 6. What Is a Jew?

1. See Lynn Spigel, *Make Room for TV: Television and the Family Ideal in Postwar America* (Chicago: University of Chicago Press, 1992), 1.

2. Morris Kertzer, *Tell Me, Rabbi* (New York: Bloch Publishing, 1976), 49.

3. Morris Kertzer, *Today's American Jew* (New York: McGraw-Hill, 1967), 228 (emphasis in original).

4. On this dynamic, see, for example, Patrick Henry, "'And I Don't Care What It Is': The Tradition-History of a Civil Religion Proof-Text," *Journal of*

the American Academy of Religion 49, no. 1 (1981): 35–47; James Hudnut-Beumler, *Looking for God in the Suburbs: The Religion of the American Dream and Its Critics, 1945–1965* (New Brunswick, NJ: Rutgers University Press, 1944); Kevin Schultz, "Religion as Identity in Postwar America: The Last Serious Attempt to Put the Question of Religion in the United States Census," *Journal of American History* 93, no. 2 (September 2006): 359–384; Stephen Whitfield, *The Culture of the Cold War* (Baltimore: Johns Hopkins University Press, 1991); and Robert Wuthnow, *The Restructuring of American Religion: Society and Faith since World War II* (Princeton, NJ: Princeton University Press, 1988).

5. "Opening Statement at Institute of Jewish Theology," March 20, 1950, Ferdinand Isserman Papers, Box 3, Folder 4, MS 6, AJA.

6. Letter from Samuel Teitelbaum to Isserman, February 3, 1950, Ferdinand Isserman Papers, Box 3, Folder 4, MS 6, AJA.

7. Letter from Isserman to Arthur Hays Sulzberger, February 16, 1950, Ferdinand Isserman Papers, Box 3, Folder 4, MS 6, AJA.

8. "Parley of Reform Rabbis Hear Bold Proposal: That Jewry Readopt Pre-Christian Proselytism," *Atlanta Southern Israelite*, March 24, 1950; "Jewish Missionary Effort Proposed at Rabbis' Meet," *Omaha Jewish Press*, March 24, 1950; "Reform Rabbis Suggest That Judaism Become Active Missionary Religion," *Jewish Floridian*, March 24, 1950; and "Urge Judaism Be Missionary Religion," *Cleveland Jewish Independent*, March 24, 1950. The *New York Times* article made only passing reference to the mission roundtable, but all of the Cincinnati papers gave broader coverage to the topic. George Dugan, "Scholars Ponder New Judaism Code," *New York Times*, March 21, 1950, 27; "Dr. Ferdinand I. Isserman," *Cincinnati Times-Star*, March 17, 1950; "Reform Jewish Theology Study Conference Set," *Cincinnati Times-Star*, March 18, 1950; "Reports of Jewish Meetings," *Cincinnati Post*, March 18, 1950; and "Modern Man Seeking Faith to Live By, Rabbi Declares," *Cincinnati Enquirer*, March 21, 1950. Copies of the newspaper articles are all in the Conversion Nearprint File, AJA.

9. This same copy is reprinted in the articles cited above from the *Cincinnati Times-Star*, the *Cincinnati Post*, the *Atlanta Southern Israelite*, the *Omaha Jewish Press*, the *Jewish Floridian*, and the *Cleveland Jewish Independent*. Also see "With All Men of Good Will," *Cleveland Jewish Independent*, March 31, 1950. All from Conversion Nearprint File, AJA.

10. Statements to the Mission Roundtable, Isserman Papers, Box 3, Folder 6, MS 6, AJA.

11. This text is found in the press release titled "Dr. Ferdinand Isserman," Isserman Papers, Box 3, Folder 4, MS 6, AJA. It was reproduced in all of the aforementioned articles about the institute.

12. Quoted in all of the March 24, 1950 articles (listed above). I was able to find out from one of his articles that Goldstein was an army chaplain: "Faith and the Army," *Jewish Spectator* 9, no. 1 (November 1943): 23–25.

13. "Cavorting with Converting," *California Jewish Voice*, March 24, 1950, Conversion Nearprint File, AJA.

14. *CCAR* 41 (1931): 193, quoted in Beth S. Wenger, *New York Jews and the Great Depression: Uncertain Promise* (New Haven, CT: Yale University Press, 1996), 166.

15. For a description of how the Great Depression affected the Reform movement, see Michael A. Meyer, *Response to Modernity: A History of the Reform Movement in Judaism* (New York: Oxford University Press, 1988), 307–309.

16. For the classic thesis that America experienced a religious depression paralleling its economic depression, see Robert T. Handy, "The American Religious Depression, 1925–1935," *Church History* 29, no. 1 (1960): 3–16. Since the publication of this article, historians have contested Handy's interpretation of Depression-era religion. Joel A. Carpenter, for example, argues that evangelical Christians established crucial institutional and popular strength during the depression. See *Revive Us Again: The Reawakening of American Fundamentalism* (New York: Oxford University Press, 1997). Beth Wenger, who has written the best and most thorough study of Jews in the Great Depression, similarly disagrees with Handy's thesis. She argues that congregational leaders went to great lengths to make synagogue and religious life relevant to Depression-era Jews, and that in doing so they significantly contributed to the development of American Judaism. Wenger, however, also acknowledges that most congregations had to trim their programming and struggle to stay afloat. See *New York Jews and the Great Depression*.

17. On these policy shifts, see Meyer, *Response to Modernity*, 294–295, 389.

18. For two thorough studies of the political and policy worlds of American Zionism, see Naomi Wiener Cohen, *American Jews and the Zionist Idea* (New York: Ktav Publishing House, 1975); and Melvin I. Urofsky, *American Zionism from Herzl to the Holocaust* (Garden City, NY: Anchor Press, 1975). For a newer study that is most successful in its analysis of the material culture of American Zionism, see Mark A. Raider, *The Emergence of American Zionism* (New York: New York University Press, 1998). Finally, for an intellectual history of nineteenth- and twentieth-century ideas about diaspora and their connection to Judaism and Jewish identity, see Arnold Eisen, *Galut: Modern Jewish Reflection on Homelessness and Homecoming* (Bloomington: Indiana University Press, 1986).

19. Although the only copy of the Wolsey letter I found was addressed specifically to Rabbi Bamberger, I think it is safe to assume, given the formulaic quality of the letter, that the other rabbis received near-identical letters. Letter from Louis Wolsey to Bernard Bamberger, April 29, 1950, Bernard Bamberger Papers, Box 3, Folder 17, MS 660, AJA.

20. Ibid.

21. Louis Wolsey, "Shall Jews Seek Converts: Let's Begin to Missionize Now," *American Judaism* 2, no. 3 (January 1953): 10–11.

22. "Report of Committee on Resolution," *CCAR* 60 (1950): 208.

23. This quote, from David Max Eichhorn, comes from William Berkowitz, ed., *Ten Vital Jewish Issues* (New York: Thomas Yoseloff, 1964), 116. The book is a transcription of lectures and classes that Berkowitz organized for his Conservative synagogue in 1960.

24. *CCARY* 60 (1950): 211.

25. Ibid., 214.

26. Ibid.

27. Ibid., 212. For information on Bernard Bamberger, see http://huc.edu/aja/BernardBamberger.html (accessed June 14, 2002), which has a full biographical sketch of him.

28. *CCARY* 60 (1950): 215.

29. Ibid.

30. This attitude was reflected in President Eisenhower's instruction that Americans should have a religion "and I don't care what it is." See Henry, "And I Don't Care What It Is," for a unique methodological approach to Eisenhower's dictate. See also Whitfield, *The Culture of the Cold War*, 88.

31. *CCARY* 60 (1950): 215.

32. Letter from David Max Eichhorn to Bernard Bamberger, June 1, 1950, Bernard Bamberger Papers, Box 3, Folder 17, MS 660, AJA.

33. Greg Palmer and Mark Zaid, eds., *The GI's Rabbi: World War II Letters of David Max Eichhorn* (Lawrence: University Press of Kansas, 2004), 178. For biographical information about Rabbi Eichhorn, see the nearprint file on him at the AJA. In an autobiographical statement he wrote in 1968, he described his chaplaincy in World War II. Eichhorn was born in Columbia, Pennsylvania, on January 6, 1906, and he received his rabbinical ordination from Hebrew Union College in 1931. He died in 1986.

34. Shaye Cohen discusses the various rabbinic opinions about converts motivated by marriage. His discussion reveals, more than anything else, that there was not one uniform view about the matter. He explains that, in B. Yevamot 24b (from the second half of the second century), Rabbi Nehemiah asserted that matrimony or financial gain would disqualify a candidate for conversion. However, there is other evidence that the rabbis were lenient in their judgments of converts' motivations. See Shaye Cohen, *The Beginnings of Jewishness: Boundaries, Varieties, Uncertainties* (Berkeley: University of California Press, 1999), 231–234. Clearly, however, a scholar's interpretation of talmudic intent is often quite different from the way that halakha functions in living communities. In 1965, Melach Schachter, an Orthodox rabbi, decried the Reform movement's approach to conversion specifically because he believed it violated Jewish law. For a conversion to be valid, he argued, "the wish to enter the Jewish fold must be motivated by conviction, by spiritual, not ulterior, purpose. Those who are prompted to embrace Judaism by the desire to contract an advantageous marriage . . . should be excluded from the Jewish fold" (9). The rabbi grounded his disapproval in rabbinic material and did not offer nearly as nuanced an interpretation as Cohen has. The complexities of the doctrine that fascinate Cohen would have undermined Rabbi Schachter's position. See Melech Schachter, *The Problem of Conversion Today* (New York: Union of Orthodox Jewish Congregations of America, 1965). Found in Max Routtenberg Papers, Box 2, Folder 9, RA.

35. As Ann Braude notes, there is a long history of men dismissing the value or importance of women's religious participation. See Ann Braude, "Women's

History *Is* American Religious History," in *Retelling U.S. Religious History,* ed. Thomas Tweed (Berkeley: University of California Press, 1997).

36. On polling and the power of social science, see Sarah Igo, *The Averaged American: Surveys, Citizens, and the Making of a Mass Public* (Cambridge, MA: Harvard University Press, 2007).

37. Eichhorn describes his method in *CCARY* 63 (1953): 171; and David Eichhorn, "Conversions to Judaism by Reform and Conservative Rabbis," *Jewish Social Studies* 16, no. 4 (October 1954): 300.

38. Eichhorn, "Conversions to Judaism by Reform and Conservative Rabbis," 310–311. Eichhorn calculated that 93.9 percent of conversions performed by Reform rabbis and 96 percent of those by Conservative rabbis were motivated by marriage. Only one out of seven or eight converts in the Conservative movement, and one out of five in the Reform movement, was male.

39. Ibid., 315.

40. Ibid., 318.

41. "American Judaism Has Gains in Converts" *Christian Century* 71, no. 46 (November 17, 1954): 1390.

42. *CCARY* 64 (1954): 118.

43. "Israelis Predict Japanese Influx," *New York Times,* March 2, 1958, copy in Conversion Nearprint File, AJA.

44. David Max Eichhorn, "Judaism and the Japanese," *Jewish Spectator* 23, no. 6 (June 1958): 22–25.

45. Robert Gordis, "Has the Time Arrived for Jewish Missionaries?" *National Jewish Monthly* 72–73 (March 1958): 6–7, 24–26; and "Japanese Jews," *Time* 74 (October 12, 1959): 75–76.

46. Eichhorn, "Judaism and the Japanese," 25.

47. Edward Ellis, "Simple Language Urged in Religion," n.p., n.d. [circa 1950s], Morris Kertzer Papers, Box 11, Folder 11, MS 709, AJA. For a study of Protestant forays into the media and the criticism they incurred, see R. Laurence Moore, *Selling God: American Religion in the Marketplace of Culture* (New York: Oxford University Press, 1994), chapter 8.

48. Morris Kertzer, "Farewell Remarks," sermon given at Park Avenue Synagogue, New York City, April 29, 1949, in Morris Kertzer Papers, Box 1, Folder 1, MS 709, AJA, 5; and "Anzio Chaplain Named as Interfaith Director," *New York Times,* April 3, 1949, Morris Kertzer Papers, Box 11, Folder 11, MS 709, AJA.

49. "Autobiography of Morris Kertzer, from Bush County to New York," December 16, 1969, Small Collections, Morris Kertzer Autobiography, AJA, 23.

50. Morris Kertzer, "What Christian Youth Know about Jews: Reporting on an Experiment in Inter-faith Education," *Community News* (Bangor, Maine), n.d. [1941], in Morris Kertzer Papers, Box 9, Folder 8, MS 709, AJA, 17. The same copy was also published in the *New York Jewish Review,* the *Montreal Canadian Jewish Chronicle,* the *Pittsburgh American Jewish Outlook,* and the *Baltimore Jewish Times.* Louis Finkelstein, along with Elliot Ross and William Adams Brown, edited the textbook used in the class, titled *Religions of Democracy* (New York: Devin-Adair, 1941).

51. See Deborah Dash Moore, *GI Jews: How World War II Changed a Generation* (Cambridge: Harvard University Press, 2004), especially chapter 5.

52. Recounted in Morris Kertzer, *What Is a Jew?* (New York: World Publishing Company, 1953), 139.

53. Morris Kertzer, *With an H on My Dog Tag* (New York: Behrman House, 1947), 127.

54. According to Leo Rosten, the editor of *Look* at the time, the magazine had a circulation of about twenty million in the early 1950s. See Leo Rosten, ed., *A Guide to the Religions of America* (New York: Simon and Schuster, 1955), xiii.

55. Ibid. This volume reprinted all the articles.

56. "Autobiography of Morris Kertzer," 33.

57. Morris Kertzer, "What Is a Jew?" *Look* (July 17, 1952).

58. Kertzer, *What Is a Jew?* 3. On the publication of *What Is a Jew?* see "Autobiography of Morris Kertzer," 33.

59. Kertzer, "What Is a Jew?" 9.

60. Ibid., 10.

61. Kertzer, *What Is a Jew?*, 28.

62. Ibid., 196.

63. Letter from DeWitt Wallace to Morris Kertzer, February 4, 1953, Morris Kertzer Papers, Box 10, Folder 4, MS 709, AJA.

64. In the preface to *What Is a Jew?*, Kertzer wrote that he received about a thousand letters, but in an interview he said he received two thousand. See Ellis, "Simple Language Urged in Religion." In February 1957, the AJC reported that it had distributed 62,950 copes of Kertzer's article. See AJC Publications Division Report for February 1957, 7; the copy can be accessed at http://ajcarchives.org/ajcarchive/DigitalArchive.aspx ("Monthly Reports, February–June 1957; accessed February 7, 2007). On his radio interview, see letters from Barry Gray of WMCA to Morris Kertzer, 1952, Morris Kertzer Papers, Box 10, Folder 4, MS 709, AJA.

65. See Braude, "Women's History *Is* American Religious History."

66. Letter from Mrs. Joseph Goodfriend (Chicago) to Morris Kertzer, June 10, 1952, Morris Kertzer Papers, Box 10, Folder 4, MS 709, AJA.

67. Letter from Charlotte Danglen (Levittown, NY) to Morris Kertzer, June 23, 1952, Morris Kertzer Papers, Box 10, Folder 4, MS 709, AJA.

68. Letter from Dr. Ira Fink (New York) to Morris Kertzer, June 3, 1952, Morris Kertzer Papers, Box 10, Folder 4, MS 709, AJA.

69. Letter from Don Haironson (Brooklyn) to Morris Kertzer, April 27, 1953, Morris Kertzer Papers, Box 10, Folder 5, MS 709, AJA.

70. Letter from Mrs. C.H. Frost (Portland, OR) to Morris Kertzer, September 26, 1952, Morris Kertzer Papers, Box 10, Folder 4, MS 709, AJA.

71. Letter from Morris Kertzer to Mrs. Ira Butler, August 5, 1952, Morris Kertzer Papers, Box 10, Folder 4, MS 709, AJA.

72. See, for example, letter from Morris Kertzer to John Markus (Bradford Woods, PA), August 5, 1952, Morris Kertzer Papers, Box 10, Folder 4, MS 709, AJA.

73. Louis Binstock, "Accurate Answers to 'What Is a Jew?'" *Chicago Sunday Tribune,* April 19, 1953, in Morris Kertzer Papers, Box 10, Folder 8, MS 709, AJA; Abraham Duker, "Kertzer, Morris N., *What Is a Jew?* [Book Review]," *Jewish Social Studies* 16, no. 2 (April 1954): 196; Ely Pilchik, "*What Is a Jew?* [Book Review]," *Judaism* 2, no. 3 (July 1953): 287; David de Sola Pool, "In the Beginning Was the Bible," *New York Times,* June 7, 1953, 29.

74. Morris Kertzer, "Milton Steinberg," sermon given at Westchester Reform Temple, New York, November 5, 1969, in Morris Kertzer Papers, Box 3, Folder 3, MS 709, AJA, 4.

75. News clipping, n.p., n.d., copy in Morris Kertzer Papers, Box 9, Folder 6, MS 709, AJA.

76. Printed in *Newsday,* June 2, 1953, copy in Morris Kertzer Papers, Box 9, Folder 6, MS 709, AJA.

77. National Conference of Christians and Jews, Field and Program Service Bulletin, June 9, 1953, Morris Kertzer Papers, Box 10, Folder 5, MS 709, AJA; and *Jewish Book Guild* 7, no. 8 (n.d.), in Morris Kertzer Papers, Box 10, Folder 8, MS 709, AJA.

78. See *Pittsburgh Post-Gazette,* November 26, 1954; *San Francisco Call-Bulletin,* February 18, 1955; *Tucson Daily Citizen,* February 3, 1955; and *Miami Daily News,* n.d. Copies of all in Morris Kertzer Papers, Box 10, Folder 9, MS 709, AJA.

79. Morris Kertzer with Lawrence Hoffman, *What Is a Jew?* (New York: Touchstone, 1996).

80. Ben Gallob, "Kertzer Father-Daughter Team Pioneers in 'Faith of a Teen-ager' TV Program," *National Jewish Post,* July 31, 1953, in Morris Kertzer Papers, Box 1, Folder 5, MS 709, AJA. In a conversation with me on July 18, 2005, Ruth Kertzer Seidman confirmed that her father had not told her what to say.

81. Technically speaking, the Kertzers performed three seders on television, but the first one, which aired on the *Home* television program in March 1956, consisted of a discussion and then brief demonstration of a seder. See AJC Mass Media Division, Radio and Television Section, Report for March 1956, 1; copy can be accessed at http://ajcarchives.org/main.php?GroupingId=1840 (accessed February 7, 2007).

82. Incidentally, the non-Jewish guest was Cathy Pike, the daughter of famed Episcopalian Bishop James Pike. *Tell Thy Son,* broadcast on CBS in the spring of 1958, copy in author's possession. Thanks to Ruth Kertzer Seidman for giving me a recording of this broadcast. A copy can also be found at http://ajcarchives.org/main.php?GroupingId=1870 (accessed February 7, 2007).

83. Morris Kertzer, "A Jewish Mission," n.d. [circa 1958], in Morris Kertzer Papers, Box 9, Folder 4, MS 709, AJA, 1 (emphasis in original).

84. He described some of his interfaith efforts in Morris Kertzer, "Cementing Jewish-Christian Relations," speech given to Hartford Chapter of the American Jewish Committee, February 25, 1954, in Morris Kertzer Papers, Box 7, Folder 6, MS 709, AJA. He also received the Pro Deo Gold Medal for his work on

Catholic-Jewish Relations. See Ari Goldman, "Rabbi Morris Kertzer Dies; Improved Interreligious Ties," *New York Times,* December 31, 1983.

85. Kertzer, *What Is a Jew?* 208.

86. "Autobiography of Morris Kertzer," 34.

87. Morris Kertzer, "A Jewish Mission," n.d. [circa 1958], Morris Kertzer Papers, Box 9, Folder 4, MS 709, AJA; Morris Kertzer, "The Burden of the Chosen," October 14, 1967, Larchmont Temple, Morris Kertzer Papers, Box 3, Folder 2, MS 709, AJA; and Morris Kertzer, "The Jews a Mission People?" n.d., Morris Kertzer Papers, Box 7, Folder 9, MS 709, AJA.

88. *CCARY* 64 (1954): 116.

89. Jakob Petuchowski, "The Jewish Mission to the Nations," *Commentary* 20, no. 4 (October 1955): 317 (emphasis in the original). Also see "What Judaism Has to Offer," *Time* 66 (October 24, 1955): 45.

90. Trude Weiss-Rosmarin, "Jews by Conversion?" *Jewish Spectator* 21, no. 10 (October 1956): 4. For more information about Weiss-Rosmarin's extraordinary life, see Deborah Dash Moore, "Trude Weiss-Rosmarin and *The Jewish Spectator,*" in *The "Other" New York Jewish Intellectuals,* ed. Carole Kessner (New York: New York University Press, 1994). I too have written a short entry about Weiss-Rosmarin in *Notable American Women,* vol. 5 (Cambridge, MA: Harvard University Press, 2005).

91. *CCARY* 65 (1955): 108.

92. "Report of the Committee on the Unaffiliated," *CCARY* 67 (1957): 99.

93. Ibid.

94. Robert Gordis, "Has the Time Arrived for Jewish Missionaries?" *National Jewish Monthly* 72–73 (March 1958): 25; and "Jewish Proselytizers?" *Time* 71 (February 24, 1958): 43. For a recent echo of this argument, see Jonathan Sarna, "Committed Today, Divorced Tomorrow," *JTS Magazine: The Journal of the Jewish Theological Seminary* 7, no. 2 (1998): 12, 23.

95. Kertzer, *Today's American Jew,* 295 (emphasis in original).

96. Petuchowski, "The Jewish Mission to the Nations," 320.

Chapter 7. A Jewish Marilyn Monroe and the Civil-Rights-Era Crisis in Jewish Self-Presentation

1. Norman Mailer, *Marilyn: A Biography* (New York: Grosset and Dunlap, 1973), 157.

2. Leslie Fiedler, *Waiting for the End* (New York: Stein and Day, 1964), 68.

3. Erich Rosenthal, "Studies of Jewish Intermarriage in the United States," in *American Jewish Year Book* (Philadelphia: Jewish Publication Society of America, 1963), 53.

4. For a copy of the conversion certificate, see Mishkan Israel, Box 31, Folder D1, MSS B54, NHCHS.

5. For a description of their wedding as well as photographs, see "Wedding Wine for Marilyn," *Life* (July 16, 1956): 113–115. Two days before their Jewish

wedding, they had been legally married in a brief civil ceremony. For reports on the civil ceremony, see "Marilyn Monroe, Arthur Miller Married in White Plains Court," *New York Times,* June 30, 1956, 19.

6. Robert Goldburg, "Intermarriage: Will Resolution Solve the Problem?" December 4, 1970, Box of Sermons, MI. Goldburg was clearly proud of his FBI file and wrote almost gloatingly about it (he used the adjective *delicious* to describe it) to his friends Arthur Miller and Howard Fast. See letter from Robert Goldburg to Arthur Miller, September 7, 1978, and letter from Robert Goldburg to Howard Fast, March 21, 1979, both located in Mishkan Israel, Box 27, Folder H, MSS B54, NHCHS.

7. Fred Lawrence Guiles, *Norma Jean: The Life of Marilyn Monroe* (New York: McGraw-Hill, 1969), 212.

8. Morton Miller, "My Moments with Marilyn. P.S. Arthur Was There, Too," *Esquire* 111–112 (June 1989): 164.

9. Paula Hyman and Deborah Dash Moore, eds., *Jewish Women in America* (New York: Routledge, 1997). Hyman and Moore were clearly aware of the challenges of determining which women merited a place in their encyclopedia, a problem they address in detail in their preface. They list a number of criteria they used to decide whether a woman was Jewish: birth, conversion, how a woman self-identified, and how contemporaries viewed her. Monroe was justifiably excluded according to the standards they stipulated. In a later recollection, Moore explains that she and Hyman deliberated over whether to include Monroe in their encyclopedia. Among the factors weighing into their decision was the fact that neither Hyman's nor Moore's children recognized Monroe as Jewish. See Deborah Dash Moore, "Jewish Women on My Mind," *Culturefront* 5, no. 3 (Winter 1997): 160–163.

10. Robert Goldburg, "Jews and the Good-will Movement," February 1958, Box of Sermons, MI.

11. Letter from Robert Goldburg to Howard Fast, March 6, 1965, Mishkan Israel, Box 27, Folder F, MSS B54, NHCHS.

12. Goldburg, "Is Judaism as Good as It Sounds?" (sermon), March 1954, Mishkan Israel, Box 27, Folder H, MSS B54, NHCHS, 5.

13. Letter from Robert Goldburg to Jacob Marcus, August 24, 1962, Small Collections 8325, AJA. Goldburg wrote Marcus about the affair on at least four separate occasions from 1962 through 1986.

14. Letter from Robert Goldburg to Jacob Rader Marcus, August 6, 1986, Small Collections 8326, AJA.

15. Letter from Goldburg to Marcus, August 24, 1962.

16. Ibid.

17. Letter from Robert Goldburg to Jacob Rader Marcus, October 4, 1973, Small Collections 8325, AJA.

18. Letter from Goldburg to Marcus, August 6, 1986.

19. See Angela Lambert, "An Intellect at Ease," *London Independent,* August 2, 1994, pp. 17, 19.

20. See Jack Hamilton, "Marilyn's New Life," *Look* 22 (October 1, 1957): 110–115; and Richard Meryman, "Marilyn Monroe: The Last Interview," *Life* 15,

no. 8 (August 1992): 72–78. Also see Susan Wender, "Marilyn Enters a Jewish Family," *Modern Screen* (November 1956): 185, reprinted in J. Hoberman and Jeffrey Shandler, eds., *Entertaining America: Jews, Movies, and Broadcasting* (Princeton, NJ: Princeton University Press, 2003).

21. Christopher Lasch, *The New Radicalism in America, 1889–1963* (New York: W. W. Norton, 1965), 319.

22. Letter from Goldburg to Marcus, August 24, 1962.

23. Ibid.

24. See Joseph A. Loftus, "Arthur Miller and Dr. Nathan Indicted on Contempt Charges," *New York Times*, February 19, 1957, 1.

25. This incident is recounted in three different letters. One from Robert Goldburg to Jacob Marcus, August 24, 1962; another from William Rosenwald, general chairman of the United Jewish Appeal, to Goldburg, March 6, 1957, Small Collections 8326, AJA; and the last from Goldburg to Jacob Rader Marcus, n.d., Small Collections 8326, AJA. For a useful context, see Ellen Schrecker, *Many Are the Crimes: McCarthyism in America* (Princeton, NJ: Princeton University Press, 1998).

26. Letter from Goldburg to Marcus, August 24, 1962.

27. According to Goldburg, he had performed two intermarriages—one for a wartime couple and the other for two elderly lovers. Robert Goldburg, "Intermarriage: Will Resolution Solve the Problem?" December 4, 1970, Box of Sermons, MI. It is possible that Goldburg was not entirely forthright about his marriage record. In 1969, the *New York Times* reported that he chanted a blessing over the union of Rachel Fast, a Jew (daughter of novelist Howard Fast), and Paul Arthur Poet, a Presbyterian. See "Rachel A. Fast Wed in Garden to Paul A. Poet," *New York Times*, June 16, 1969, located in Intermarriage Nearprint File, AJA.

28. Robert Goldburg, "Intermarriage: Will Resolution Solve the Problem?"

29. Ibid.

30. See Guiles, *Norma Jean*, 292. See also Louis Calta, "Marilyn Monroe to Divorce Miller," *New York Times*, November 12, 1960, pp. 1, 14.

31. Recollected in Robert Goldburg's letter to Bertram Korn, September 7, 1962, Marilyn Monroe, Small Collections 8325, AJA.

32. See Richard Cramer, *Joe DiMaggio: The Hero's Life* (New York: Simon and Schuster, 2000), chapter 16.

33. Arthur Miller, *Timebends* (New York: Penguin, 1995), 482. For other reflections on Miller's relationship to Monroe, see Mel Gussow, *Conversations with Miller* (New York: Applause Theatre and Cinema Books, 2002); and Arthur Miller, *After the Fall* (New York: Viking Press, 1964).

34. Morris Kertzer, *The Art of Being a Jew* (New York: World Publishing Company, 1962), 58.

35. On Orthodox attitudes to intermarriage, see David Ellenson, "The Development of Orthodox Attitudes to Conversion in the Modern Period," *Conservative Judaism* 36, no. 4 (Summer 1983): 57–73.

36. Seminar under the Auspices of the Synagogue Commission of Federation, (May 6, 1958), Intermarriage Nearprint File, Box 2, AJA, 4. For

information about Leo Jung, see Jacob Schacter, *Reverence, Righteousness, and Rahamanut: In Memory of Rabbi Dr. Leo Jung* (New Jersey: J. Aronson, 1992).

37. Norman Lobsenz, "How Successful Are Interfaith Marriages?" *Redbook* 107 (October 1956): 37.

38. Ibid., 39.

39. Levi Olan, "Marrying a Person of Another Faith," December 11, 1960 (sermon broadcast on WFAA in Dallas, TX), Box 26, Folder 6, MS 181, AJA.

40. James Bossard, "Eight Reasons Why Marriages Go Wrong," *New York Times,* June 24, 1956, 21. See also Eleanor Stoker Boll, and James Bossard, *One Marriage Two Faiths: Guidance on Interfaith Marriage* (New York: Ronald Press Company, 1957).

41. For historical analyses of American conceptions of childhood, see Steven Mintz, *Huck's Raft: A History of American Childhood* (Cambridge, MA: Harvard University Press, Belknap Press, 2004); and Peter Stearns, *Anxious Parents: A History of Modern Childrearing in America* (New York: New York University Press, 2003).

42. Ardis Whitman, "Children of Interfaith Marriage," *Redbook* 121, no. 2 (June 1963): 112.

43. Bernard J. Bamberger, "Plain Talk about Intermarriage," *Reconstructionist* 15, no. 16 (December 16, 1949): 12.

44. Eleanor Felder, "My Child: Jew or Christian?" *Commentary* 14, no. 3 (November 1952): 232.

45. Ibid.

46. Ibid., 234.

47. Letters to the editor, *Commentary* 14, no. 5 (November 1952): 502.

48. Ibid.

49. Richard Goldhurst, "Growing Up between Two Worlds," *Commentary* 16, no. 1 (July 1953): 30.

50. Ibid., 32.

51. Ibid., 33.

52. Ibid.

53. Letters to the editor, *Commentary* 16, no. 4 (October 1953): 377.

54. Eugene Fleming and George Walsh, "Mixed Marriage," *Cosmopolitan* 141, no. 5 (November 1956): 72.

55. Ibid., 73.

56. Lobsenz, "How Successful Are Interfaith Marriages?" 96.

57. Whitman, "Children of Interfaith Marriage," 113.

58. Felder, "My Child: Jew or Christian?" 231.

59. Marshall Sklare, "Intermarriage and the Jewish Future," *Commentary* 37, no. 4 (April 1964): 51. For biographical information about Sklare, see Marshall Sklare, *Observing America's Jews* (Hanover, NH: University Press of New England, Brandeis University Press, 1993), chapter 1; and Jonathan Sarna, "Marshall Sklare (1921–1992)," *Proceedings of the American Academy of Jewish Research* 58 (1992): 33–35.

60. Clark Vincent, "Interfaith Marriage: Problem or Symptom?" in *Religion and the Face of America: Papers of the Conference*, ed. Jane Zahn (Berkeley: University Extension, University of California, 1958), 69.

61. Whitman, "Children of Interfaith Marriage," 113.

62. Marc Dollinger persuasively makes this case. See *Quest for Inclusion: Jews and Liberalism in Modern America* (Princeton, NJ: Princeton University Press, 2000).

63. Bamberger, "Plain Talk about Intermarriage," 11.

64. Milton Barron, "Research on Intermarriage: A Survey of Accomplishments and Prospects," *American Journal of Sociology* 57, no. 3 (November 1951): 255.

65. Hershel Shanks, "Jewish-Gentile Intermarriage: Facts and Trends," *Commentary* 16, no. 4 (October 1953): 374.

66. Thomas Morgan, "The Vanishing American Jew," *Look* 28 (May 5, 1964): 42.

67. Milton Gordon, *Assimilation in American Life: The Role of Race, Religion, and National Origins* (New York: Oxford University Press, 1964), 263.

68. Albert I. Gordon, *Intermarriage: Interfaith, Interracial, Interethnic* (Boston: Beacon Press, 1964), 368.

69. Sklare, "Intermarriage and the Jewish Future," 46.

70. Nathan Hurvitz, "Sixteen Jews Who Intermarried," *YIVO Annual of Jewish Social Science* 13 (1965): 173–174.

71. Maria Levinson and Daniel Levinson, "Jews Who Intermarry: Sociopsychological Bases of Ethnic Identity and Change," *YIVO Annual of Jewish Social Science* 12 (1958–59): 103–130.

72. Hurvitz, "Sixteen Jews Who Intermarried," 153.

73. Sklare, "Intermarriage and the Jewish Future," 52.

74. Whitman, "Children of Interfaith Marriage," 119.

75. Lobsenz, "How Successful Are Interfaith Marriages?" 95.

76. Monford Harris, "On Marrying Outside One's Existence," *Conservative Judaism* 20, no. 2 (Winter 1966): 61.

77. Deborah Dash Moore, *GI Jews: How World War II Changed a Generation* (Cambridge, MA: Harvard University Press, 2004).

78. For copies of the conversion certificates and marriage license, see Material on Conversions of Sammy Davis Jr. and May Britt, Small Collections 2489, AJA.

79. See "Jewish Negro," *Time* 75 (February 1, 1960): 38; Sammy Davis Jr., "Why I Became a Jew," *Ebony* 15, no. 4 (February 1960): 62–64, 66, 68–69; Sammy Davis Jr., Jane Boyar, and Burt Boyar, *Yes I Can: The Story of Sammy Davis Jr.* (New York: Farrar, Straus and Giroux, 1965); and Sammy Davis Jr., Jane Boyar, and Burt Boyar, *Why Me? The Sammy Davis, Jr. Story* (New York: Farrar, Straus and Giroux, 1989).

80. "Chicky Baby Davis Honeymoons Solo," *Los Angeles Herald and Express*, November 14, 1960, A-3, Material on Conversions of Sammy Davis Jr. and May Britt, Small Collections 2489, AJA.

81. Letter from Jacob Rader Marcus to William Kramer, February 7, 1961, Material on Conversions of Sammy Davis Jr. and May Britt, Small Collections 2489, AJA.

82. Letter from Sidney Brown (of South Houston, TX) to Rabbi William Kramer (Hollywood, CA), November 15, 1960, Material on Conversions of Sammy Davis Jr. and May Britt, Small Collections 2489, AJA. A Jewish woman, who was married to a black man, also commented on the reluctance among many Jews to accept dark-skinned Jews. See Inge Lederer Gibel, "The Negro-Jewish Scene: A Personal View," *Judaism* 14, no. 1 (1965): 12–21.

83. See letter from William Kramer to May Britt, January 16, 1961, which contained a copy of a letter the rabbi received praising the interracial Jewish marriage, Material on Conversions of Sammy Davis Jr. and May Britt, Small Collections 2489, AJA.

84. In 1967, the Supreme Court ruled in *Loving v. Virginia* that statutes prohibiting marriage across the color line were unconstitutional. Until the court ruling, every state below the Mason-Dixon Line, except Maryland (which had repealed its law just prior to the verdict), had antimiscegenation laws on the books. Between 1952 and 1966, fourteen other states repealed their laws. See David Hollinger, "Amalgamation and Hypodescent: The Question of Ethnoracial Mixture in the History of the United States," *American Historical Review* 108, no. 5 (December 2003): 1365. Also see Peggy Pascoe, "Miscegenation Law, Court Cases, and Ideologies of 'Race' in Twentieth-Century America," *Journal of American History* 83, no. 1 (June 1996): 44–69; and Peter Wallenstein, *Tell the Court I Love My Wife: Race, Marriage, and Law—an American History* (New York: Palgrave Macmillan, 2002).

85. Werner Cahnman, "The Interracial Jewish Children," *Reconstructionist* 33, no. 8 (June 9, 1967): 9.

86. On Jewish involvement in the civil rights movement, see Dollinger, *Quest for Inclusion,* chapters 7 and 8; and Debra Schultz, *Going South: Jewish Women in the Civil Rights Movement* (New York: New York University Press, 2001).

87. An excerpt from this letter, which is undated but likely from the 1960s, can be found in a packet of materials about intermarriage prepared for the 1972 CCAR meeting, copy in Morris Kertzer Papers, Box 14, Folder 4, MS 709, AJA.

88. Quoted in Cahnman, "The Interracial Jewish Children," 10.

89. For an insightful discussion about the costs that Jews incurred in insisting upon their non-race-based identities, see Eric Goldstein, *The Price of Whiteness: Jews, Race, and American Identity* (Princeton, NJ: Princeton University Press, 2006). Also see Susan Kahn, "The Multiple Meanings of Jewish Genes," *Culture, Medicine, and Psychiatry* 29, no. 2 (June 2005). I should note that there are a number of black Jewish groups, many dating back to the 1920s. For a compelling discussion of the intersection of race and religion, see Henry Goldschmidt, *Race and Religion: Among the Chosen Peoples of Crown Heights* (New Brunswick, NJ: Rutgers University Press, 2006), chapter 5.

90. See Sander Gilman, *The Jew's Body* (New York: Routledge, 1991).

91. Quoted in Murray Rothman, "1972 Convention Statement: A Complex Phenomenon," *CCAR Journal* (Spring 1973): 17.

92. John Neufield's letter, *Commentary* 3, no. 38 (September 1964): 10.

93. Herbert Gans, "Symbolic Ethnicity: The Future of Ethnic Groups and Cultures in America," in *On the Making of Americans: Essays in Honor of David Riesman*, eds. Nathan Glazer, Herbert Gans, Joseph Gusfield, and Christopher Jencks (Philadelphia: University of Pennsylvania Press, 1979), 213. On symbolic Judaism, see Herbert Gans, "American Jewry: Present and Future," *Commentary* 21, no. 5 (May 1956): 427.

94. Michael Staub has discussed the many sides of this intracommunal culture war. See Michael Staub, *Torn at the Roots: The Crisis of Jewish Liberalism in Postwar America* (New York: Columbia University Press, 2002).

95. Burt Siegel, "Officiating at Mixed Marriages," *CCAR Journal* (April 1971): 82.

96. For an insightful discussion about gender politics and American Jewish stereotypes, see Riv-Ellen Prell, *Fighting to Become Americans: Jews, Gender, and the Anxiety of Assimilation* (Boston: Beacon Press, 1999). Also see Joyce Antler, *You Never Call! You Never Write! A History of the Jewish Mother* (New York: Oxford University Press, 2007).

97. Sidney Goldstein and Calvin Goldscheider, "Social and Demographic Aspects of Jewish Intermarriages," *Social Problems* 13, no. 4 (Spring 1966): 399.

98. Henry Cohen, "Mixed Marriage and Jewish Continuity," *CCAR Journal* (April 1972).

99. The late sociologist Egon Mayer was the most outspoken proponent of this school of thought. See, for example, his "Outreach to Intermarried Adds Strength to Jewish Community," *Jewish Exponent* 192, no. 19 (November 6, 1992).

100. Alan Chenkin and Fred Massarik, "United National Population Study: A First Report," *American Jewish Year Book* 74 (1973): 292.

101. As I noted in chapter 3, modern Jewish historians have generally agreed that Jewish women have had higher rates of endogamy than Jewish men, except for a period of time in late-eighteenth-century Berlin. See Deborah Hertz, *Jewish High Society in Old Regime Berlin* (New Haven, CT: Yale University Press, 1988); and Todd Endelman, ed., *Jewish Apostasy in the Modern World* (New York: Holmes and Meier, 1987).

102. Goldstein and Goldscheider, "Social and Demographic Aspects of Jewish Intermarriages," 396.

103. Cohen, "Mixed Marriage and Jewish Continuity," 50.

104. See the first page of the packet of material compiled by the CCAR Committee on Mixed Marriage, in Morris Kertzer Papers, Box 14, Folder 4, MS 707, AJA.

105. *CCARY* 83 (1973), copy at http://data.ccarnet.org/cgi-bin/resodisp .pl?file=mm&year=1973 (accessed February 12, 2007).

106. The advertisement appeared on September 4, 1974, copy in Intermarriage Nearprint File, AJA.

107. Louis Berman, "Decorum, Prudery, and Intermarriage," *Reconstructionist* 34, no. 8 (May 31, 1968): 7.

108. William Abrams, "Intermarriage: Catastrophe or Challenge," *United Synagogue Review* (Spring 1973): 13.

109. Ibid., 27.

110. For discussions of programs that catered specifically to Jewish youth in the 1960s and beyond, see Saul Kelner, "Almost Pilgrims: Authenticity, Identity, and the Extra-Ordinary on a Jewish Tour of Israel" (PhD diss., City University of New York, 2002); Riv-Ellen Prell, "Summer Camp, Postwar American Jewish Youth, and the Redemption of Judaism," in *The Jewish Role in American Life: An Annual Review,* ed. Bruce Zuckerman and Jeremy Schoenberg (Los Angeles: University of Southern California Casden Institute, 2006), 79; Edward Shapiro, *A Time for Healing: American Jewry since World War II* (Baltimore: Johns Hopkins Press, 1992): and Jack Wertheimer, "Jewish Education in the United States: Recent Trends and Issues," *American Jewish Year Book* 99 (1999): 3–114.

Conclusion

1. The old Mishkan Israel building, erected in 1897, still stands on the corner of Audubon Street and Orange Street in New Haven. The synagogue relocated to Hamden in 1960. See "Mishkan Israel 1840–1975 Houses of Worship," Mishkan Israel, Box 30, Folder B, MSS B54, NHCHS.

2. Arthur Miller, "A Talk on Peace and Justice," *Jewish Currents* 48, no. 6 (June 1994): 5.

3. Ibid., 6.

4. Ibid.

5. Abraham Joshua Heschel, *God in Search of Man: A Philosophy of Judaism* (New York: Noonday Press, 1955), 3. For accounts of Heschel's life before and after he left Europe, see Edward Kaplan and Samuel Dresner, *Abraham Joshua Heschel: Prophetic Witness* (New Haven, CT: Yale University Press, 1998); and Edward Kaplan, *Spiritual Radical: Abraham Joshua Heschel in America, 1940–1972* (New Haven, CT: Yale University Press, 2007). For a useful essay, see Edward Kaplan, "The American Mission of Abraham Joshua Heschel," in *The Americanization of the Jews,* ed. Norman Cohen and Robert Seltzer (New York: New York University Press, 1995).

6. This conception of religion was contrary to the theories that had emerged from within the social sciences, but resembled a phenomenological approach (such as Rudolph Otto's) to religion. In the United States, Reinhold Niebuhr was one of the most important champions of neoorthodoxy. In his biography of Niebuhr, Richard Fox provides an excellent discussion about the movement. It also so happens that Heschel and Niebuhr were close friends and found quite a bit to admire in one another. See Richard Fox, *Reinhold Niebuhr: A Biography* (New York: Pantheon Books, 1985); Ursula Niebuhr,

"Notes on a Friendship: Abraham Joshua Heschel and Reinhold Niebuhr," in *Abraham Joshua Heschel: Exploring His Life and Thought*, ed. John Merkle (New York: Macmillan, 1985); and Rudolph Otto, *The Idea of the Holy* (New York: Oxford University Press, 1958).

7. Heschel explores this component of his theology in *God in Search of Man*.

8. For an excellent study that reveals just how individual-based Jewishness had become in the last decades of the twentieth century, see Steven M. Cohen and Arnold Eisen, *The Jew Within: Self, Family, and Community in America* (Bloomington: Indiana University Press, 2000).

9. My thinking on this has been informed by philosopher Kwame Anthony Appiah's work on cosmopolitanism. He argues that individuals have an ethical and moral responsibility to see themselves as part of something larger than their tribal or ethnic affiliations, but that it is impossible for individuals to perceive the world without being grounded in the particularities of their identity. The problem, however, is, how does one preserve the particularity of identity and still participate in the globalized—or interconnected—world? See *Cosmopolitanism: Ethics in a World of Strangers* (New York: Norton, 2006).

10. Cohen and Eisen, *The Jew Within*, chapter 2.

11. Pierre Bourdieu asks whether it is legitimate to rely on people's own explanations of themselves as a guide for understanding human society, though of course importing an outsider's explanation carries a whole host of problems as well. See *The Logic of Practice* (Stanford, CA: Stanford University Press, 1990), 17–18. For a useful guide to Bourdieu, see Richard Jenkins, *Key Sociologists: Pierre Bourdieu* (New York: Routledge, 1992).

12. Sarah E. Richards, "You Don't Have to Be Jewish to Love JDate," *New York Times*, December 5, 2004; Eric Fingerhut, "Not Just Js in JDate," *Washington Jewish Week*, October 23, 2007.

13. Nathaniel Popper, "Birthright Israel Builds a Solid Foundation," *Forward* (November 11, 2005) accessed at http://www.forward.com/articles/2237/ (October 4, 2008).

14. Barbara Babcock, "Reflexivity: Definitions and Discriminations," *Semiotica* 30 (1980): 1–14. Also see Elaine J. Lawless, *Holy Women, Wholly Women: Sharing Ministries of Wholeness through Life Stories and Reciprocal Ethnography* (Philadelphia: University of Pennsylvania Press, 1993).

Selected Bibliography

Archives

American Jewish Archives, Hebrew Union College, Cincinnati, OH
American Jewish Committee Information Center and Digital Archives, New York
American Jewish Historical Society, New York
City College of the City University of New York, Division of Archives and Special Collections
Connecticut College Archives, New London
Jewish Chautauqua Society Archives, Union of American Hebrew Congregations, New York
Mishkan Israel, Hamden, CT
New Haven Colony Historical Society, New Haven, CT
Ratner Archives, Jewish Theological Seminary, New York
Regenstein Library, University of Chicago
Smith College Archives, Northampton, MA
Stanford University Libraries Special Collections
Yale University Manuscripts and Archives

Articles and Chapters

Abrams, Nathan. "'America Is Home': *Commentary* Magazine and the Refocusing of the Community of Memory, 1945–1960." In *Commentary in American Life*, ed. Murray Friedman. Philadelphia: Temple University Press, 2005.
Allen, Barbara. "Story in Oral History: Clues to Historical Consciousness." *Journal of American History* 79, no. 2 (September 1992): 606–611.

Babcock, Barbara. "Reflexivity: Definitions and Discriminations." *Semiotica* 30 (1980): 1–14.

Bailey, Beth. "Scientific Truth . . . and Love: The Marriage Education Movement in the United States." *Journal of Social History* 20 (Summer 1987): 711–732.

Ball, Terrence. "The Politics of Social Science in Postwar America." In *Recasting America: Culture and Politics in the Age of Cold War,* ed. Lary May. Chicago: University of Chicago Press, 1989.

Bannister, Robert. "Principle, Politics, Profession: American Sociologists and Fascism, 1930–1950." In *Sociology Responds to Fascism,* ed. Stephen Turner and Dirk Käsler. New York: Routledge, 1992.

Bellah, Robert. "Civil Religion in America." *Daedalus* 96 (Winter 1967): 1–21.

Berman, Lila Corwin. "Mission to America: The Reform Movement's Missionary Experiments, 1919–1960." *Religion and American Culture* 13, no. 2 (2003): 205–239.

———. "Sociology, Jews, and Intermarriage in Twentieth-Century America." *Jewish Social Studies* 14, no. 2 (Winter 2008): 32–60.

Beuttler, Fred. "For the World at Large: Intergroup Activities at the Jewish Theological Seminary." In *Tradition Renewed: A History of the Jewish Theological Seminary,* ed. Jack Wertheimer. New York: Jewish Theological Seminary of America, 1997.

Braude, Ann. "Women's History *Is* American Religious History." In *Retelling U.S. Religious History,* ed. Thomas Tweed. Berkeley: University of California Press, 1997.

Cahnman, Werner. "Sociology." *Encyclopaedia Judaica* 15 (1971): 62–69.

Davis, Rebecca. "'Not Marriage at All, but Simple Harlotry': The Companionate Marriage Controversy." *Journal of American History* 94, no. 4 (March 2008): 1137–1163.

Diner, Hasia. "Introduction to the Transaction Edition." In *The Ghetto,* by Louis Wirth. New Brunswick, NJ: Transaction Publishers, 1998.

Eisen, Arnold, and Noam Pianko, eds. "Mordecai Kaplan's *Judaism as a Civilization:* The Legacy of an American Idea." Special issue, *Jewish Social Studies* 12, no. 2 (Winter 2006).

Ellenson, David. "The Development of Orthodox Attitudes to Conversion in the Modern Period." *Conservative Judaism* 36, no. 4 (Summer 1983): 57–73.

Endelman, Todd. "Anglo-Jewish Scientists and the Science of Race." *Jewish Social Studies* 11, no. 1 (Fall 2004): 52–92.

Feingold, Jessica. "Up from Isolation—Intergroup Activities at the Seminary." *Judaism* 27, no. 3 (Summer 1978): 283–291.

Frank, Geyla. "Jews, Multiculturalism, and Boasian Anthropology." *American Anthropologist* 99, no. 4 (1997): 731–745.

Gerstle, Gary. "Liberty, Coercion, and the Making of Americans." *Journal of American History* 84, no. 2 (September 1997): 524–558.

Gjerde, Jon. "New Growth on Old Vines—the State of the Field: The Social History of Immigration to and Ethnicity in the United States." *Journal of American Ethnic History* 18, no. 4 (Summer 1999): 40–66.

Gleason, Philip. "American Identity and Americanization." In *Harvard Encyclopedia of American Ethnic Groups*, ed. Stephan Thernstrom. Cambridge, MA: Harvard University Press, 1980.

Glenn, Susan. "In the Blood? Consent, Descent, and the Ironies of Jewish Identity." *Jewish Social Studies* 8, no. 2–3 (Winter–Spring 2002): 139–152.

———. "The Vogue of Jewish Self-Hatred in Post–World War II America." *Jewish Social Studies* 12, no. 3 (Spring–Summer 2006): 95–136.

Goldstein, Eric. "'Different Blood Flows in Our Veins': Race and Jewish Self-Definition in Late Nineteenth Century America." *American Jewish History* 85, no. 1 (March 1997): 29–55.

Greene, Daniel. "A Chosen People in a Pluralist Nation: Horace Kallen and the Jewish-American Experience." *Religion and American Culture* 16, no. 2 (June 2006): 161–193.

Handy, Robert T. "The American Religious Depression, 1925–1935." *Church History* 29, no. 1 (1960): 3–16.

Henry, Patrick. "'And I Don't Care What It Is': The Tradition-History of a Civil Religion Proof-Text." *Journal of the American Academy of Religion* 49, no. 1 (1981): 35–47.

Hirsch, Richard. "American Jewish Life since 1935: A Reconstructionist Retrospective." *Reconstructionist* 70, no. 1 (Fall 2005): 5–14.

Hollinger, David. "How Wide the Circle of the 'We'? American Intellectuals and the Problem of the Ethnos since World War II." *American Historical Review* 98, no. 2 (April 1993): 317–337.

———. "Amalgamation and Hypodescent: The Question of Ethnoracial Mixture in the History of the United States." *American Historical Review* 108, no. 5 (December 2003): 1363–1390.

Jaher, Frederic Cople. "The Quest for the Ultimate *Shiksa*." *American Quarterly* 35, no. 5 (Winter 1983): 518–542.

Janowitz, Morris. Introduction to *Introduction to the Science of Sociology*, ed. Ernest Burgess and Robert Park. Chicago: University of Chicago Press, 1969 [1921].

Joselit, Jenna Weissman. "By Design: Building the Campus of the Jewish Theological Seminary." In *Tradition Renewed: A History of the Jewish Theological Seminary*, ed. Jack Wertheimer. New York: Jewish Theological Seminary of America, 1997.

Kahn, Susan. "The Multiple Meanings of Jewish Genes." *Culture, Medicine, and Psychiatry* 29, no. 2 (June 2005): 179–192.

Kang, Joon-Mann. "Franklin D. Roosevelt and James L. Fly: The Politics of Broadcast Regulation, 1941–1944." *Journal of American Culture* 10, no. 2 (Summer 1987): 23–33.

Kaplan, Dana Evan. "W. E. Todd's Attempt to Convert to Judaism and Study for the Reform Rabbinate in 1896." *American Jewish History* 83, no. 4 (December 1995): 429–444.

Kaplan, Edward. "The American Mission of Abraham Joshua Heschel." In *The Americanization of the Jews*, ed. Norman Cohen and Robert Seltzer. New York: New York University Press, 1995.

Kazal, Russell. "Revisiting Assimilation: The Rise, Fall, and Reappraisal of a Concept in American Ethnic History." *American Historical Review* 100, no. 2 (April 1995): 437–471.

Konvitz, Milton. "Horace M. Kallen." In *The "Other" New York Jewish Intellectuals,* ed. Carole Kessner. New York: New York University Press, 1994.

Kraut, Benny. "A Wary Collaboration: Jews, Catholics, and the Protestant Goodwill Movement." In *Between the Times: The Travail of the Protestant Establishment in America, 1900–1960,* ed. William Hutchison. New York: Cambridge University Press, 1989.

Laipson, Peter. "'Kiss without Shame, for She Desires It': Sexual Foreplay in American Marital Advice Literature, 1900–1925." *Journal of Social History* 29, no. 3 (Spring 1996): 507–525.

Laslett, Barbara. "Gender in/and Social Science History." *Social Science History* 16, no. 2 (Summer 1992): 177–195.

Levenson, Alan. "Reform Attitudes, in the Past, toward Intermarriage." *Judaism* 38, no. 3 (Summer 1989): 320–332.

Levin, Leonard. "The Legacy of Milton Steinberg." *Conservative Judaism* 32, no. 4 (Summer 1979): 81–87.

Levinger, Lee. "The Theology of Kaufmann Kohler." *CCAR Journal* no. 24 (January 1959): 10–14, 27.

Marvick, Elizabeth Wirth. "Biographical Memorandum on Louis Wirth." In *Louis Wirth on Cities and Social Life,* ed. Albert J. Reiss. Chicago: University of Chicago Press, 1964.

Matthews, Fred. "Louis Wirth and American Ethnic Studies: The Worldview of Enlightened Assimilationism, 1925–1950." In *The Jews of North America,* ed. Moses Rischin. Detroit: Wayne State University Press, 1987.

Merwin, Ted. "The Performance of Jewish Ethnicity in Anne Nichols' *Abie's Irish Rose.*" *Journal of American Ethnic History* 20, no. 2 (Winter 2001): 3–37.

Meyerowitz, Joanne. "Beyond the Feminist Mystique: A Reassessment of Postwar Mass Culture, 1946–1958." *Journal of American History* 79, no. 4 (March 1993): 1455–1482.

Miller, Zane. "Pluralism, Chicago Style: Louis Wirth, the Ghetto, the City, and 'Integration.'" *Journal of Urban History* 18, no. 3 (May 1992): 251–279.

Mishler, Elliot. "The Analysis of Interview-Narratives." In *Narrative Psychology: The Storied Nature of Human Conduct,* ed. Theodore Sarbin. New York: Praeger, 1986.

Moore, Deborah Dash. "Trude Weiss-Rosmarin and *The Jewish Spectator.*" In *The "Other" New York Jewish Intellectuals,* ed. Carole Kessner. New York: New York University Press, 1994.

———. "Jewish Women on My Mind." *Culturefront* 5, no. 3 (Winter 1997): 160–163.

———. "Jewish GIs and the Creation of the Judeo-Christian Tradition." *Religion and American Culture* 8, no. 1 (Winter 1998): 31–53.

Moore, R. Laurence. "Secularization: Religion and the Social Sciences." In *Between the Times: The Travail of the Protestant Establishment in America, 1900–1960,* ed. William Hutchinson. Cambridge: Cambridge University Press, 1989.

Neuhaus, Jessamyn. "The Importance of Being Orgasmic: Sexuality, Gender, and Marital Sex Manuals in the United States, 1920–1963." *Journal of the History of Sexuality* 9, no. 4 (October 2000): 447–473.

Niebuhr, Ursula. "Notes on a Friendship: Abraham Joshua Heschel and Reinhold Niebuhr." In *Abraham Joshua Heschel: Exploring His Life and Thought,* ed. John Merkle. New York: Macmillan, 1985.

"Oral History Symposium." *Journal of American History* 86, no. 2 (September 1999): 698–733.

Pascoe, Peggy. "Miscegenation Law, Court Cases, and Ideologies of 'Race' in Twentieth-Century America." *Journal of American History* 83, no. 1 (June 1996): 44–69.

Prell, Riv-Ellen. "Summer Camp, Postwar American Jewish Youth, and the Redemption of Judaism." In *The Jewish Role in American Life: An Annual Review,* ed. Bruce Zuckerman and Jeremy Schoenberg. Los Angeles: University of Southern California Casden Institute, 2006.

Reinharz, Shulamit. "Sociology." In *Jewish Women in America,* ed. Paula Hyman and Deborah Dash Moore. New York: Routledge, 1997.

Rose, Anne. "'Race' Speech—'Culture' Speech—'Soul' Speech: The Brief Career of Social-Science Language in American Religion during the Fascist Era." *Religion and American Culture* 14, no. 1 (Winter 2004): 83–108.

Rosenfeld, Leonora Cohen. "The Judaic Values of a Philosopher: Morris Raphael Cohen, 1880–1947." *Jewish Social Studies* 42, no. 3–4 (Summer–Fall 1980): 189–202.

Sarna, Jonathan. "The American Jewish Response to Nineteenth-Century Christian Missions." *Journal of American History* 68, no. 1 (1981): 35–51.

———. "Marshall Sklare (1921–1992)." *Proceedings of the American Academy of Jewish Research* 58 (1992): 33–35.

———. "Church-State Dilemmas of American Jews." In *Jews and the American Public Square: Debating Religion and Republic,* ed. Alan Mittleman, Jonathan D. Sarna, and Robert Licht. New York: Rowman and Littlefield, 2002.

Scheper-Hughes, Nancy. "Hortense Powdermaker, the Berkeley Years (1967–1970)." *Journal of Anthropological Research* 47, no. 4 (Winter 1991): 457–471.

Schultz, Kevin. "Religion as Identity in Postwar America: The Last Serious Attempt to Put the Question of Religion in the United States Census." *Journal of American History* 93, no. 2 (September 2006): 359–384.

Shandler, Jeffrey, and Elihu Katz. "Broadcasting American Judaism: The Radio and Television Department of the Jewish Theological Seminary." In *Tradition Renewed: A History of the Jewish Theological Seminary,* ed. Jack Wertheimer. New York: Jewish Theological Seminary of America, 1997.

Shumsky, Neil Larry. "Zangwill's *the Melting Pot:* Ethnic Tensions on Stage." *American Quarterly* 27, no. 1 (March 1975): 29–41.

Silk, Mark. "Notes on the Judeo-Christian Tradition in America." *American Quarterly* 36, no. 1 (Spring 1984): 65–85.

Silverberg, Helene. "Introduction: Toward a Gendered Social Science History." In *Gender and American Social Science: The Formative Years,* ed. Helene Silverberg. Princeton, NJ: Princeton University Press, 1998.

Simmons, Christina. "Companionate Marriage and the Lesbian Threat." *Frontiers* 4, no. 3 (Fall 1979): 54–59.

Smith, Charles, and Lewis Killian. "Black Sociologists and Social Protest." In *Black Sociologists: Historical and Contemporary Perspectives,* ed. James Blackwell and Morris Janowitz. Chicago: University of Chicago Press, 1974.

Sol, Adam. "Longings and Renunciations: Attitudes toward Intermarriage in Early Twentieth Century Jewish American Novels." *American Jewish History* 89, no. 2 (June 2001): 215–230.

Solomon, Barbara Miller. "A Portrait of Oscar Handlin." In *Uprooted Americans: Essays to Honor Oscar Handlin,* ed. Richard L. Bushman, Neil Harris, David Rothman, Barbara Miller Solomon, and Stephan Thernstrom. Boston: Little, Brown and Company, 1979.

Steinberg, Jonathan. "Milton Steinberg, American Rabbi—Thoughts on His Centenary." *Jewish Quarterly Review* 95, no. 3 (Summer 2005): 579–600.

Strauss, Lauren. "Staying Afloat in the Melting Pot: Constructing an American Jewish Identity in the *Menorah Journal* of the 1920s." *American Jewish History* 84, no. 4 (December 1996): 315–331.

Thomson, Alistair. "Fifty Years On: An International Perspective on Oral History." *Journal of American History* 85, no. 2 (September 1998): 581–595.

Toll, William. "Ethnicity and Freedom in the Philosophy of Horace M. Kallen." In *The Jews of North America,* ed. Moses Rischin. Detroit: Wayne State University Press, 1987.

Ueda, Reed. "Immigration and the Moral Criticism of American History: The Vision of Oscar Handlin." *Canadian Review of American Studies* 21, no. 2 (Fall 1990): 183–201.

Volkov, Shulamit. "German Jews between Fulfillment and Disillusion." In *In Search of Jewish Community: Jewish Identities in Germany and Austria, 1918–1933,* ed. Michael Brenner and Derek Penslar. Bloomington: Indiana University Press, 1998.

Wertheimer, Jack. "The Conservative Synagogue." In *The American Synagogue,* ed. Jack Wertheimer. Hanover, NH: Brandeis University Press, 1987.

———. "Jewish Education in the United States: Recent Trends and Issues." *American Jewish Year Book* 99 (1999): 3–114.

Wyler, Marjorie. "*The Eternal Light:* Judaism on the Airwaves." *Conservative Judaism* 39, no. 2 (Winter 1986–87): 18–22.

Zipperstein, Steven. "*Commentary* and American Jewish Culture in the 1940s and 1950s." *Jewish Social Studies* 3, no. 2 (Winter 1997): 18–28.

Books and Dissertations

Abbott, Andrew. *Department and Discipline: Chicago Sociology at One Hundred.* Chicago: University of Chicago Press, 1999.

Abell, Aaron Ignatius. *American Catholicism and Social Action: A Search for Social Justice, 1865–1950.* Garden City, NY: Hanover House, 1960.

Ahlstrom, Sydney. *A Religious History of the American People.* New Haven, CT: Yale University Press, 1972.

Alexander, Michael. *Jazz Age Jews.* Princeton, NJ: Princeton University Press, 2001.

Antler, Joyce. *You Never Call! You Never Write! A History of the Jewish Mother.* New York: Oxford University Press, 2007.

Appiah, Kwame Anthony. *Cosmopolitanism: Ethics in a World of Strangers.* New York: Norton, 2006.

Ariel, Yaakov. *Evangelizing the Chosen People: Missions to the Jews in America, 1880–2000.* Chapel Hill: University of North Carolina Press, 2000.

Ausmus, Harry. *Will Herberg: From Right to Right.* Chapel Hill: University of North Carolina Press, 1987.

Baldwin, Neil. *Henry Ford and the Jews: The Mass Production of Hate.* New York: Public Affairs, 2001.

Bannister, Robert. *Sociology and Scientism.* Chapel Hill: University of North Carolina Press, 1987.

Barkan, Elazar. *The Retreat of Scientific Racism: Changing Concepts in Britain and the United States between the World Wars.* New York: Cambridge University Press, 1992.

Bederman, Gail. *Manliness and Civilization: A Cultural History of Gender and Race in the United States, 1880–1917.* Chicago: University of Chicago Press, 1995.

Bernstein, Philip. *Rabbis at War: The CANRA Story.* Waltham, MA: American Jewish Historical Society, 1971.

Beuttler, Fred. "Organizing an American Conscience: The Conference on Science, Philosophy, and Religion, 1940–1968." PhD diss., University of Chicago, 1995.

Biale, David. *Power and Powerlessness in Jewish History.* New York: Schocken Books, 1986.

Birnbaum, Pierre, and Ira Katznelson, eds. *Paths of Emancipation: Jews, States, and Citizenship.* Princeton, NJ: Princeton University Press, 1995.

Blackwell, James, and Morris Janowitz, eds. *Black Sociologists: Historical and Contemporary Perspectives.* Chicago: University of Chicago Press, 1974.

Bloom, Alexander. *Prodigal Sons: The New York Intellectuals and Their World.* New York: Oxford University Press, 1986.

Bourdieu, Pierre. *The Logic of Practice.* Stanford, CA: Stanford University Press, 1990.

Brinkley, Alan. *The End of Reform: New Deal Liberalism in Recession and War.* New York: Knopf, 1995.

Brumberg, Stephan. *Going to America, Going to School: The Jewish Immigrant Public School Encounter in Turn-of-the-Century New York City.* New York: Praeger, 1986.

Buhle, Paul, ed. *Jews and American Popular Culture*. Westport, CT: Praeger, 2006.

Butler, Jon. *Becoming America: The Revolution before 1776*. Cambridge, MA: Harvard University Press, 2000.

Carlebach, Elisheva. *Divided Souls: Converts from Judaism in Germany, 1500–1750*. New Haven, CT: Yale University Press, 2001.

Carpenter, Joel A. *Revive Us Again: The Reawakening of American Fundamentalism*. New York: Oxford University Press, 1997.

Casey, Edward. *Remembering: A Phenomenological Study*. Bloomington: Indiana University Press, 1987.

Cohen, Lizabeth. *Making a New Deal: Industrial Workers in Chicago, 1919–1939*. New York: Cambridge University Press, 1990.

Cohen, Mark. *Under Crescent and Cross: The Jews in the Middle Ages*. Princeton, NJ: Princeton University Press, 1994.

Cohen, Naomi Wiener. *Not Free to Desist: The American Jewish Committee, 1906–1966*. Philadelphia: Jewish Publication Society, 1972.

———. *American Jews and the Zionist Idea*. New York: Ktav Publishing House, 1975.

———. *Encounter with Emancipation: The German Jews in the United States, 1830–1914*. Philadelphia: Jewish Publication Society, 1984.

Cohen, Shaye. *The Beginnings of Jewishness: Boundaries, Varieties, Uncertainties*. Berkeley: University of California Press, 1999.

Cohen, Steven M., and Arnold Eisen. *The Jew Within: Self, Family, and Community in America*. Bloomington: Indiana University Press, 2000.

Cooney, Terry. *The Rise of New York Intellectuals: Partisan Review and Its Circle*. Madison: University of Wisconsin Press, 1986.

Coser, Lewis. *Masters of Sociological Thought: Ideas in Historical and Social Context*. New York: Harcourt Brace Jovanovich, 1977.

Cott, Nancy F. *Public Vows: A History of Marriage and the Nation*. Cambridge, MA: Harvard University Press, 2000.

Cramer, Richard. *Joe DiMaggio: The Hero's Life*. New York: Simon and Schuster, 2000.

Cross, Robert D. *The Emergence of Liberal Catholicism in America*. Cambridge, MA: Harvard University Press, 1958.

Davidman, Lynn. *Tradition in a Rootless World*. Berkeley: University of California Press, 1991.

Davis, Moshe. *The Emergence of Conservative Judaism*. Philadelphia: Jewish Publication Society, 1963.

Davis, Rebecca. "'The Wife Your Husband Needs': Marriage Counseling, Religion, and Sexual Politics in the United States, 1930–1980." PhD diss., Yale University, 2006.

D'Emilio, John, and Estelle Freedman. *Intimate Matters: A History of Sexuality in America*. Chicago: University of Chicago Press, 1997.

Diner, Hasia. *A Time for Gathering: The Second Migration, 1820–1880*. Baltimore: Johns Hopkins University Press, 1992.

———. *The Jews of the United States, 1654–2000*. Berkeley: University of California Press, 2004.

Dinnerstein, Leonard. *Antisemitism in America*. New York: Oxford University Press, 1994.

Dinnerstein, Leonard, and Gene Koppel. *Nathan Glazer: A Different Kind of Liberal*. Tucson: University of Arizona, 1973.

Dollinger, Marc. *Quest for Inclusion: Jews and Liberalism in Modern America*. Princeton, NJ: Princeton University Press, 2000.

Dorman, Joseph. *Arguing the World: The New York Intellectuals in Their Own Words*. New York: Free Press, 2000.

Douglas, Ann. *The Feminization of American Culture*. New York: Avon Books, 1978.

Douglas, Mary. *Purity and Danger*. New York: Praeger, 1966.

Dubofsky, Melvyn. *The State and Labor in Modern America*. Chapel Hill: University of North Carolina Press, 1994.

Dudziak, Mary L. *Cold War Civil Rights: Race and the Image of American Democracy*. Princeton, NJ: Princeton University Press, 2000.

Efron, John M. *Defenders of the Race: Jewish Doctors and Race Science in Fin-de-Siècle Europe*. New Haven, CT: Yale University Press, 1994.

Eisen, Arnold. *The Chosen People in America: A Study in Jewish Religious Ideology*. Bloomington: Indiana University Press, 1983.

———. *Galut: Modern Jewish Reflection on Homelessness and Homecoming*. Bloomington: Indiana University Press, 1986.

———. *Rethinking Modern Judaism: Ritual, Commandment, Community*. Chicago: University of Chicago Press, 1998.

Elazar, Daniel Judah, and Rela Mintz Geffen. *The Conservative Movement in Judaism: Dilemmas and Opportunities*. Albany: State University of New York Press, 2000.

Endelman, Todd. *The Jews of Georgian England, 1714–1830: Tradition and Change in Liberal Society*. Philadelphia: Jewish Publication Society of America, 1979.

———, ed. *Jewish Apostasy in the Modern World*. New York: Holmes and Meier, 1987.

———. *Radical Assimilation in English Jewish History, 1656–1945*. Bloomington: Indiana University Press, 1990.

Faber, Eli. *A Time for Planting: The First Migration, 1654–1820*. Baltimore: Johns Hopkins University Press, 1992.

Feiner, Shmuel. *The Jewish Enlightenment*. Translated by Chaya Naor. Philadelphia: University of Pennsylvania Press, 2004.

Feingold, Henry. *A Time for Searching: Entering the Mainstream, 1920–1945*. Baltimore: Johns Hopkins University Press, 1992.

Fermaglich, Kirsten. *American Dreams and Nazi Nightmares: Early Holocaust Consciousness and Liberal America, 1957–1965*. Waltham, MA: Brandeis University Press, 2006.

Fiedler, Leslie. *Waiting for the End*. New York: Stein and Day, 1964.

Fox, Richard. *Reinhold Niebuhr: A Biography*. New York: Pantheon Books, 1985.

Fraser, Steve, and Gary Gerstle, eds. *The Rise and Fall of the New Deal Order, 1930–1980*. Princeton, NJ: Princeton University Press, 1989.

Gerstle, Gary. *Working-Class Americanism: The Politics of Labor in a Textile City, 1914–1960*. New York: Cambridge University Press, 1989.

———. *American Crucible: Race and Nation in the Twentieth Century*. Princeton, NJ: Princeton University Press, 2001.

Gillman, Neil. *Conservative Judaism: The New Century*. West Orange, NJ: Behrman House, 1993.

Gilman, Sander. *The Jew's Body*. New York: Routledge, 1991.

Glick, Leonard. *Abraham's Heirs: Jews and Christians in Medieval Europe*. Syracuse, NY: Syracuse University Press, 1999.

Goldman, Karla. *Beyond the Synagogue Gallery: Finding a Place for Women in American Judaism*. Cambridge, MA: Harvard University Press, 2000.

Goldschmidt, Henry. *Race and Religion: Among the Chosen Peoples of Crown Heights*. New Brunswick, NJ: Rutgers University Press, 2006.

Goldstein, Eric. *The Price of Whiteness: Jews, Race, and American Identity*. Princeton, NJ: Princeton University Press, 2006.

Gorelick, Sherry. *City College and the Jewish Poor: Education in New York, 1880–1924*. New Brunswick, NJ: Rutgers University Press, 1981.

Goren, Arthur A. *New York Jews and the Quest for Community: The Kehillah Experiment, 1908–1922*. New York: Columbia University Press, 1970.

———. *The Politics and Public Culture of American Jews*. Bloomington: Indiana University Press, 1999.

Gould, Joseph. *The Chautauqua Movement: An Episode in the Continuing American Revolution*. New York: State University of New York Press, 1961.

Greek, Cecil. *The Religious Roots of American Sociology*. New York: Garland Publishing, 1992.

Greenbaum, Michael. *Louis Finkelstein and the Conservative Movement: Conflict and Growth*. Binghamton, NY: Global Publications, 2001.

Greene, Daniel. "The Crisis of Jewish Freedom: The Menorah Association and American Pluralism, 1906–1934." PhD diss., University of Chicago, 2004.

Grossman, James. *Land of Hope: Chicago, Black Southerners, and the Great Migration*. Chicago: University of Chicago Press, 1989.

Guiles, Fred Lawrence. *Norma Jean: The Life of Marilyn Monroe*. New York: McGraw-Hill, 1969.

Gurock, Jeffrey S. *The Men and Women of Yeshiva: Higher Education, Orthodoxy, and American Judaism*. New York: Columbia University Press, 1988.

Hart, Mitchell. *Social Science and the Politics of Modern Jewish Identity*. Stanford, CA: Stanford University Press, 2000.

Haskell, Thomas. *The Emergence of Professional Social Science: The American Social Science Association and the Nineteenth-Century Crisis of Authority*. Urbana: University of Illinois Press, 1977.

Hayes, Christine. *Gentile Impurities and Jewish Identities: Intermarriage and Conversion from the Bible to the Talmud*. New York: Oxford University Press, 2002.

Heil, Alan. *Voice of America: A History*. New York: Columbia University Press, 2003.

Heinze, Andrew. *Jews and the American Soul: Human Nature in the Twentieth Century.* Princeton, NJ: Princeton University Press, 2004.

Herman, Ellen. *The Romance of American Psychology: Political Culture in the Age of Experts.* Berkeley: University of California Press, 1995.

Hertz, Deborah. *Jewish High Society in Old Regime Berlin.* New Haven, CT: Yale University Press, 1988.

Hess, Jonathan. *Germans, Jews, and the Claims of Modernity.* New Haven, CT: Yale University Press, 2002.

Higham, John. *Strangers in the Land: Patterns of American Nativism, 1860–1925.* New York: Atheneum, 1963.

Hinchman, Lewis P., and Sandra K. Hinchman, eds. *Memory, Identity, Community: The Idea of Narrative in the Human Sciences.* Albany: State University of New York Press, 1997.

Hoberman, J., and Jeffrey Shandler, eds. *Entertaining America: Jews, Movies, and Broadcasting.* Princeton, NJ: Princeton University Press, 2003.

Hodes, Martha. *White Women, Black Men: Illicit Sex in the Nineteenth Century South.* New Haven, CT: Yale University Press, 1993.

Hollinger, David. *Morris R. Cohen and the Scientific Ideal.* Cambridge, MA: MIT Press, 1975.

———. *Science, Jews, and Secular Culture: Studies in Mid-Twentieth-Century American Intellectual History.* Princeton, NJ: Princeton University Press, 1996.

Holloway, Jonathan. *Confronting the Veil: Abram Harris Jr., E. Franklin Frazier, and Ralph Bunche, 1919–1941.* Chapel Hill: University of North Carolina Press, 2002.

Hopkins, Charles Howard. *The Rise of the Social Gospel in American Protestantism, 1865–1915.* New Haven, CT: Yale University Press, 1940.

Horowitz, Daniel. *Vance Packard and American Social Criticism.* Chapel Hill: University of North Carolina Press, 1995.

Hudnut-Beumler, James. *Looking for God in the Suburbs: The Religion of the American Dream and Its Critics, 1945–1965.* New Brunswick, NJ: Rutgers University Press, 1994.

Hutchison, William. *The Modernist Impulse in American Protestantism.* Cambridge, MA: Harvard University Press, 1976.

———. *Errand to the World: American Protestant Thought and Foreign Missions.* Chicago: University of Chicago Press, 1987.

———. *Religious Pluralism in America: The Contentious History of a Founding Ideal.* New Haven, CT: Yale University Press, 2003.

Hyman, Paula. *Gender and Assimilation in Modern Jewish History: The Roles and Representation of Women.* Seattle: University of Washington Press, 1995.

———. *The Jews of Modern France.* Berkeley: University of California Press, 1998.

Igo, Sarah. *The Averaged American: Surveys, Citizens, and the Making of a Mass Public.* Cambridge, MA: Harvard University Press, 2007.

Jackson, Kenneth T. *Crabgrass Frontier: The Suburbanization of the United States.* New York: Oxford University Press, 1985.

Jackson, Walter. *Gunnar Myrdal and America's Conscience: Social Engineering and Racial Liberalism, 1938–1987.* Chapel Hill: University of North Carolina Press, 1990.

Jacobson, Matthew Frye. *Whiteness of a Different Color: European Immigrants and the Alchemy of Race.* Cambridge, MA: Harvard University Press, 1998.

———. *Barbarian Virtues: The United States Encounters Foreign Peoples at Home and Abroad, 1876–1917.* New York: Hill and Wang, 2000.

———. *Roots Too: White Ethnic Revival in Post–Civil Rights America.* Cambridge, MA: Harvard University Press, 2006.

Jay, Martin. *The Dialectical Imagination: A History of the Frankfurt School and the Institute of Social Research, 1923–1950.* Boston: Little, Brown and Company, 1973.

Joselit, Jenna Weissman. *The Wonders of America: Reinventing Jewish Culture, 1880–1950.* New York: Hill and Wang, 1994.

Jumonville, Neil. *Critical Crossings: The New York Intellectuals in Postwar America.* Berkeley: University of California Press, 1991.

Kaplan, Edward. *Spiritual Radical: Abraham Joshua Heschel in America, 1940–1972.* New Haven, CT: Yale University Press, 2007.

Kaplan, Edward, and Samuel Dresner. *Abraham Joshua Heschel: Prophetic Witness.* New Haven, CT: Yale University Press, 1998.

Kaplan, Marion. *The Making of the Jewish Middle Class: Women, Family and Identity in Imperial Germany.* New York: Oxford University Press, 1991.

Katz, Jacob. *Out of the Ghetto: The Social Background of Jewish Emancipation, 1770–1870.* Cambridge, MA: Harvard University Press, 1973.

Kelner, Saul. "Almost Pilgrims: Authenticity, Identity, and the Extra-Ordinary on a Jewish Tour of Israel." PhD diss., City University of New York, 2002.

Klingenstein, Susanne. *Jews in the American Academy, 1900–1940: The Dynamics of Intellectual Assimilation.* Syracuse, NY: Syracuse University Press, 1998.

Konvitz, Milton. *Nine American Jewish Thinkers.* New Brunswick, NJ: Transaction Publishers, 2000.

Kosek, Joseph. "Spectacles of Conscience: Christian Nonviolence and the Transformation of American Democracy, 1914–1956." PhD diss., Yale University, 2004.

Kraut, Benny. *From Reform Judaism to Ethical Culture: The Religious Evolution of Felix Adler.* Cincinnati: Hebrew Union College Press, 1979.

Kuznitz, Cecile. "The Origins of Yiddish Scholarship and the YIVO Institute for Jewish Research." PhD diss., Stanford University, 2000.

Lasch, Christopher. *The New Radicalism in America, 1889–1963.* New York: W. W. Norton and Company, 1965.

Laslett, John, and Seymour Martin Lipset, eds. *Failure of a Dream? Essays on the History of American Socialism.* New York: Anchor Press/Doubleday, 1974.

Lawless, Elaine. *Holy Women, Wholly Women: Sharing Ministries of Wholeness through Life Stories and Reciprocal Ethnography.* Philadelphia: University of Pennsylvania Press, 1993.

Lears, T. J. Jackson. *No Place of Grace: Antimodernism and the Transformation of American Culture: 1880–1920*. New York: Pantheon Books, 1981.

Lederhendler, Eli. *New York Jews and the Decline of Urban Ethnicity, 1950–1970*. Syracuse, NY: Syracuse University Press, 2001.

Lemire, Elise. *"Miscegenation": Making Race in America*. Philadelphia: University of Pennsylvania Press, 2002.

Liberles, Robert. *Salo Wittmayer Baron: Architect of Jewish History*. New York: New York University Press, 1995.

Lipset, Seymour Martin, and David Riesman. *Education and Politics at Harvard*. New York: McGraw-Hill, 1975.

Lipsitz, George. *A Rainbow at Midnight: Labor and Culture in the 1940s*. Urbana: University of Illinois Press, 1994.

Mailer, Norman. *Marilyn: A Biography*. New York: Grosset and Dunlap, 1973.

Marrus, Michael. *The Politics of Assimilation: A Study of the French Jewish Community at the Time of the Dreyfus Affair*. Oxford: Clarendon Press, 1971.

Marsden, George M. *Fundamentalism and American Culture: The Shaping of Twentieth-Century Evangelicalism, 1870–1925*. New York: Oxford University Press, 1980.

Matthews, Fred. *Quest for an American Sociology: Robert E. Park and the Chicago School*. Montreal: McGill-Queen's University Press, 1977.

May, Elaine Tyler. *Great Expectations: Marriage and Divorce in Post-Victorian America*. Chicago: University of Chicago Press, 1980.

———. *Homeward Bound: American Families in the Cold War Era*. New York: Basic Books, 1988.

May, Henry Farnham. *Protestant Churches and Industrial America*. New York: Harper, 1949.

McClain, Charles J. *In Search of Equality: The Chinese Struggle against Discrimination in Nineteenth-Century America*. Berkeley: University of California Press, 1994.

McGinity, Keren. "Still Jewish: A History of Women and Intermarriage in America." PhD diss., Brown University, 2005.

Mendes-Flohr, Paul, and Jehuda Reinharz, eds. *The Jew in the Modern World*. New York: Oxford University Press, 1980.

Meyer, Michael A. *Response to Modernity: A History of the Reform Movement in Judaism*. New York: Oxford University Press, 1988.

Michels, Tony. *A Fire in Their Hearts: Yiddish Socialists in New York*. Cambridge, MA: Harvard University Press, 2005.

Miller, Perry. *Errand into the Wilderness*. Cambridge, MA: Harvard University Press, Belknap Press, 1956.

Mintz, Steven. *Huck's Raft: A History of American Childhood*. Cambridge, MA: Harvard University Press, Belknap Press, 2004.

Moore, Deborah Dash. *At Home in America: Second Generation New York Jews*. New York: Columbia University Press, 1981.

———. *B'nai B'rith and the Challenge of Ethnic Leadership*. Albany: State University of New York Press, 1981.

———. *GI Jews: How World War II Changed a Generation*. Cambridge, MA: Harvard University Press, 2004.

Moore, R. Laurence. *Religious Outsiders and the Making of Americans*. New York: Oxford University Press, 1986.

———. *Selling God: American Religion in the Marketplace of Culture*. New York: Oxford University Press, 1994.

Moskowitz, Eva. *In Therapy We Trust: America's Obsession with Self-Fulfillment*. Baltimore: Johns Hopkins University Press, 2001.

Myers, David. *Re-inventing the Jewish Past: European Intellectuals and the Zionist Return to History*. New York: Oxford University Press, 1995.

Ngai, Mae. *Impossible Subjects: Illegal Aliens and the Making of Modern America*. Princeton, NJ: Princeton University Press, 2004.

Noveck, Simon. *Milton Steinberg: Portrait of a Rabbi*. New York: Ktav Publishing House, 1978.

Novick, Peter. *That Noble Dream: The "Objectivity Question" and the American Historical Profession*. New York: Cambridge University Press, 1988.

O'Neill, William. *American High: The Years of Confidence, 1945–1960*. New York: Free Press, 1986.

Pearl, Jonathan, and Judith Pearl. *The Chosen Image: Television's Portrayal of Jewish Themes and Characters*. Jefferson, NC: McFarland, 1999.

Pearlstein, Peggy Kronsberg. "Understanding through Education: One Hundred Years of the Jewish Chautauqua Society, 1893–1993." PhD diss., George Washington University, Washington, DC, 1993.

Peffer, George Anthony. *If They Don't Bring Their Women Here: Chinese Female Immigration before Exclusion*. Urbana: University of Illinois Press, 1999.

Peiss, Kathy Lee. *Cheap Amusements: Working Women and Leisure in Turn-of-the-Century New York*. Philadelphia: Temple University Press, 1986.

Penslar, Derek. *Shylock's Children: Economics and Jewish Identity in Modern Europe*. Berkeley: University of California Press, 2001.

Persons, Stow. *Ethnic Studies at Chicago, 1905–1945*. Chicago: University of Illinois Press, 1987.

Pianko, Noam. "Diaspora Jewish Nationalism and Identity in America, 1914–1967." PhD diss., Yale University, 2004.

Porter, Jack. *The Jew as Outsider: Historical and Contemporary Perspectives, Collected Essays, 1974–1980*. Washington, DC: University Press of America, 1981.

Prell, Riv-Ellen. *Fighting to Become Americans: Jews, Gender, and the Anxiety of Assimilation*. Boston: Beacon Press, 1999.

Putney, Clifford. *Muscular Christianity: Manhood and Sports in Protestant America, 1880–1920*. Cambridge, MA: Harvard University Press, 2003.

Raider, Mark A. *The Emergence of American Zionism*. New York: New York University Press, 1998.

Rieser, Andrew. *The Chautauqua Movement: Protestants, Progressives, and the Culture of Modern Liberalism*. New York: Columbia University Press, 2003.

Rischin, Moses. *The Promised City: New York's Jews, 1870–1914*. Cambridge, MA: Harvard University Press, 1962.

Ritterband, Paul, and Harold S. Wechsler. *Jewish Learning in American Universities: The First Century.* Bloomington: Indiana University Press, 1994.

Rodgers, Daniel. *Atlantic Crossings: Social Politics in a Progressive Age.* Cambridge, MA: Harvard University Press, Belknap Press, 1998.

Rogow, Faith. *Gone to Another Meeting: The National Council of Jewish Women, 1893–1993.* Tuscaloosa: University of Alabama Press, 1993.

Romano, Renee. *Race Mixing: Black-White Marriage in Postwar America.* Cambridge, MA: Harvard University Press, 2003.

Rose, Anne C. *Beloved Strangers: Interfaith Families in Nineteenth-Century America.* Cambridge, MA: Harvard University Press, 2001.

Rosenzweig, Roy. *Eight Hours for What We Will: Workers and Leisure in an Industrial City, 1870–1920.* New York: Cambridge University Press, 1983.

Ross, Dorothy. *The Origins of American Social Science.* New York: Cambridge University Press, 1991.

Rothman, Ellen. *Hands and Hearts: A History of Courtship in America.* New York: Basic Books, 1984.

Salerno, Robert. *Louis Wirth: A Bio-Bibliography.* New York: Greenwood Press, 1987.

Salyer, Lucy E. *Laws Harsh as Tigers: Chinese Immigrants and the Shaping of Modern Immigration Law.* Chapel Hill: University of North Carolina Press, 1995.

Sarna, Jonathan. *JPS: The Americanization of Jewish Culture, 1888–1988.* Philadelphia: Jewish Publication Society, 1989.

———. *American Judaism: A History.* New Haven, CT: Yale University Press, 2004.

Satlow, Michael. *Jewish Marriage in Antiquity.* Princeton, NJ: Princeton University Press, 2001.

Savage, Barbara. *Broadcasting Freedom: Radio, War, and the Politics of Race.* Chapel Hill: University of North Carolina Press, 1999.

Schachter, Daniel. *The Seven Sins of Memory: How the Mind Forgets and Remembers.* Boston: Houghton Mifflin, 2001.

Schacter, Jacob. *Reverence, Righteousness, and Rahamanut: In Memory of Rabbi Dr. Leo Jung.* New Jersey: J. Aronson, 1992.

Schechter, Ronald. *Obstinate Hebrews: Representations of Jews in France, 1715–1815.* Berkeley: University of California Press, 2003.

Schneider, Susan Weidman. *Intermarriage: The Challenge of Living with Difference between Christians and Jews.* New York: Free Press, 1989.

Schorsch, Ismar. *Jewish Reactions to German Anti-Semitism, 1870–1914.* New York: Columbia University Press, 1972.

———. *From Text to Context: The Turn to History in Modern Judaism.* Hanover, NH: Brandeis University Press, 1994.

Schrecker, Ellen. *Many Are the Crimes: McCarthyism in America.* Princeton, NJ: Princeton University Press, 1998.

Schultz, Debra. *Going South: Jewish Women in the Civil Rights Movement.* New York: New York University Press, 2001.

Scott, Daryl Michael. *Contempt and Pity: Social Policy and the Image of the Damaged Black Psyche, 1880–1996*. Chapel Hill: University of North Carolina Press, 1997.

Scult, Mel. *Judaism Faces the Twentieth Century: A Biography of Mordecai M. Kaplan*. Detroit: Wayne State University Press, 1993.

Shapiro, Edward. *A Time for Healing: American Jewry Since World War II*. Baltimore: Johns Hopkins Press, 1992.

Silk, Mark. *Spiritual Politics: Religion and America since World War II*. New York: Simon and Schuster, 1988.

Simpson, Jeffrey. *Chautauqua: An American Utopia*. New York: Harry N. Abrams, 1999.

Slezkine, Yuri. *The Jewish Century*. Princeton, NJ: Princeton University Press, 2004.

Sollors, Werner. *Beyond Ethnicity: Consent and Descent in American Culture*. New York: Oxford University Press, 1986.

Sorin, Gerald. *A Time for Building: The Third Migration, 1880–1920*. Baltimore: Johns Hopkins University Press, 1992.

———. *Irving Howe: A Life of Passionate Dissent*. New York: New York University Press, 2002.

Sorkin, David. *The Transformation of German Jewry, 1780–1840*. New York: Oxford University Press, 1987.

Spickard, Paul. *Mixed Blood: Intermarriage and Ethnic Identity in Twentieth-Century America*. Madison: University of Wisconsin Press, 1990.

Spigel, Lynn. *Make Room for TV: Television and the Family Ideal in Postwar America*. Chicago: University of Chicago Press, 1992.

Staub, Michael. *Torn at the Roots: The Crisis of Jewish Liberalism in Postwar America*. New York: Columbia University Press, 2002.

Stave, Bruce. *The Making of Urban History: Historiography through Oral History*. Beverly Hills: Sage Publications, 1977.

Stearns, Peter. *Anxious Parents: A History of Modern Childrearing in America*. New York: New York University Press, 2003.

Steinberg, Stephen. *The Academic Melting Pot: Catholics and Jews in American Higher Education*. New York: McGraw-Hill, 1974.

———. *The Ethnic Myth: Race, Ethnicity, and Class in America*. New York: Atheneum, 1981.

———. *Turning Back: The Retreat from Racial Justice in American Thought and Policy*. Boston: Beacon Press, 1995.

Steinweis, Alan. *Studying the Jew: Scholarly Antisemitism in Nazi Germany*. Cambridge, MA: Harvard University Press, 2006.

Stern, Alexandra Minna. *Eugenic Nation: Faults and Frontiers of Better Breeding in Modern America*. Berkeley: University of California Press, 2005.

Stocking, George W. *Race, Culture, and Evolution: Essays in the History of Anthropology*. Chicago: University of Chicago Press, 1982.

Stoltzfus, Nathan. *Resistance of the Heart: Intermarriage and the Rosenstrasse Protest in Nazi Germany*. New York: Norton, 1996.

Svonkin, Stuart. *Jews against Prejudice: American Jews and the Fight for Civil Liberties.* New York: Columbia University Press, 1997.

Synnott, Marcia Graham. *The Half-Opened Door: Discrimination and Admissions at Harvard, Yale, and Princeton, 1900–1970.* Westport, CT: Greenwood Press, 1979.

Takaki, Ronald T. *Strangers from a Different Shore: A History of Asian Americans.* New York: Penguin Books, 1990.

Tomasi, Luigi, ed. *The Tradition of the Chicago School of Sociology.* Brookfield, VT: Ashgate, 1998.

Ueda, Reed. *Post-War Immigrant America: A Social History.* Boston: St. Martin's Press, Bedford Books, 1994.

Urofsky, Melvin I. *American Zionism from Herzl to the Holocaust.* Garden City, NY: Anchor Press, 1975.

Wald, Alan. *The New York Intellectuals: The Rise and Decline of the Anti-Stalinist Left from the 1930s to the 1980s.* Chapel Hill: University of North Carolina Press, 1987.

Wallenstein, Peter. *Tell the Court I Love My Wife: Race, Marriage, and Law—an American History.* New York: Palgrave Macmillan, 2002.

Walzer, Michael. *On Toleration.* New Haven, CT: Yale University Press, 1997.

Webb, Clive. *Fight against Fear: Southern Jews and Black Civil Rights.* Athens: University of Georgia Press, 2001.

Weiner, Hollace Ava. "The Jewish Junior League: The Rise and Demise of the Forth Worth National Council of Jewish Women, 1901–2002." Master's thesis, University of Texas, Arlington, 2005.

Wenger, Beth S. *New York Jews and the Great Depression: Uncertain Promise.* New Haven, CT: Yale University Press, 1996.

Whitfield, Stephen. *The Culture of the Cold War.* Baltimore: Johns Hopkins University Press, 1991.

Wilford, Hugh. *The New York Intellectuals: From Vanguard to Institution.* New York: Manchester University Press, 1995.

Wilson, Charles Reagan. *Baptized in Blood: The Religion of the Lost Cause, 1865–1920.* Athens: University of Georgia Press, 1980.

Wuthnow, Robert. *The Restructuring of American Religion: Society and Faith since World War II.* Princeton, NJ: Princeton University Press, 1988.

Zeitz, Joshua. *White Ethnic New York: Jews, Catholics, and the Shaping of Postwar Politics.* Chapel Hill: University of North Carolina Press, 2007.

Zerubavel, Eviatar. *The Fine Line: Making Distinctions in Everyday Life.* Chicago: University of Chicago Press, 1991.

Index

Washington, Booker T., 38
Weinstein, Jacob, 51–52, 64–65, 68–69
Weiss-Rosmarin, Trude, 140
Wenger, Beth, 220n16
"What Is a Jew?" (article; Kertzer), 132–35
What Is a Jew? (book; Kertzer), 130, 133, 135–36, 138, 148
"Why the Jews Are Not Missionaries" (*Literary Digest*), 18–19
Wiener, Max, 180n15
Wirth, Louis, 34, 35, 36, 43*fig.*, 93, 94; background, 36–37; *The Ghetto*, 34, 39, 40–42, 45, 51, 52, 195n70; legacy of, 51–52; marriage, 34, 42, 190n25; at 1945 Conference on Jewish Adjustment, 96; view of the role of social science, 43, 51, 52, 191n30
Wissenschaft des Judentums, 44–45
With an H on My Dog Tag (Kertzer), 131
Wolfson, Harry, 46
Wolsey, Louis, 28, 124–25
Woman's Home Companion, 153
women: concerns about feminization of American society and institutions, 183n48, 184n59; as conferrers of

Jewish identity, 69; female converts to Judaism, 22, 23, 127, 138, 165; viewed as responsible for social-religious regulation, 65, 68–69, 155, 199–200n51. *See also* gender disparities
women's magazines: articles on intermarriage in, 68–69, 153, 156
World Publishing: *What Is a Jew?*, 133, 135–36
World War II, 169; impact on Jewish soldiers, 132; Jewish assimilation and, 160; Jewish chaplains, 69–70, 88, 127, 129, 131–32; missionary Judaism and, 127, 131–32. *See also* Holocaust

Yale Divinity School, 68
Yiddish Scientific Institute (YIVO), 107, 192n37
YIVO Annual of Jewish Social Science, 50

Zeitlin, Joseph, 178n15
Zionism, 56; endogamy and, 56, 196n9; Glazer's student activities, 102–3; missionary Judaism and, 124; Reform position on, 124. *See also* Israel

Text: 10/13 Galliard
Display: Galliard
Compositor: International Typesetting and Composition
Indexer: Thérèse Shere
Printer and binder: Sheridan Books, Inc.